Asian Values and
Vietnam's Development
in Comparative Perspectives

T0351933

NATIONAL CENTER FOR SOCIAL SCIENCES AND HUMANITIES

INTERNATIONAL CONFERENCE

ASIAN VALUES AND

VIETNAM'S DEVELOPMENT

IN COMPARATIVE PERSPECTIVES

(Selected Papers)

HANOI - 2000

Asian Values and Vietnam's Development
in Comparative Perpectives: Selected Papers
Edited by Irene Nørlund and Nguyen Duc Thanh

First published in 2000 by the
National Center for Social Sciences and Humanities (NCSSH)
in association with the
Nordic Institute of Asian Studies (NIAS)

Reprinted in 2004 by NIAS Press
Nordic Institute of Asian Studies
Leifsgade 33, DK–2300 Copenhagen S, Denmark
tel: (+45) 3532 9501 • fax: (+45) 3532 9549
E–mail: books@nias.ku.dk • Website: www.niaspress.dk

Original edition printed in Vietnam
Cover design by Nguyen Thi Hoa
Photographs by Nguyen Van Ku, Nguyen Thanh Liem and Nguyen Nhu Thiet

This reprinted edition printed in Great Britain
Production by Bookchase
Cover design by NIAS Press

British Library Cataloguing in Publication Data
A catalogue record for this book is available from the British Library

ISBN 87-87062-97-6 (NIAS edition)

List of Contents

Community and Family Perspectives

Development and Culture

History and Tradition

Introduction

Irene Norlund

*M*earby the beautiful French-built opera house, one of the classical buildings of Hanoi today, and the newly built neighbouring Hanoi Hilton, attempting to fit into the 19th century style, the conference about Asian values and Vietnam's development was organised in the Army Guesthouse - where even the interior also is inspired by the 19th century Europe. Few hundred metres away the busy 'old city', the trade guild's headquarters of Hanoi revived in commerce during the *doi moi* renovation. In another direction new modern buildings of glass and steel have been erected with offices and international style of the 20th almost 21st century. Hanoi is one of the remaining signs of the crossroads of the East and the West, the traditional and the colonial culture still remains - more than in most other Asian cities - and today meet with the modern global society.

Asian values and Vietnam development in comparative perspective was chosen as subject for the conference, because of the engagement of researchers in the topic of Asian values both in East and West, with considerations of both tradition and modernity, governance and family, policy and economics and not least East and West. Vietnam was a core consideration, because it has not participated so much in the ongoing debate internationally, and has a special history of great power impact from both the East and the West. The National Center for Social Sciences and Humanities and the Nordic Institute of Asian Studies decided to arrange the seminar as a follow up of their cooperation agreement with the purpose to involve scholars from various disciplines and countries.

In the light of the recent financial and economic crisis in Asia, some arguments have to be reconsidered in the debate, as the new strength of some of the Asian economies suddenly appeared to have weaknesses as well. Those who had thought that Asian societies had found a synthesised way out of the dilemma of tradition and modernity in development, had to reconsider and it has had an important impact on some of the discussions in Asia.

At any rate the purpose was not so much to discuss the fairly stereotype features of Asian values, as suggested by the political leaders like Le Kuan

Yew of Singapore and others, who mainly stress the necessity of strong and authoritarian Asian governments in the process of development. The purpose was rather to go beyond the debate and deeper into the history and tradition on one hand, and to consider the influences at society from other cultures both though history and in contemporary global society with the purpose of a more profound understanding of the interaction of the various cultures and cross-cultural interactions.

The presentations during the conference showed a broad spectrum of foci and approaches, from the acceptance of values as mainly universal to the more culturally oriented analysis. Interesting is it that the dividing lines in the debate did not go between Vietnamese and foreign researchers, or between even Asian and European scholars – the dividing lines went across cultures. Robert Cribb pointed out in the beginning how culture is a changeable concept, and that the various scientific approaches might be build on so different understandings that they barely deal with the same subject, and as such the debate of Asian values as an antithesis of globalisation is not fruitful to pursue. The papers published in this publication, show, however, that in spite of the various approaches and viewpoints, there is a common ground for discussion. Both the most universal approaches presented, and most of the culturally based perspectives opened up for a dialogue.

An important characteristic of the Vietnamese scholars presentations is that they are based in a tradition of a society which have been influenced by many cultures from outside. Confucianism is one of the most profound influences, and scholars are now investigating both other Confucian societies as well as the Vietnamese, their values and traditions, what the influences are today and how Confucian values are merged and accommodated in the Vietnamese society. Still most of the Vietnamese scholars hold a position that the revolution in Vietnam could not have been carried out based on Confucianism, the Western values were introduced by the French colonialist and by anti-colonial ideas of the revolutionaries, who maintained national independence as a lead theme. Another central theme is the relation between the individual and the collective of society. The various approaches are summarised in a condensed way by Vu Khieu, who finds that where is not absolute opposition between the Asian and the European values.

The position on the importance of the traditional values versus the outside values among the Vietnamese scholars depends largely on the type of subjects they do research into. Those working on subjects related to the micro level tends to focus more on the importance of 'Asian values' (probably more correctly called Vietnamese values), like the papers by Do Thi Binh, on the family, Phan Dai Doan and Ngo Duc Thinh, who looks at aspects of the communal conventions and customary law. The scholars who look into the history are also much concerned about Confucian thinking, and other traditional values, like Dang Thanh Le, who compares the national consciousness in several Asian countries, Phan Ngoc, who presents an important distinction between Confucianism and Confucius's doctrines and by that touch on the fundamental of what 'Confucianism' represents in his colourful espistimological study of Confucius' doctrine, and the linguist Cao Xuan Hao, who suggests that Vietnamese linguistics have to develop a system of analysis not based on European linguistics, which might help in the analysis of the Vietnamese culture.

The presentations of issues related to governance, legislation and economic development point to the advantage of the 'Asian' values in some respects and as a part of the development and change, but concludes that more Western oriented values are important for building a society in the modern world, based on regulations of society more than traditions. This approach includes the presentation by Pham Duc Thanh about culture and development in East Asia, and Dan Tri Uc and Le Minh Thong who made a survey of Oriental and Western Law values in the Vietnamese laws. Bui Huy Khoat's paper about EU-ASEAN relations points, however, more to the need of less value-based and more *real-politik* in relations between the two sides in order not to challenge the positive interaction.

The non-Vietnamese scholars are represented by some who have carried out research in Europe, others who studies Asia and some who compare the approaches and conditions in both Asia and Europe. Jan Ifversen's paper deals with European and universal values, the latter which he suggests exist as common values in freedom and equality. However, he also suggests that it is necessary for all to relativise their universal values in cross-cultural debates. Peter Bugge searches for the origin of Asia as Europe's "other" and demonstrates how such stereotypes have often had negative connotations and effects. Instead of speaking of "European" or "Asian values" as some reified property of the two continents he suggests that a dialogue should be based on an open discussion of "values in Europe" and "values in Asia" as they are expressed today. Hans Gullestrup presents a model of how culture is integrated in societal and historical structures, but fully base his approach in individual society and in that way avoids the dichotomy between Europe and Asia.

A number of papers compared the situation in both the East and the West, among which Li Narangoa explores the first deliberate Japanese search for learning and not learning from the West and how to integrate into the Japanese society through a high-ranking mission to Europe in the 1870's. Geir Helgesen analyses the perception of Nordic and Asian citizens' idea on governance and concludes that there are significant differences. Hatla Thelle looks at the social policy in China and Denmark, and point to the collectivitist ideas in both societies. At present some apparent tendencies of decreasing rights and social security in both countries takes place in the social field, which might be due to the impact of global trends towards liberalisation.

The chapters on community and family by Elena Samorante, Uichol Kim and Pirom Chantaworn are based on studies and ideas in the societies where the scholars originate (The Philippines, South Korea and Thailand), but in various ways shows that the relation between the individual and the family is essential for the socialisation of children into society, a point also brought out in Do Thi Binh's paper. Pirom Chantaworn is, however, more concerned with the relation between the community and the individual. In various ways they suggest not to follow too narrowly the Western ideas of development based on liberal ideas, because is has costs to the individual and their core values. Uichol Kim moreover adds a section about the Asian crisis and some of the problems in South Korea which he finds is caused by traditional thinking and social relations. The paper by Irene Norlund deals with a large Swedish supported development project in the 1980's and the relation to the Vietnamese reform process in order to explore how the 'business cultures' and 'system cultures' interacted.

The ideas of 'Asian values' in a more profound understanding had clearly had an impact on the thinking among Vietnamese scholars, but more surprisingly, the crisis has had a more profound impact than expected on the discussion in Vietnam. Most Vietnamese scholars would not talk about 'Asian values' but rather Vietnamese values, because the Asian impact was transformed in the Vietnamese setting. Those dealing with modern society tended to perceive the Western value impact as positive and universal. If there has been a period of much concern with the 'Asian values', particularly the Confucian one's, the pendulum seems for most of the Vietnamese participants to go back to perceive Westerns values as the future, but certainly some found the strength in the Vietnamese – or even Asian? – values. The foreign participants were after all representing the largest diversity from almost total universal approaches to the almost total rejection of the universal.

Hanoi and Copenhagen, December 1999

Research of Asian Values —
Problems and Perspectives

Le Huu Tang
National Center for Social Sciences and Humanities

*I*t's a great honour for me, on behalf of the Vietnam National Center for Social Sciences and Humanities, to welcome and say thanks to the international and domestic colleagues who attend this Seminar and will discuss a subject that is attracting the attenition of many people, i.e. "Asian Values Vietnam's Development in Comparative Perspectives".

As partly presented in the invitation letter to the delegates, I would like to emphasise now again, that for a long time, the world's renowned ideologists, sociologists and humanists have been attached to the differences between the Occidental and Oriental cultures, of which the values play a key role.

Together with the incredible advances of Japan, and later of the "Asian tigers", people not only spoke of the differences of the economies, but emphasised the role of the Asian values, considering them impetus, and even the prime important factor, to the unexpected and marvellous development in Asia over the past dozens of years. Quite a few Western scholars, who saw the obstacles for socio-economic development in their countries, came to the Orient and carried out research. They concluded that it's time for the Westerners to learn something from the Easterners.

Ezra F. Vogel, an American scientist, after more than 20 years of research, wrote that the Americans believed in the superiority of the Occidental civilisation and they saw themselves as the "Number One", which hampered their acknowledgement of the fact that, in reality, there was much they had to learn from the Easterners.

E.F. Vogel's observation was not the only one of the kind.

Over the past years, there have been carried out a number of projects and translations in Vietnam to introduce the achievements and analyse the reasons for the results that led to great successes of Japan and other Asian tigers. Of these reasons, the authors paid special attention to the impetus to socio-economic development of the Asian values, including patriotism, national pride, communal spirit, family relations, industriousness, thrift, etc. The Vietnamese Ex-Ambassador to Japan, Dao Huy Ngoc, drew out four lessons about Japan's miracles in his book "Thinking over Japan's miracles"[1], of which the third one is that "the educational-cultural element always takes the lead". The author remarked that inheritance and development of the national culture, together with a highly developed education system, is one of the basic elements boosting Japanese socio-economic development. Director of Singapore Policy Research Institute and ex-Ambassador to the United States, Tommy Koh, set forth 10 values which became a solid foundation of strength and success of the East Asian countries.

They are:

1. The East Asian people do not accept the extreme of individualism applied in the West.

2. The East Asian people respect the family, seeing it a support pillar of the society.

3. Unlike the Westerners, the East Asian people respect the study.

4. Unlike the lifestyles of consumption of the Westerners, the East Asian people love a life of thrift and simplicity.

5. The East Asian people see hard work as a valuable character.

6. The East Asian people uphold the communal spirit and cooperation in work.

7. There are conventions between the State and the people, upon which the State retains laws and social order, and ensures its citizens the basic necessity, including employment, housing, education and healthcare. In turn, the citizens implement the laws, work hard, practice thrift, and encourage the children to study and rely on one's own strength.

---

[1] (Hanoi: Su That Publishing House and Hanoi Institution of International Relations. 1991).

8. In some Asian countries, the authorities try to help each citizen to become a shareholder in his country.

9. The East Asian people want to maintain a social environment with healthy morality.

10. The well-managed authorities in East Asian countries want to have a free press, but unlike the westerners, they see it not as an absolute power.

These 10 values, according to the author, are combined and support the East Asian societies to have a prosperous economy and a stable, harmonious society. We may or may not approve all, or part of the above-mentioned ideas. But this shows the fact that over the past years, both Occidental and Oriental scientists have not only paid attention to, but also deeply researched and identified the Asian values and their impetus in socio-economic development, which helps discovering the Oriental potential.

The same has happened in Vietnam, and it could be said that the Asian values became positive factors to promote research of the role of culture in development. Especially the relations between tradition and modernity started a hot debate. However, that took place in the time of the success of the "Asian tigers". Since the monetary and financial crisis occurred in various countries in Asia, such as South Korea, Japan, Indonesia, etc., the question had to be raised: Are Asian values still important and what is their true role? Some Western scholars spoke of the "breakdown of Asian values" but many others said that it's time now for the Asian values to be upheld in order to overcome the crisis.

So how should this problem be perceived?

The aim of our Seminar is to help find out appropriate solutions for the question. To reach this goal, we should focus on following issues:

1. Are there "Asian values"? If there are, what are they? What is the foundation for their establishment? What are the relations between "Asian values" and "Oriental values"? What are their similarities and differences compared to the "Occidental values"?

2. What is the true role of Asian values in socio-economic development in Asia in general, in Japan and "Asian tigers" in particular, through thousands of years of history, and over the recent dozens of years?

3. What are the relations between the "Asian values" and the "Vietnamese values?" What are their roles in the development of Vietnam in the past and at the present national construction of an equitable, prosperous and civilised Vietnam?

4. What is our attitude towards "Asian values", "Oriental values" and "Occidental values?"

What I have said so far are just a few items on our agenda on "Asian values and development in Vietnam in a comparative perspectives". I hope that the papers delivered at this Seminar, together with the discussion among the participants, will help to find out the answers to the above-mentioned questions, which I believe are not only urgent issues in Vietnam, but also of the other countries in the region. I wish the Seminar great success, and hope it helps to boost the exchange of values among nations and further our friendly relationship as well as foster the values we have earned.

On behalf of the National Center for Social Sciences and Humanities of Vietnam and the Organising Committee, I would like to thank you for your wholehearted participation in the event, and especially thank the Royal Ministry of Foreign Affairs of Denmark and the Royal Danish Embassy to Vietnam for help and financial support to the workshop.

Thank you for listening.

Moderators of the Conference

A View of the Conference

Participants at the Conference

A View of the Conference

Asian Values and Scientific Discourse - Some Reflections

Robert Cribb
Nordic Institute of Asian Studies

do not normally begin my scientific papers by quoting from the Bible, but let me cite just a few words from Paul's first letter to the Corinthians (1:22): discussing techniques for winning new converts to Christianity, he wrote: "For Jews demand signs and Greeks seek wisdom." Paul was not making an anthropological point, of course, but his remark reflects the fact that one of the ancient features of human philosophy is a consciousness that ethnic differences are a matter not just of clothing and food, music and games, but of deep-seated attitudes to the world and the cosmos. We might therefore wonder why we have gathered close to the end of the twentieth century to consider the question of Asian values. How could it possibly be that scholars doubt the importance of culture in political, social and economic behaviour?

Let me offer part of an answer to this question with some historical ethnography. Once upon a time, there were two large ethnic groups on the mainland of Northwestern Europe. One of these ethnic groups was widely thought of as hard, cold and scientific, good in war and in planning, and inclined to authoritarian politics, but rather deficient when it came to the finer things of life. They had culture of course, but it tended to be sterile and formalistic. The other ethnic group, by contrast, was ramshackle and chaotic in its politics, incompetent in warfare and management, but they were a people who knew how to have a good time, to eat and drink and make merry.

At the end of the 20th century, there would be no doubt that these descriptions referred respectively to the Germans and the French, the Germans with their hard rationality and the supposedly soft romantic French. Yet only two hundred years ago, these two sets of national characteristics were completely reversed. The France of Louis XIV, Voltaire and Rousseau and later of Napoleon, was a militaristic, expansionist power feared by its neighbours; its experts were second to none in finding military applications for science and philosophy. The Germans, by contrast, were divided into an impossible patchwork of small states; they were producing great music, great wine and the concept of *Gemütlichkeit*, but they seemed congenitally unable to turn their abilities to great, or at least more dangerous, things.

Another part of the answer to the question, "How is it possible to ignore culture?", also involves the Germans. During the early twentieth century, a debate known as *Zivilisationskritik* took place in Germany.[1] The terms of that debate where highly reminiscent of today's Asian Values debate. Rather than contrast Asia and the West, proponents of *Zivilisationskritik* contrasted Western *Zivilisation* (Civilization) with German *Kultur* (Culture). *Kultur* emphasised family values, patriarchal authority, discipline, politics based on an articulation of national consensus by leaders, rather than the hurly-burly and conflict of democratic politics. Although there are still some observers who would accept such a distinction between Germany and the more westerly parts of Europe, for the most part Germany now seems to be a bulwark of *Zivilisation* rather than *Kultur*.

The point in both cases is that if culture is so changeable in the space of a few generations, then the image which some of those on the culturalist side present of culture as a deep and immutable set of values must be at least partly flawed. Such dramatic change in such a short time suggests that culture, rather than controlling societies and setting the framework within which they operate, is really just a flexible coat which societies put on and take off in response to other, more profound influences at work on them.

Rather than tackling directly such difficult issues as the nature of Asian values, the role which they may have played in Asia's economic performance in during the last few decades, and the role which they may or may not play in Vietnam's development in the future, I would like to consider the Asian values debate from a slightly more detached point of view. What are the issues at stake, intellectually and methodologically in the debate? And is there anything in the circumstances of the debate which can help us when we engage in the debate itself?

I would like to approach this question at three levels. First, how does the

---

[1] For a major statement in complicated debate over civilisation and culture in German, see Norbert Elias, *Über den Prozeß der Zivilisation* Bd. 1 (Frankfurth: Suhrkamp, 1997).

debate measure against the standard of scientific discourse? Second, what are the social and political implications of the debate? And third, how does the debate fit into the sociology of academic discussion?

The conceptual model for science was once based on the inductivist techniques of Francis Bacon. Bacon put forward what still seems to be the common sense view that science was a matter of careful, prolonged and dispassionate observation. Once enough cases had been studied, he maintained, it was possible to generalise a conclusion which would have the force of scientific authority. Bacon's approach still informs a significant part of the research done in both the natural and the social sciences. Almost any piece of research which depends on field observation and which makes use of the hunches and memory of the researcher is Baconian in spirit. Baconian science is cumulative, and authority tends to be linked to the mastery of knowledge. To know a vast amount of detail, or to know details which no-one else has access to, or (as a third, lesser choice) to combine knowledge of different fields in an unusual way, these are the paths to respect in the Baconian world. Baconian science tends to be theoretically unreflective, and its feuds tend to be ferociously personal rather than detached and intellectual, perhaps because the source of each fact is remote and the main guarantee of truth is the reliability of the scientist who asserts it.[2]

· In both the natural and social sciences, the Baconian approach stands not only as a model of impressive rigour but also as a discredited and naive misunderstanding of the nature of knowledge. Karl Popper comprehensively demolished the philosophical underpinnings of Baconian science by demonstrating that the mere accumulation of data of itself proves nothing. He cited the celebrated mediaeval European philosophical proposition that if you see enough white swans you can eventually conclude by induction that all swans are white. Popper, however, visited Australia and there saw the black swans, which had also astounded early European explorers. Millions of white swans, he concluded, were not enough to make safe the proposition that all swans were white. What he proposed instead was that the scientific validity of a statement be judged by its capacity to resist refutation. In other words, a scientific statement gathers authority to the extent that scientists try and fail to

---

[2]See Max Charlesworth, *Science, non-science and pseudo-science: Bacon, Popper, Lakatos, Kuhn and Feyerabend on defining science* (Waurn Ponds, Vic.: Deakin University Press, 1982).

refute it.[3]

Powerful through it was, Popper's critique suffered from what is often said to be a shortcoming of history of science, namely that it did not reflect what scientists actually did. A vast number of facts were not constructed as falsifiable propositions at all but, rightly or wrongly, as statements of truth. Did this disqualify them as scientific? Moreover, Popper's critique begged the question of where falsifiable propositions came from if not from induction. In answer to these objections, Thomas Kuhn constructed the notion of scientific revolutions.[4] He maintained that the vast bulk of science – 'normal science' as he called it – involved the collection and explanation of facts within a theoretical paradigm. The paradigm acted as a largely unspoken theoretical framework for science, setting the terms and language of discourse. Normal science, then, was a process in which new Baconian 'facts' were systematically embedded within a paradigm (which of course also tended to dictate what facts were looked for). Kuhn was especially interested in how scientists coped with facts which appeared inconsistent with the paradigm. Contrary to Popper's proposition, they did not discard a theory in the face of a single contradictory fact. Rather, they would tinker with both theory and fact to make the two consistent. Kuhn gave as his example the elaborate system of complicated orbits which pre-Copernican astronomers used to incorporate their growing knowledge of the planets into the paradigm which placed the Earth at the centre of the universe. Kuhn's successors invoke some of the ingenious arguments advanced to incorporate all physiological and psychological features of all organisms into a single theory of evolution.

Kuhn maintained, however, that this process of incorporation eventually produced so many implausible formulations that it collapsed under its own intellectual weight in what he called a scientific revolution. The old paradigm was swept away and a new one, dramatically more powerful was put in its place. The Copernican, Darwinian and Einsteinian revolutions are the clearest and strongest examples of such revolutions.

Where, then, does the Asian Values debate stand in this scheme of

---

[3] See Karl R. Popper, *The logic of scientific discovery* (London: Hutchinson, 1972).

[4] Thomas S. Kuhn, *The structure of scientific revolutions* (Chicago: University of Chicago Press, 2nd ed., 1970).

scientific knowledge? It seems plausible to suggest that one reason for the vigour of the dispute and its apparent inability to reach a conclusion is that the different sides reflect not just honest but divergent understandings of the evidence but different philosophies of science.

The opponents of Asian values as an analytical tool are, at least in philosophical terms, supporters of a grand unified paradigm. They share the long-standing interest of many physicists in particular in unifying all knowledge of the world into a single comprehensive theory. As many of you will know, it is a source of considerable frustration to many physicists that there appear to be four fundamental physical forces at work in the cosmos. The physicists would be much happier with just one single force, and they put a great deal of effort into working out what it is.

In the social sciences, for much of the twentieth century Marxism had the most commanding claim to be a unified theory of everything. Its complex system of base and superstructure and of different historical stages gave it a powerful analytical force in uniting economics, politics, culture and society. It is notable that Marxism was rather unfriendly to the idea that cultural values might play a major role in determining the economic success of society. Yet, in the late twentieth century Marxism's claims to comprehensiveness were placed under strain by the willingness of some prominent Marxist theorists to concede the 'relative autonomy' of the state and to allow that economic determinism operated only 'in the last instance'. From the point of view of Kuhn's analysis, Marxism had become a paradigm struggling with evidently indigestible facts.

Marxism's intellectual opponents made something of a virtue of not offering a grand unified paradigm. Although they were willing to concede occasional links – in both directions – between culture and economics, they were willing for the most part to concede economics to economists, politics to political scientists, history to historians and so on. With the retreat of Marxism, however, aspirations for a grand unified paradigm have emerged with new force amongst economists with what I will call for the purposes of this paper, 'rational economism'. By rational economism I mean the philosophy whose basic unit is the individual who makes rational decisions in the light of his/her circumstances and the information then available. In this view, the rationality of decisions is driven by universal human characteristics, so that all human behaviour is explicable in the same terms. 'Culture' does exist for the proponents of rational economism, but it is not especially relevant to analysis, perhaps no more than the subjective beauty of a butterfly's wings is relevant to an analysis of display as part of a strategy for insect survival and reproduction.

19

By contrast, the proponents of cultural analysis are not offended by the lack of unified paradigm. Indeed, rather like the Baconians, they rejoice in an infinity of knowledge and they argue that culture is an appropriate tool of analysis in its own right. For some, the argument is that you don't need to know the physics of motion to ride a bicycle. Even though the physics of motion is knowable and in a sense basic to riding a bike, it is only one of the things which is worth investigating. The culturalists, in other words, apply a rather utilitarian criterion to their approach: Does it help to explain events? What the rational economists see as a distraction, therefore, the culturalists see as a part of the rich tapestry of scientific investigation. For other social scientists, this formulation is perhaps too close to suggesting that their research might be a form of art, perhaps comparable to angling, but even those social scientists can point to the field of fluid mechanics, in which a vast range of events are still technically unexplained and in which the basic analytical tools of physicists are neither derived from nor dependent on the 'fundamental' knowledge of particle physics.

If this analysis is correct, then the debate over the role of culture in politics and economics is not likely to conclude quickly. Regardless of the evidence which either side can bring to bear, the fundamental goals of their investigations are different, and a reconciliation is unlikely.

The second level of analysis which I suggested we should apply to the Asian Values debate is that of its social and political implications. This level of analysis is a sensitive one, because it generally implies at best bad judgement on the part of one side or the other. Let me leap in, therefore, and offer the positive and negative implications of the culturalist position and of its alternative.

On the one hand the culturalist position is a scientific affirmation of cultural diversity, and a legitimation of self-determination. The culturalist analysis is a friend of nations and of traditions. On the other hand, these characteristics mean that it also undermines the notion of universal human values. Of course to undermine or limit is not to reject, but the culturalists stand for a point of view which leads easily to legal discrimination between ethnic groups and to the application of different standards of human rights to different countries. Culturalism points towards a justification for slavery and colonialism, towards an acceptance of Pol Pot, for instance, as an acceptable manifestation of Cambodian culture.

And what of rational economism? On the positive side, it is an affirmation of human free will and of universal human values. Yet it seems to make the dubious judgement that 'we' of the West are without culture and that the values and norms which are presented as fundamental human values have no specific roots in Western culture. The rational economists also tend to reject cavalierly the importance of structures and constraints. In asserting human freedom, they tend to ignore the extent to which people are shackled in one way or another by their circumstances. If culturalism leads in the direction of slavery and colonialism, rational economism leads with equal energy in the direction of globalisation, the Multilateral Agreement on Investments (MAI) and utter subordination to global capital.

Of course, very few scholars on either side are interested in carrying their approach to the extremes I have outlined, but the possibility of those extremes makes the debate over culture all the sharper. It is easy to accuse one side of pandering to the interests of Asian dictators and the other side of being a tool of the imperialism of multi-national corporations.

At both levels I have discussed so far, my conclusion has been somewhat pessimistic: At one level there are fundamentally different understandings of the most appropriate form which knowledge can take, and at the other level each side tends to assume either nefarious motives of wilful naivete on the part of its opponents.

At the third level, however, I think that we can be more optimistic for two reasons. First, it is relatively rare for an academic debate in the social sciences to spill over into the broader public arena. For the most part, the process happens in reverse: Biting issues of concern to society are carried into the realm of social science, but the findings of social science have relatively little impact on the debate. A characteristic example is the debate in Europe and America over punishment. Sociological investigation of the consequences of different styles of punishment has, it seems, only a marginal impact on the public debate. In the Asian Values controversy, on the other hand, expert analysis by academics is a central part of the debate, along with the contribution of politicians and philosophers. Whatever our position on the issues involved, we are likely to be unhappy with some of the conclusions which result from such debate, but we should applaud the fact that debate is taking place in this way.

Second, we should recognise in the current form of the Asian Values debate, specifically the Huntingtonian 'Clash of Civilisations' idea[5], a commonly found element in academic which, for want of a more scientific-sounding term, I will call a Good Idea. Good Ideas are propositions which say something novel, insightful and incisive about some aspect of human existence. They are typically couched in a way that lets people read a lot or a little into them, and for this reason alone they tends to generate first excitement and expectation, then controversy and scepticism. As the controversy matures, it spawns workshops and books, but the Good Idea characteristically shrinks in importance rather rapidly (at least if one compares it with real theorising). It can be useful to think of the Good Idea as having a 'half-life', like radioactive material, denoting the period during which the Good Idea becomes half as useful and half as frequently cited as it did at its people. The reason for this decay in utility, as opposed to radioactivity, is that analytical propositions need empirical information to feed upon, and Good Ideas tend only to feed on existing knowledge, rather than suggesting effective lines for new research.

Our work is clear. We are part of the process which determines what the half-life of the Asian Values idea will be. We contribute to this process by close examination of the idea as it applies to the concrete problems of Vietnam's development.

---

[5] Samuel P. Huntington, *The Clash of Civilizations and the Remaking of World Order* (New York: Simon & Schuster, 1996).

Vietnam vis-a-vis Asian and European values

Vu Khieu
National Centre for Social Sciences and Humanities

Today, we discuss an issue that has been paid much attention to in Vietnam as well as all over the world. It is values. Are there differences in relation to this issue, first of all the difference between the Asian and European values, and the difference between the two cultures, life styles and ways to evaluate the problems?

Is it true that the time has passed when Europeans considered the Occidental values a symbol of the highest civilisation of mankind and a goal for all nations? Is it true that the Asian countries, in their turn, got rid of the European values and only affirmed the good qualities of the Asian values after they broke the colonialist domination? Is it true that Asian values have replaced European values and really met the new demands of Asia and mankind on the road of development? Quite a number of people think that the "Asian dragon" countries developed rapidly over the last decades thanks to their Asian values. If this is true, how can we explain the long-standing stagnation of other countries with Asian values in their histories spanning thousands of years? And how to explain the defeat of the countries with Asian values under the aggression and cruel domination of the countries with European values?

If Asian values played a great role in the development of many Asian countries over the last decades, do they bear any responsibility for the financial crisis which took place in these countries recently? We think that each nation has its own typical characteristics, in terms of geography and history, social and economic organisations, which create distinctive habits, customs, psychology and ways of life. In short, each nation has its own values which have been preserved and developed through their historical stages.

However the development of each nation must be looked at together with its relations with other nations, especially those in the region. Luckily, Vietnam is a country having a multi-cultural mixture, first of all, the mixture between the

East Asian and Southeast Asian cultures, then the Indian and Chinese cultures; the Asian and European cultures in modern times; and recently the socialist and capitalist cultures.

Vietnamese culture has developed unceasingly and created its long-lasting national values by virtue of its correct attitude, bringing into full play its own values, at the same time receiving the good values of other countries. Vietnam is situated in Asia and has quite a number of similarities with other Asian countries, in terms of the geographical conditions, the socio-economic circumstances, the characters of morality and religious belief. If the Asian countries have typical Asian values, then of course, Vietnam also has them. Nevertheless, it is not appropriate to say that these values have affected the movement and development of Vietnamese society.

In its long-standing history, the Vietnamese nation has tried to learn and acquire many material and spiritual values of other countries. But it must be said that the values acquired from outside, including the so-called Asian values, have been Vietnamised throughout its history of thousands of years, i.e. they have been selected to become Vietnamese values, suitable to the Vietnamese social and economic situations and the sentiment, ambition and principles of life of the Vietnamese people.

Buddhism and Confucianism, the religious and ideological source of high Asian values, entered Vietnam in the first centuries of the millennium. In the hard time under foreign domination, Vietnam adopted Buddhism more easily than Confucianism. The Confucian followers at that time were trained to serve the State of the invaders, while those who disseminated Buddhism lived closely with the people, preaching to them the Buddhist idea of benevolence.

However, it must be said that the compassionate love among the people in Vietnam was not created by Buddhism, but first of all, it was a moral requirement and a condition for the people to survive from the harsh challenges of the natural disasters and the enemy's destruction. It is impossible to say simply that Buddhism brought benevolence to the Vietnamese people. It is only possible to say that Vietnamese people's benevolence has been enhanced by the Buddhist dogmas. It was the available national tradition that integrated easily with the Buddhist doctrins, creating an active humanism, full of Vietnamese identity, a long-lasting factor in the Vietnamese outlook.

Buddhism itself, when doing away with its limits, entered into the real world from an unreal life, changing from being submissive and passive to the enemy to becoming combative and ready to sacrifice itself for the country. The heroic kings of the nation and those leaders who lead the people in the struggle against the aggressors are symbolic of the spirit of Buddhism in Vietnam, a Buddhism with Vietnamese values.

Confucianism is a moral and social doctrine which has had a deep and wide impact on many Asian countries, but in Vietnam it developed only in the Ly and Tran dynasties and since Vietnam regained national sovereignty (11th century). The Vietnamese authorities actively received Confucius' doctrine and considered it the superstructure of Vietnam and a Vietnamized type of Confucianism. Through one thousand years, the Vietnamese people's lifestyle was consolidated by numerous Confucian viewpoints, which contributed to maintaining their national independence, sovereignty and territory, retaining morality and culture in the families and villages, and reminding the people of their responsibilities for the fatherland and compatriots.

President Ho Chi Minh remarked: "*Confucius' doctrine has a good point, i.e. the nurture of individual morality.*" He knew well that Confucian ideas constituted great strength in the cultural life of some Asian countries. However, he also said: "*Confucianism is only suitable to a stable and unchanged society.*"

This stable and unchanged society, a society of the Asian mode of production and Oriental culture, faced its greatest-ever challenges in history, i.e. the aggression of the imperialist Western countries. Soon aware of the danger of the time, Japan under the rule of Emperor Minh Tri quickly adopted the good points of Occidental culture in the fields of industry, science and technique, with which it created its own economic and military strength.

During this time, Vietnam, China and Korea, with a pride in their Asian values, became extremely conservative, continuing to believe blindly in the endless strength of the sages and saints, and consider the Oriental culture a justice, Confucianism an eternality, and Confucius, a teacher of uncountable generations. The above mentioned countries considered European countries "brutal white demons", which only relied on weapons and machines, and were examples of a terrible and dishonoured culture. Lulling themselves into a conservative atmosphere of Asian values, these countries, in turn, fell into the enslaved position of colonial and semi-colonial countries. They could not have liberated themselves if they had kept their so-called Asian values, without acquiring the advanced achievements of mankind, including the values called European values.

In Vietnam, the value which is considered the highest and most long-lasting value, which affected people's thought, sentiment and actions for thousands of years, is independence and freedom. When President Ho Chi Minh said: *"Nothing is more precious than independence and freedom"*, this is the value that we constantly fight to obtain, and is the long-standing desire of the whole nation, the first condition in the human right to live and the strength and honour of Vietnam.

We know that for Europe, freedom is the highest value and that you had to sacrifice much blood and sweat to obtain and retain it. In Enlightenment Period, the struggle for freedom was linked closely to the humane idea of freedom, equality and fraternity, and subsequently with the declaration of independence of the United States of America and the declaration of human rights and civil rights of the French Revolution.

These above-mentioned matters have really encouraged Vietnam, inspiring us in our long struggle for independence and freedom. But for us, freedom must be put behind independence, which is considered a priority. President Ho Chi Minh, the soul of the Vietnamese revolution, devoted all his life to freedom, which he considered the goal of his life. No brutal force could conquer his will for freedom. All the Vietnamese remember his immortal verses:

There is untold bitterness in life

Nothing is more bitter than the loss of independence

Perhaps the European people do not understand so well the bitterness of the loss of freedom which an independent nation suffers.

Vietnam carried out a thousand-year struggle against the domination of foreign aggressors, then a thousand-year struggle to defend their national independence, and sacrifice their blood and sweat to fight against the French colonialists, the Japanese fascists and the US imperialists. We carried out these struggles not just for human rights but, first of all, the peoples' right to live in an independent country. That is why, for us, independence is the highest value and the first condition of all the other values of the people.

But does Vietnam only consider independence a value, paying no attention to other specific values of the people? No. We strive for the freedom and happiness of those who live in independence, so that they can master their country, develop their intellect and talent, and live in peace and friendship with the whole of mankind. But all these values and rights of the people can only be acquired when their country is free from political and economic oppression and ideological enslavement of other countries.

In Vietnamese history, each time the foreign aggressors were swept away, our State focused on caring for the people's life, giving them the human's minimum values, both material and spiritual. The State organised the building of dikes to prevent floods, ensuring the people a stable life, free from want and care. The State also helped the people develop good habits and customs as well as a passionate love among them, organised special classes for the people to learn, from the central to local levels. Independence is not the last goal, but a prerequisite to build a free and happy life for the people. President Ho Chi Minh once said that if independence did not bring freedom and happiness to the people, it was meaningless. This is the very reason why Vietnam, on the basis of independence, strives for the good values that each nation and the whole of mankind tries to obtain.

In line with tradition, Vietnamese people always put the interests of the society above those of the family and of themselves. The rights of each individual are respected on condition that they are not opposite to those of the family, village and country. If an individual is ready to sacrifice himself for the country, it does not mean that he is forced to do so; rather, he volunteers, considering it a right to devote his life to the fatherland and people.

In turn, the State and society must always pay attention to the personal life of the people, compensating the losses that they have suffered while serving the country, society and people. With this spirit, we do not accept those individual interests, which are opposite to the social interests. We always consider that correct relationships between society and the individual a good value in the Vietnamese tradition.

Vietnamese people do not accept that there is an absolute opposition between Asian and European values. We stand firmly on our land to preserve the national identity while receiving the values of mankind, including both Asia and Europe. It is lucky that our nation had Ho Chi Minh, an initiator and leader of the Vietnamese revolution, a man with a serious attitude to national and human values, to the so-called Asian and European values. If he had not acquired the Vietnamese values in Vietnamese historical and cultural circumstances, he would not have selectively received the values that mankind has acquired. If he had not spent 36 years going to all continents to find a way to save his country, nor acquired the values of Europe and humanity, the

Vietnamese revolution would not have been successful and there could not be the country like that of Vietnam of today.

Following are President Ho Chi Minh's words, symbolic of the Vietnamese spirit in the relationship between a nation and people, between Asia and Europe:

Confucius' doctrine has a good point, i.e. the nurture of individual morality. Christian religion has a good point, i.e. a noble benevolence. Marx's doctrine has a good point, i.e. a dialectical working method. Sun Yi Xian's doctrine has a good point, i.e. its policy is suitable to our country's condition. I try to be a little pupil of all these above-mentioned men...

With Vietnamese and Asian values, President Ho Chi Minh acquired the good points of Confucius' doctrine, i.e. the individual moral upbringing. But this upbringing was not enough to fight against the colonialist domination. He left Asia to make a study of European values. He overcame the Asian prejudices and affirmed the good point of Christian religion, i.e. noble benevolence. But this benevolence was not strong enough to help mankind escape from the sufferings caused by oppression and exploitation. He studied Marxism and received its good point, i.e. a dialectical working method. However, he received Marxism, not with a dogmatic attitude, but with a creative spirit. Right from 1924, he considered Marxism a doctrine formed on the basis of an Occidental society and tradition, and he affirmed that it should be supplemented with Oriental knowledge.

Returning to the Orient he saw that Sun Yi Xian's doctrine had a good point, i.e. its policy was suitable to the Vietnamese conditions, but he did not imitate his policy and experiences because there were differences between the Vietnamese and Chinese situations. President Ho Chi Minh's success lay in the fact that he knew how to combine national values with universal values to create new values suitable to the Vietnamese development in modern times. Vis-à-vis Asian and European values, the Vietnamese people forever remember Ho Chi Minh's immortal words: *"Vietnamese culture is a blend of Oriental and Occidental cultures. Whatever good the Orient or Occident has, we should learn from it to create a Vietnamese culture."*

An Analytical Model for Understanding the Complexity of Intercultural Communication in Cross-Cultural Management

Hans Gullestrup
Center of International Studies, Aalborg University

I. INTRODUCTION AND THE CONCEPT OF CULTURE

When talking about "intercultural communication" and "cross-cultural management" we more or less have to accept that culture does exist at least as an abstract concept or as an abstract "unit".

By treating culture as a unit, one can analyse and try to understand it and, by seeing culture as a unit with some kind of vague or undefined borderlines, one can begin to understand what separates one culture from another. These cultural borderlines - which might move from time to time and from situation to situation - can, however, be crossed for various reasons, such as in connection with all kinds of intercultural co-operation, international tourism, cross-cultural management etc. And intercultural communication - of course - is important in all these situations.

One of my basis statements for this paper, therefore, is that it is meaningful - from an abstract as well as from an empirical point of view - to consider "culture" as a continuously changeable unit, which contents can be analysed and compared with the contents of other cultures.

My understanding of culture will be covered by the following definition:

Culture is the philosophy of life, the values, norms and rules, and actual behaviour - as well as the material and immaterial products from these - which is taken over by man from the past generations, and which man wants to bring forward to the next generation - eventually in a different form - and which in one way or another separates individuals belonging to the culture from

29

individuals belonging to other cultures.

By basing this paper - as well as my ongoing research on culture and cross-cultural management - on this statement and the presented definition of culture, I first of all decline to be placed as a member of *one* specific scientific school, as I consider the study of culture as far too complex to be studied only from the viewpoint of *one* specific, scientific school, or to be based on *one* specific paradigm. I *believe* that one can base his or her work on different paradigms and different understanding of culture in different situations and for different purposes.

By focussing on the dynamics of culture and by focussing on the basic philosophy of life, the values and norms - "which is taken over by man from the past generations, and which man wants to bring forward to the next generation - eventually in a different form" - I find myself in company with Clifford Geertz, when he defines culture as: "A historically transmitted pattern of meanings.[1] And when I add to the basic philosophy of life, the values and norms: "Rules and actual behaviour, as well as the material and immaterial products from these", I also find myself in company with Geertz and the following part of his definition: "Embodied in symbols, a system of inherited conceptions expressed in symbolic forms by means of which man communicate, perpetuate, and develop their knowledge about and attitudes toward life" (p. 89). A point that I shall come back to in a little while, is that I consider the basic philosophy of life and values as being the core of any culture. However, I also consider the manifestation of this core culture - in expressed meanings, in behaviour, in structures and in material and immaterial products, or as one might say: The symptoms or symbols of the core culture - as more or less equal important parts of the culture. They are important

1. Partly because the manifest components of the culture is an important part of the conscious elements of life for people belonging to a particular culture. That is, what we see, touch, hear, etc.

2. Partly because the manifest components of the culture is that part of the culture in which we first of all register equalities and/or differences between various cultures (how we eat, work, speak, etc.).

3. Partly - but not insignificant - because we only have the manifest culture

---

[1] Clifford Gertz, *The Interpretation of Culture* (London: Basic Books, 1973), p. 89.

as a kind of gate to the understanding of other people's core culture - or even to the understanding of our own core culture.

To me, therefore, culture consists both of "shared meanings" as they conceptualise themselves in basic philosophy of life and values among a group of people, and of the way in which these shared meanings visualise or manifest themselves in people's social interactions and the results of that.

However, I also find myself linked to a phenomenological tradition, as I fully accept the fact that one can only understand other cultures through ones own culture - through ones own cultural foundation or ones own cultural glasses; and that one's own cultural foundation will be influenced by interaction with people from other cultures in the same way as their cultural foundations are influenced by their interaction with me.

Finally, I also feel myself in family with a functionalistic understanding of culture, as I also see culture as a particular group of people's consideration or unconscious attempt to find a way - maybe just one way among different other ways - to meet their social and physical needs as a group of individuals, or as an organisation - or even as a nation - under certain environmental conditions, which to a certain degree are given for the individuals at a certain time. We see this from many anthropological studies (e.g.: studies of the Samoan people in Oceania and of the Inuit people in the Arctic) as well as from many studies of organisational cultures in different social and physical environments.

My definition of culture is a general definition, which might be accepted for various social units, and in different situations - and, therefore, also when we are studying cross-cultural management as well as intercultural communication in Vietnam and between Vietnamese and people from other parts of the World.

I see many different places or areas, in which cross-cultural management takes place, and in which cross-cultural or intercultural communication plays a big role:

a. Management of organisations in other countries with different cultures from that of ones own, e.g. Danish companies operating in Vietnam, South Africa or elsewhere.

b. Management of organisations, employing people from different cultures, e.g. Transnational Corporations (TNCs), IBM, Maersk Line, Shell, Volvo etc.

c. Management of international organisations, e.g. UN, EU, WHO etc.

31

In order to understand cross-cultural management and intercultural communication both as abstract concepts and as empirical phenomena, we need to create theories and analytical models enabling us:

1. To perceive and understand important elements of culture as well as the interrelations between them.

2. To perceive and understand the complexity of cultural as well as of the complexity of cross-cultural studies.

II. IMPORTANT ELEMENTS OF CULTURE

Regarding the problem of how to know which of the many observations - or elements - of a particular culture we have to consider as the most important ones to be studied more deeply, we have to accept that this is not to be decided once and for all, as that is a function not only of

1. The culture in focus for the study

2. The aim of the study

3. The cultural foundation of the researcher or the actor

4. The research methods and techniques to be used

We need, therefore, to reflect a little more on each of these four factors.

With regard to the first, in connection with empirical studies, it might create difficulties just to delimit and define the culture we want to study. For example, how do we define "Danish Culture"? Is Danish Culture the same as the culture for all people living in Denmark? Or only the culture of people born in Denmark, whether they are still living in Denmark or elsewhere? Does Danish Culture include all people living in the Kingdom of Denmark, including those in Greenland and the Faeroe Islands? And what about the people living north and south of the borderline between Germany and Denmark?

As for the second factor, what is the actual purpose of the study? Do we only wish "to understand" the other culture in order to know more about the people? Or do we wish to know them better in order to try to change parts of their culture in such a way that they:

a. Might wish to buy our products?

b. Might fit better into our organisations?

c. Fit better into our way of living like we often want the immigrants to do? And so on.

32

Regarding the third factor, by being aware of the influences of the cultural actor himself, I am *not* only thinking on the influences of the national culture of the actor (as earlier European studies of African cultures in last century were very much influenced by the general, European view on Africans) but also on the actor's scientific paradigm, and his professional background etc. (However, I will look more into that problem later on).

And finally, regarding the fourth factor, by mentioning the influences of the many different research methods and techniques (like interviews, observation, reading of existing reports, etc.), I am thinking on the very fact that each method and each technique focuses more specifically on some elements of the culture and less on others. This then gives alternative pictures of the culture in focus.

This understanding of mine that all cultural studies are unique studies, depending on the contents of such factors as the four just mentioned, leads me to the conclusion that no cultural - or cross-cultural study - can claim to be *the* study. And that no cultural study can claim to show how this or that culture has to be seen and understood - as an objective factum! We have to conclude that each cultural study - and each cross-cultural study - has to be considered as only one study among others, and that the results of each study has to be seen as a function of the four factors just mentioned above, in addition - perhaps - with a fifth factor: The resources available for the study.

This factor might determine some way that the culture is studied and exclude others. For individuals - whether they are researchers or practical managers - who have to use cultural studies made by other people - what many of us have to do many times in our lifetime - it is advisable, then, to:

a. Try to know as much as possibly of the background of such studies (factors 1-5)

b. Try to read as many different studies - or to talk with as many different persons with different knowledge about the culture - as possible, these based on as many different paradigms or research schools as possible.

The various studies might be very different, but there might also be some kind of overlapping between the various studies, which might lead to some kind equality and cultural understanding at a higher level.

So much about my first claim to theories and models for cultural and cross-cultural studies, now a few comments to the second claim: To perceive and understand the complexity of cultural studies as well as the complexity of cross-

33

cultural studies.

III. THE COMPLEXITY OF CROSS-CULTURAL STUDIES

The complexity of cross-cultural studies - as well as of cultural studies as such - are especially related to the following observations or "facts":

1. *The relativity of each culture.* (The cultural hierarchy, e.g. Danish, Scandinavian, or European culture).

2. *The co-incidence of the cultures.* (The cultural categories).

3. *The changeability of each culture.* (The cultural dynamic).

4. *The ethical problems related to cross-cultural studies.* (What can we allow ourselves to do in other cultures?)

For these reasons I strongly believe that we need theoretical and analytical models for cultural and cross-cultural studies formulated as frame models - or as a kind of skeleton - where each researcher (or cultural actor) can relate their own data, observations and experiences to each other, in trying to create an understanding of a particular cross-cultural situation, according to his or her needs and the contents of the four factors mentioned above. My presentation of such an analytical frame for cross-cultural studies will begin with a discussion of the first two of the four "facts" in the complexity of cross-cultural studies: *The relativity of the cultures and the co-incidence of the cultures.*

After that I will present an analytical frame for how one might study and understand *a* culture as an abstract unit at a given point of time - a static model consisting of two cultural dimensions:

a. The *horizontal* cultural dimension.

b. The *vertical* cultural dimension.

After that I will turn to the third of the four "facts" in the complexity of cross-cultural studies: *The changeability of each culture.* In doing so I will turn the static model of culture into a dynamic model of culture by introducing the third cultural dimension into the model: *The dynamic cultural dimension.*

Finally I will put these three "cultural dimensions" and the "complexity facts" together into an analytical frame for cross-cultural studies. Unfortunately, The fourth of the four "facts' - *The ethical problems related to cross-cultural studies*, has to be left out of this paper because of space limitations.

34

The relativity and co-incidence of culture

The definition of what should be considered as *a culture* is very relative, as individuals consider themselves as part of - or member of - different cultures in different situations, (or they are considered - by others - as being members of different cultures depending of the situation and the character of their intercultural relations). This situation is due to two different - but interrelated - aspects of the complexity of cross-cultural relations:

1. *The relativity of the cultures.*

2. *The co-incidence of the cultures.*

The relativity of the cultures

Within that category of culture which we might call "National culture" or "Macro-culture" (like the Geert Hofstede –concept of "culture" when talking about Danish, Swedish or Vietnamese cultures) both the individuals themselves and others might consider them as being representatives of different layers of culture within the category of "macro culture" (for instance, me – the author seen as a Dane, as a Scandinavian, or just as a European - or even as a "Northern Jutlander").

This can be illustrated (Fig. 1). In this way we can talk about a cultural hierarchy within a specific category of culture consisting of different layers of culture (John Kuada and Hans Gullestrup, 1998).

By category of culture I mean:

A set of interrelated units of culture which, at a general (or higher) level of aggregation, can be meaningfully described, analysed and understood as one distinct cultural unit, which can then be broken down into its component units (cultural dimensions) for a more detailed analysis for specific purposes.

By layers of culture I understand:

A number of units of culture within a given cultural category, which together can be meaningfully described as a distinct cultural unit at a higher level of aggregation; this unit forms - together with other units at the same level of aggregation - another cultural unit at a still higher level of aggregation within the same cultural category, etc.

In this way - theoretically as well as empirically - we have to count with a hierarchy of different layers within a certain category of culture. And we never know if the involved people in a cross-cultural relation consider each other to be on the same layer in the hierarchy.

Figure 1.

Analytical Framework for Understanding Philippine Values

Orientation	Asian Ethic	Asian Manifestation	Western Ethic or Input	Western Manifestation
Philosophical orientation	Pessimism	Affectivity (Bahalana)	Optimism	Affective Neutrality
	Ascription	Rigid class structure	Achievement	Upward/downward mobility
	Superstition	Religiosity	Scientific	Secularism
	Leisure	Suwerte	Hard work	Just reward
Sociology		Uran na loob	Utang na loob	
	Loyalty	Blow-out (Balaro)	Cash employment	Geographic mobility
	Obedience	Diffuse relationships	Increased urbanization	Special relationships
		Pakikisama		Individualism
Psychological/ Social-Psychological orientation	Humility	Amor propio	Western education	Worth of individual
	Harmony	Hospitality	Use of English Western example	Western prejudice Self-determinism
	Modesty	Hiya	Media	Non-conformity

The co-incidence of the cultures

The complexity of cross-cultural relations is also caused by the fact that people are not only to be considered as members - or part - of *one* category of culture, but of many different cultural categories at the same time (Fig. 2).

This means that even though we want to analyse differences in macro/national cultures - like Hofstede's studies - we also have to recognise the fact, that people at the same time are reflecting other cultural categories than the macro/national culture - each of them with their own hierarchy of cultural layers.

When understanding culture - as well as cross-cultural relations and management - in this way, one might expect that individuals (or groups of individuals) have to be understood as belonging to a number of potential cultures in a number of different hierarchies within different categories of culture. Which culture of the many cultures one might expect to be the most important one for understanding the people involved in the actual cross-cultural relations, will - of course - depend on the actual situation, and might change rather rapidly.

However, the intercultural actor - or manager - will have to predict which of the actual cultural categories, and which layers in the relevant hierarchy he has to estimate as being the potentially relevant culture(s) - and which cultures he might try to understand according to this estimations.

Each of these potential and/or relevant cultures then has to be analysed as an empirical unit in accordance with the analytical, theoretical cultural frame model - or some other models.

Cultural dimensions

As mentioned before, a particular culture might be described and understood at a given time by way of two cultural dimensions: The horizontal cultural dimension and the vertical cultural dimension.

The horizontal cultural dimension

Common to all living beings is the fact that their survival as individuals or as a species depends on the relationship between their own fundamental biological needs (the need for food, the need for protection against the climate, and the need for a possibility to bring up new generations, etc.) and the opportunities offered to them by the natural and social environment surrounding them.

If more than one human being is present at the same time in nature, man will try to fulfil his or her fundamental needs in a kind of *joint action*, which may be characterised by social cooperation and solidarity or by some kind of oppression and exploitation. Even though the natural conditions are the same, the actual ways of fulfilling the fundamental needs and the actual ways in which the joint action is organised may thus vary considerably over time and space, from one group of people to another - or from one culture to another. So one might be able to observe differences and variations in the way in which the individual cultures try to fulfil their fundamental human needs.

At the same time, however, it will also be possible to observe a certain pattern in the tasks or functions that make up the central parts - or the central *cultural segments* - in this human joint action. In this connection it is meaningful to operate with eight such cultural segments which will all be manifested in any culture, but which may individually and in relation to each other manifest themselves in very different ways.

The eight cultural segments mentioned below jointly make up what I call the horizontal dimension of culture - horizontal, because the eight cultural segments are manifested at the same level, and because they are all of equal importance to the cultural understanding:

1. How nature is processed (technology).

2. How the output is distributed (economic institutions).

3. How the individuals live together (social institutions).

4. Who controls whom (political institutions).

5. How knowledge, ideas and values are disseminated among individuals and groups (language and communication in the widest sense).

6. How the individuals and the unity are integrated, kept up and developed (reproduction and socialisation).

7. How a common identity is created and preserved (ideology).

8. How the view of the relationship between life and death is manifested (religious institutions).

The individual segments may be manifested in numerous ways and be combined in different ways. As an example, nature may be processed via fishing, agriculture or heavy industry based on the culture's own raw materials, and the output of such processing may be distributed via free market forces, or via some kind of planned economy as in the former Soviet Union, by market intervention as in the case of the present common agricultural policy of the EU;

or via cultural traditions. In principle, the individual segments may manifest themselves independently of each other and of nature, but in practise it is a fact that in the same way as a given nature offers certain opportunities and sets certain limitations for the processing of nature - e.g., it is not possible to set up farming in Greenland, nor is it possible to extract iron ore in the islands of Polynesia - then in the same way the actual manifestation of the individual cultural segments will offer certain opportunities and set up certain limits for the manifestation of the other segments of the culture.

The vertical cultural dimension

When meeting a foreign culture, some immediately sensed impressions will push more to the front than others, and thereby create a kind of initial picture of the culture observed. Actual behaviour, clothing and various kinds of existing products will form the basis of such first-hand pictures. Soon after, however, the underlying norms of morality and social structures, more difficult to observe, will stand out and in many ways introduce variation in the initial picture of the culture.

For these reasons, not every observation is as decisive as others for the understanding of the culture. Some, especially the immediately "visible" cultural traits, may only be an expression of - or symbol or symptom - of the more fundamental cultural traits such as attitudes and values, at the same time as they may have (and usually do have) importance for the cultural understanding in themselves. It is therefore meaningful to talk about a hierarchy of observations - a vertical cultural dimension - in which a deeper penetration from the "immediately observable symbols" to the "fundamental legitimating values" and the "fundamental philosophy of life" will create a continuously deeper insight into the culture observed.

It has been meaningful for me to work with six different levels of culture, even though I do realise that this stratification is based on an assessment. Three of these levels belong to the visible part of the culture - *the manifest culture* - whereas the other three levels represent the more hidden but also more fundamental *core culture*. The six levels of culture can be characterised in the following way:

1. The level of immediately observable symbols or symptoms.

2. The structures that are difficult to observe.

3. The governing morals, patterns and norms.

4. The partially legitimating values.

5. The general accepted highest values.

6. The fundamental philosophy of life.

As already mentioned, human behaviour and its material output are important elements within the level of *immediately observable symbols*. However, this behaviour is only rarely coincidental. It is rather based on more or less fixed patterns within the *structures* that are difficult to observe. The individuals within the culture behave differently in a certain way towards other individuals according to the age and status within society of these individuals, etc., just as they follow certain rules and laws to a certain extent, if for no other reason then to avoid sanctions from others. In this way certain connections and systems are created which somehow form a skeleton of the culture observed. These *patterns and norms* whose structures and contents vary from one culture to another are very central to the understanding of a given culture. Even if they cannot be seen or heard, the knowledge of their existence and contents may be inferred from an empirical analysis, and together with the other two cultural levels mentioned above they make up the *manifest part of the culture*.

Among the *partially legitimating values*, are these values that comprise only part of the culture (such as general values concerning competition and trade); in contrast the *general accepted highest values* comprise values that are valid for the entire culture. An example could be individual versus community rights. The *fundamental philosophy of life* says something about man's view on other human beings; about man's relation to nature; about man's attitude towards life and death and about the relations to the past, present and future. The three last-mentioned levels make up the *core culture*.

By means of the horizontal and the vertical cultural dimensions - or rather by trying to describe and understand the individual segments and levels of the two cultural dimensions - the actor or manager will be able to obtain a *static snapshot* of a given culture at a given time. What information and data should be included in such an analysis, and which segments and levels might be relevant will depend both on the object of the actual cultural analysis and of the resources that are available as mentioned above.

Thus, the static cultural model introduced here is an abstract cultural model which - as already mentioned - needs to be made more concrete in connection with a concrete analysis and empirical field of analysis. As examples of such studies, the models have formed the basis of a comparative analysis of management theories developed in the West and management cultures in Ghana and Kenya (Kuada, 1995), of Danish playground technology and the differences between French, German and Dutch child culture (Gram, 1995 and 1999)(See Fig. 3).

The dynamics or changeability of culture

However, a culture is not static. Quite the contrary, actually. It is constantly subjected to pressure for change from both external and internal factors - from what I will refer to as *initiating factors of change*. The reason why they are called "initiating" factors of change is that they may well push and press for changes in the culture, but they do not in the same way determine whether or not a change will actually take place in the culture observed. Whether a change does happen, and the direction in which such a change is going to take, will be determined by another set of factors, the *determining factors of change*.

Among the *external*, initiating factors of change in a culture are both changes in natural conditions and conditions in other cultures. The mere fact that nature constantly changes with or without the interference of man means that the joint action of man whose explicit object is to make it possible for a group of people to exist under certain given natural conditions is also subjected to a pressure for change. Thus, any culture is in a kind of double relationship towards nature. On the one hand nature forms the framework, to which the culture - i.e. the total complex of cultural segments and levels developed by a group of people over time - will have to adapt to; and on the other hand, this culture at the same time - for better or worse - is involved in changing the very same nature. Research, technological development and trade and industry also play decisive roles in this double relationship, and the same applies to their relationship with other cultures from which new input within the three areas may have a very change initiating effect on the culture observed.

The *internal* initiating factors of change are - as the term signifies - initiating factors which have developed within the culture observed. All kinds of internal research, technological development, trade and industry as such, are internal, initiating factors of change.

Factors *determining* change decide whether an action for change will actually lead to a change in the culture observed. Decisive factors in this understanding will be the *degree of integration* - applying to the existing values

- and the *degree of homogeneity* of the culture in question, but also the existing *power structure within the culture* plays a part. The degree of integration is an expression of the degree of conformity between the different values within the culture, whereas the degree of homogeneity is an expression of the width and depth of the total knowledge and insight of the culture observed.

In a strongly integrated culture, almost everybody agrees on the value of, e.g. "technological development at all cost", about the "prioritisation of *economic gain* over *resource gain*" and about the "individual's right to consume and the freedom of the individual in general". Or - conversely - about the "individual's responsibility towards or dependence on the group or the 'whole'", whether this 'whole' is based on a strong religion, a strong family or on fixed organisational relations. Usually, modern industrial cultures are very integrated around liberal freedom values, about economic values and about individualistic freedom values.

By synthesising the three cultural dimensions - the horizontal, vertical, and dynamic cultural dimensions - into a kind of dynamic whole, we get a picture of a part of the "cultural reality" (as shown in Fig. 4). And by synthesising the three cultural dimensions and the cultural categories and hierarchies we get a picture of a more complex, cultural reality, of which trade and industry form part, and - at the same time - are contributing to changes in the cultures. But we will also achieve a picture of the cultural reality, which - indirectly and for better or worse - governs the very same trade and industry and the development of the societies as such (Fig.5).

Conclusion

The aim of this paper has been to present an analytical model for understanding the complexity of cross-cultural relations theoretically as well as in the "real world" in very few pages. It has been stated many times that each cross-cultural relation is not only a *complex* situation, it is also a *unique* situation, which has to be understood individually in each case. Consequently the presented model is more like a kind of a "frame model" acting as a skeleton, which has to be completed by specific data and information for each specific study. The model has been used for studying intercultural relations between many different cultures in the past, and I do hope that it might contribute just a little for a better understanding of the various intercultural possibilities of Vietnam's development in the future.

LITERATURE

1. Geertz, Clifford, The Interpretation of Culture (London: Basic books, 1973).

2. Gram, Malene, Grounds to Play - Culture-specific Ideals in the Upbringing of Children in France, Germany and the Netherlands (Aalborg: Aalborg University, 1999).

3. Gullestrup, Hans, *Kultur, Kulturanalyse og kulturetik - eller hvad adskiller og forener os?* [Culture, Cultural Analyse and Cultural Ethics] (Copenhagen: Academic Press,1992).

4. Hofstede, Geert, Cultures and Organizations - Software of the Mind (London: McGraw-Hill, 1980).

5. Kuada, John, Managerial Behaviour in Ghana and Kenya - A Cultural Perspective (Aalborg: Aalborg University Press, 1994).

6. Kuada, John and Hans Gullestrup, "Cultural Categories and Profiles: A Framework for Studying Individuals' Behaviour in Organizations", in: Lauristin and Rahnu, *Intercultural Communication and Changing National Identities* (Tartu, Estonia: Tartu University Press, 1999).

7. Kuada, John and Hans Gullestrup, "The Cultural Context of Corporate Governance, Performance, Pressures and Accountability", in: Istemi Demiraq: *Corporate Governance, Accountability, and Pressures to Perform an International Study* (London: JAI-Press, 1998).

Figure 2

Culture hierarchy

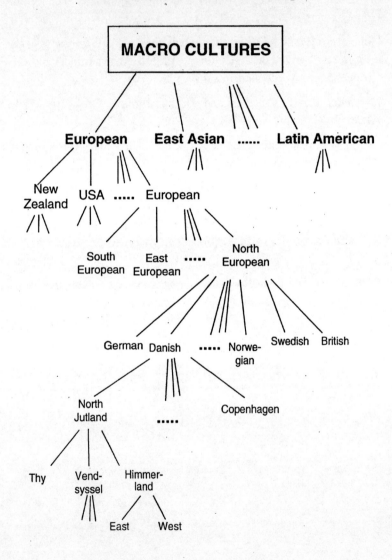

Figure 3

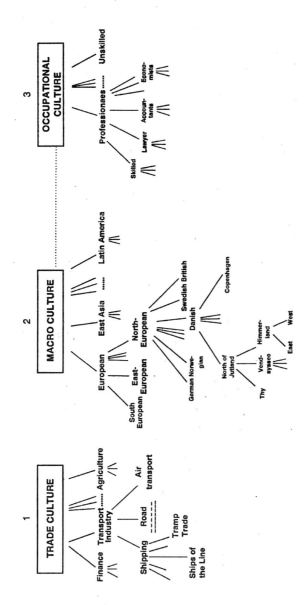

Figure 4

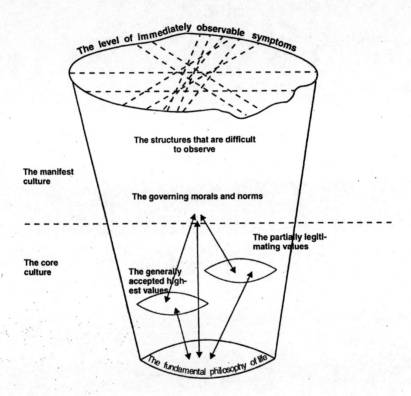

The level of immediately observable symptoms

The structures that are difficult
to observe

The manifest
culture

The governing morals and norms

The partially legiti-
mating values

The core
culture

The generally
accepted high-
est values

The fundamental philosophy of life

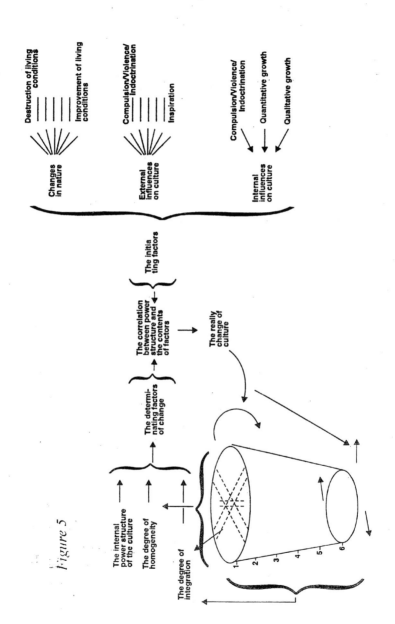

Figure 5

Changes in nature
- Destruction of living conditions
- Improvement of living conditions

External influences on culture
- Compulsion/Violence/Indoctrination
- Inspiration

Internal influences on culture
- Compulsion/Violence/Indoctrination
- Quantitative growth
- Qualitative growth

The initiating factors

The correlation between power structure and the contents of factors

The really change of culture

The determinating factors of change

The internal power structure of the culture

The degree of homogeneity

The degree of integration

47

European Values and Universal Values

Jan Ifversen
Centre for European Studies, University of Aarhus

*P*artly spurred by the European Union, there has been a growing interest, in the question of European identity and European values in recent years. But one event, the fall of the Berlin wall in 1989, really aroused a new, energetic search for 'Europeanness' in the different European countries. From one perspective the event could be presented in the form of a narrative of the triumphant West, and from yet another perspective as a story of a home-coming to Europe of the estranged communist East. The Western perspective tended to stress the expansive and universalist features of European democracy and capitalism, whereas the 'Eastern' perspective underlined the spiritual values of European intellectual life.[1]

EUROPEAN VALUES

In this paper, I intend first to look into some of the histories of European and Western identity[2] to see which values are singled as core values, and secondly to discuss whether these values can be universalised. Two works are prominent poles of orientation in the debate. The first is the book by Francis Fukuyama, *The End of History and the Last Man*, published in 1992. With

---

[1] To speak of an Eastern perspective is in fact dubious since the whole idea behind the perceptions of Europe coming from the former communist countries is to eliminate the Eastern denotation. The locus classicus of this effort is Milan Kundera's article *The Tragedy of Central Europe* from 1984. For a broader discussion of the concept of Central Europe and its relation with the former Eastern countries, see Peter Bugge, "The Use of the Middle", in *European Review of History*, vol. 6, no.1,1999.

[2] I am aware that Europe is not synonymous with the West, but for my purpose the discussion of the difference between the two concepts is not important.

48

Fukuyama's book, the narrative of the triumphant West received a philosophical foundation. Fukuyama linked the political development towards liberal democracy in Europe to a philosophical anthropology (man's universal drive for recognition) and to a philosophy of history (history as a progressive realisation of freedom). Even though much can be held against his philosophical construction and its empirical validation, by focusing on the universal elements of the West, Fukuyama forcefully reopened the debate on European values.

The content of Fukuyama's position on universalism can be summarised in three claims:

1. Democracy is a universal form of social co-existence that expresses man's universal striving for happiness.

2. Whereas economic modernisation based on capitalism tends to be universal there is no essential relation between capitalism and democracy. Economic modernisation, therefore, does not lead to the realisation of true universal values. Capitalism is essential to modernisation.

3. The world today is divided into two parts, a traditional part and a modern, post-historical part where the traditional, non-democratic forces (e.g. nationalism and religion) have been left behind. Fukuyama crystallises this point in a metaphor of "a long wagon train strung out along the road" (Fukuyama 1992, p. 338).

Two things are worth noting in these claims: First, that economic modernisation is degraded to a second order universalism allowing for a wide range of different political regimes; second, that all aspects of cultural diversity are relegated to the traditional and backward part of the world.[3] Fukuyama views the culture argument and culturalist thinking as either products of traditional resistance to modernisation or as an illusion of European provenance caused by the experience of colonisation and decolonisation (Fukuyama 1992, p. 338).

---

[3] This is not completely correct. Fukuyama acknowledges the importance of "group-oriented cultures" in Asia based on "Asia's confucian heritage" in the political development of this region, Fukuyama, *The End of History and the Last Man* (London: Hamish Hamilton 1992), pp.238-244. But culture is still seen as a traditional force of resistance against universal development.

The other pole in the debate is marked by Huntington's paradigm of the clash of civilisations presented in his book bearing this title.[4] Huntington is precisely advocating the cultural relativism denounced by Fukuyama. For Huntington the only perspective that can explain the changing world order is cultural: He locates the states of the world in large cultural units or civilisations defined by traditional cultural criteria such as ethnicity, language, religion and way of life,[5] and supports this culturalist approach with a simple anthropological claim about people always being tempted to divide themselves into us and them (Huntington 1996, p. 32).

Huntington's approach is not only culturalist, it is emphatically anti-universalist. In his frontal attack on universalism he shoots both at globalisation (the claim of a progressive homogenisation of the world) and at the idea of universal values put forward by Fukuyama and others. His central claim is almost the complete opposite of Fukuyama's: "The concept of a universal civilisation is a distinctive product of Western civilisation" (*ibid*, p. 66).

Huntington seeks to refute all claims of globalisation and global culture by pointing to the existing cultural diversity. From his point of view globalisation and its universalist ideology is seen as Westernisation, and the reactions as defensive cultural responses against a form of cultural imperialism. Consequently, there are neither universal values nor global homogenisation, but a clash between civilisations. In his denunciation of universalism as Western cultural imperialism Huntington seems to join a traditionally Third World critique (tiersmondism) of Western dominance.[6] But his purpose is only to create a separation between "the West and the rest" in order to place the West as the best.

Huntington does not, however, disregard all ideas of a general process of modernisation. He introduces modernisation into his scheme of civilisation as an underlying, almost structural movement in the development of all societies related to "industrialisation, urbanisation, increasing levels of literacy,

---

[4] Samuel P. Huntington, *The Clash of Civilisations and the Remaking of World Order* (New York: Simon & Schuster 1996).
[5] The idea of using a concept of civilisation to designate large cultural units goes back to 19th Europe. For an overview of the historical meanings of civilisation, see Jan Ifversen, "The Meaning of European Civilisation. A Historical-conceptual Approach", in *European Studies Newsletter*, vol.1, no.2, 1998.
[6] For a critique of tiersmondism from a universalist point of view, see Alain Finkelkraut, *La défaite de la pensée* (Paris: Gallimard 1987).

education and social mobilisation" (*ibid*, p. 68). But at the same time, when he states that 'modern cultures' are as diverse as were traditional cultures (ibid.), he places culture at the fundamental level thereby staying on safe cultural grounds so that he make claims for the "West [being] the West long before it was modern" (ibid. p. 69).[7]

In Huntington's world order, history takes the form of a clash and a race between civilisations. The West dominated the world from the 16th century to the beginning of the 20th century, which has seen a gradual decline in Western dominance. From 1989 the Rest[8] strikes back. The cause for Western dominance has to be sought in a unique composition of social, political and technological factors. But in order to present an age-old Western civilisation, Huntington relate these factors to different layers of cultural values which manifest themselves through time.

Let us now have a look at the values that make up Huntingston's grand narrative of the West.[9] As in the traditional national-cultural paradigm these values are defined in opposition to non-Western civilisations:

1. A strong *sense of community*. Christianity developed a strong sense of community (*a Gemeinschaft*) based on differences to different non-Christian groups.

2. 2. *Cultural pluralism* based on the diversity of European languages which differs from the "core languages" of other civilisations. The argument only holds, of course, if by languages is understood state languages.

3. *Social pluralism* (or civil society) based on the existence and recognition of voluntary associations within states. These associations

---

[7] The argument has the advantage of countering the culturalist argument, as it is expounded for example in the idea of Asian values, where modernisation is referred to specific cultural values, but it leaves open the question of how then to explain modernisation as different from Westernisation.

[8] In the scholarly discussion, the term 'Rest' is meant as non-European as in the expression "the West and the Rest" (editors note).

[9] The tradition of designating European values by the construction of a common European history goes back to the development of the historicist paradigm of the early 19th century. For a critical survey of the standard narratives of Western history, see David Gress, *From Plato to NATO* (New York: The Free Press 1998).

are then related to a diversity of classes in the European societies.[10] Neither associations (civil society) nor classes are to be found in "centralised, bureaucratic states" outside the West.[11]

4. *Political pluralism* which is divided into two parts. Pluralism appears as a dualism in the form of a separation of spiritual and temporal power as distinct from the theocratic structure of the non-European empires. But pluralism also directly asserts itself in the form of representative bodies for the social classes.

5. Pluralism points in the direction of democracy. In order to arrive at this point Huntington needs something more. Subsequently, he adds *the rule of law*, which leads to constitutionalism and ultimately to human rights. The Roman idea of law, he claims, contributed to mark the difference to the non-Western world where the law was of lesser importance.

6. 6. The final and most important value in the construction of Western distinctness is based on *individualism*, which establishes a tradition of individual rights.

The different values, all being interrelated, constitute a pattern around democracy where pluralism leads to representation, temporal authority supported by the rule of law leads to rights, and individualism gives the final touches on it all. It is neither my intention to demonstrate the internal inconsistency of the arguments nor to pile up counter examples from the non-European civilisations that go against his claims. A few remarks will suffice to show that Huntington is walking on thin ice. Take for example the claim that the separation of temporal and spiritual power will bring along freedom. It is possible to imagine the completely opposite situation of a state not tempered by moral norms.[12] Huntington would probably reply that this factor cannot be seen in isolation, as he actually does when he simply concludes that it is the combination of all the factors that produces the unique result (*ibid*, p. 72). In

---

[10] It does not seem to make a difference for his argument whether the groups mentioned are defined sociologically as classes (e.g. peasants) or as associations (e.g. guilds).

[11] It must either be assumed that bureaucrats are not a class, or even less probable, that there were only bureaucrats in these empires.

[12] And it is in fact possible to come up with examples of rather untempered states in European history such as the absolutist state where rule of law certainly was influenced by the ruling legislator.

52

the above mentioned case the temporal state would thus be tempered by the rule of law. Apart from the fact that the combination is left for the reader to make it does not solve our problem of possible other (non-democratic) scenarios in the West. Huntington gets around the problem by making his combination develop in time. First there is the separation of temporal and spiritual power followed by the rule of law which later on unites with representation, and so on. Through this procedure he can get rid of all the misfits and false directions (such as for example the absolutist state and the hierarchical society) which would make the West resemble the Rest.

Huntington's simplification of the Western narrative is nothing compared to the reductions he imposes on the non-Western civilisations. The example of the separation of religion and state clearly demonstrates this reduction. In Huntington's view the case can be cut down to two possibilities: Either we have separation and consequently freedom, or we have theocracy and therefore despotism. The possibility of any other relationship between religion and state is ruled out.

Huntington leaves out some essential elements in his narrative of Western civilisation, such as science, technology and capitalism. The reason seems to be that these factors would complicate his version of Western civilisation as freedom. It has often been argued that capitalism is linked to democracy by the notion of individual freedom, but the argument demands a rather restricted definition of capitalism, which tends to underscore such structural aspects as accumulation and exploitation.[13] Even more complicated is the relation between science and democracy. Evidently, science needs a space free from religious control to develop itself, but nothing indicates that this kind of freedom has to be honoured by democracy.[14]

---

[13] Fukuyama is very clear on this point when he says that "(t)here is no democracy without democrats" (Fukuyama, op.cit. 1992, p. 134) meaning that democracy cannot be explained only by referring to a process of capitalist modernisation, Fukuyama op.cit. 1992, pp. 134-35.

[14] Alain-Marc Rieu argues, not very convincingly, for an epistemological relation between the experimental method of science, the ideal of individual freedom and democracy the key being a new idea of "the power of the human mind". See Alain Marc Rieu: Scientific Revolutions and the Idea of democracy, in Gérard Duprat et al. (eds.), *European Democratic Culture* (Milton Kenyes: The Open University 1993), pp.15-58.

Instead of locating these factors within Western civilisation, Huntington's trick is to place them in a process of modernisation which is maybe not universal, but nor is it expressively Western. Modernisation is not Westernisation, Huntington claims. Precisely what is meant by this claim is somewhat unclear, however; Huntington only refers very vaguely to economic growth and technical modernisation. But the principal message is that modernisation can be attained by different cultures. The idea that any modernisation should follow a Western pattern is dismissed by Huntington as a Western illusion that attempts to dominate the rest of the world: "At the end of the twentieth century the concept of universal civilisation helps justify Western cultural dominance of other societies" (*ibid.* p. 66). Cultural imperialism has thus replaced 19th century political imperialism with its racial ideology. In this view Huntington comes very close to the position taken by leading proponents of Asian values (such as former prime minister of Singapore Lee Kuan Yew, who rejects any connection between economic modernisation and Western ideas of political liberty). Huntington does not have to agree with Lee's proposition that positive characteristics of a Confucian culture are more dynamic than Western individualism. It is enough to see this position as an independent cultural expression taken within a successful process of modernisation.[15]

It seems commonplace, like Huntington does, to distinguish between Western culture and the general process of modernisation, thereby discrediting Westernisation as a form of cultural imperialism.[16] This distinction, however, does not tell us what belongs to culture and what does not. Do democracy and individualism belong to the Western world as Huntington claims, or are they 'tools of modernity' which people will be using to shape their culture without thereby becoming Western? The latter viewpoint is held by the Danish historian David Gress, who argues for leaving only a historical pole position to the West: "The West was simply the first of several cultures to have undergone the revolutions of modernity" (Gress 1998, p. 20).

---

[15] Since the outbreak of the crisis in the Asian economies the question of success might be doubted.
[16] Seen from a perspective critical towards the potential Westernisers in the non-Western world Westernisation "is a mimic and mechanical adoption of some superficial and trivial aspects of the way of life in Western societies, doing things in a way that has no relation to reality." Mehdi Mozafarri: *Can a Declined Civilisation be Re-constructed?* (Department of Political Science, Aarhus University 1998), p. 23.

54

Huntington's cultural-relativist position seems the easy one where every civilisation is formed by its own historical culture, the only problem being to dig it out and mark out the boundaries between different cultures. Though cast in rather vague terms Huntington still acknowledges a process of modernisation which does not fit into a paradigm of cultural relativism where normally there is no room for transcultural and transhistorical movements. Gress' stand is more logical when he says that modernity was invented in Western culture for subsequent apprehension and reworking by other cultures. Perhaps it would make things more clear if we distinguish between a Western *modernity* and a *modernisation* process of modelling and reworking in all societies.[17] But even with this distinction it gets difficult to avoid a eurocentric perspective where the rest of the world is reduced to *receive* and *re*work a Western experience (or at least some of it). Would it not be possible to argue, as do the proponents of Asian values, that elements of modernisation could be produced by non-Western cultures. The historical case of an autonomous Chinese capitalism could support this argument.[18]

Where does all this leave us? I think it is possible to find a way among the different positions outlined so far by pointing at two emergency exits. The first one is to make a difference within European civilisation of the universal and the universalisable. The second one is to develop a generalised concept of modernisation (in line with globalisation).

UNIVERSALISM AND UNIVERSABILITY

It must be clear by now that to claim a universality for Western/European civilisation is problematic. Any universal *discourse* is embedded in culture and history. First of all, not every discourse is universal. We therefore need to determine whether a discourse has universal pretensions or not. A discourse is universal when its subject is of universal scope, for example by using universal denominators such as human nature, reason, mankind or the world. This leaves out all the discourses that only refer to a limited subject, be that a specific nation, Europe, the white race, the working class etc. The universal subjects are

---

[17] This distinction is proposed by the Swedish historian of ideas, Sverker Sörlin: "Modernity is European. It is from it that the Europeans have approached the world. Modernisation has today spread far beyond Europe. (...) on the other continents, modernity is still only vaguely and undecidedly received" (Sverker Sörlin: "Signalement af Europa" in *Nordrevy* 1990 (4), p. 19-20).
[18] For an argument along these lines, see Jack Goody, *The East in the West* (Cambridge University Press 1996).

linked to specific topics or objects.[19] Mankind or humanity will appear in anthropological discourses which try to delineate a human nature, or in moral discourses where rules and norms of justice are claimed to be universally valid. These discourses can then be transferred to other fields. Anthropological statements can be used to 'explain' cultural expressions. An illustration of this could be the efforts to see more fundamental community structures (ethnies) behind the European nation-building process,[20] or the similar claim by Huntington that *"people are always* tempted to divide into us and them" (my italics). Apparently, such an implicit anthropology often comes up when cultural matters are treated.[21] Moral statements enter the political field through several channels. The prime European example is, of course, the declaration of human rights by which a moral idea of human justice (right) - through the intermediary of a legal discourse (right*s*) - is attached to democracy (popular sovereignty).[22] Another interesting case is the debate launched after World War I on civilisation standards in international politics where cultural, moral and political topics intersect.[23]

Yet another type of universal discourse is related to the spatial concept of the world whatever the form of worldliness might be. Any talk of world trade, world opinion, global village and the like produces statements of the world as a *place* of global action. As we shall see many of these statements get together in a discourse on globalisation.

Universalisation through universal discourses makes it possible for a culture to transcend its own limited sphere. However, not all topics in a culture can reasonably be given a universal status. Some are so bound up with specific cultural subjects that it makes no sense to try to place them on a world scale,

---

[19] For the use of the terms subject and object to analyse discourses, see Michel Foucault, *L'Archéologie du savoir* (Paris: Gallimard, 1969).

[20] This is the position taken by Anthony Smith in his analysis of European nation building, see Anthony Smith: *Nations and Nationalism in a Global Era* (Cambridge: Polity Press, 1995). Smith alternates between anthropological statements (concerning all human coexistence) and historical statements ("deep structures", "layers").

[21] Though seldom so overtly as when David Gress asserts that "(d)emocracy and capitalism were (...) in harmony with human nature" (Gress, op.cit. 1998, p.18).

[22] For a discussion of the complex linking of morality and democracy, see Jürgen Habermas, *Faktizität und Geltung* (Frankfurt a/M: Suhrkamp 1992).

[23] Gerrit W. Gong: *The standard of "civilisation" in international society* (Oxford: Clarendon Press, 1984).

take for example the Danish idea of popularity (*folkelighed*) which cannot even be translated properly into English. Furthermore, we will have to distinguish between what I will call **open** and **closed** universalisation. By closed universalisation I understand a universal discourse the purpose of which it is to *exclude* other universal discourses. A case in point is the elevation of the idea of national self-determination to a universal principle in 1918. Taken in itself the idea only links up the nation with the democratic principle of popular sovereignty, but in the European context nation would also mean a unity defined by criteria of culture and ethnicity. The truly European idea of the *Kulturnation* thus became a principle for a political world order excluding other forms of unity. One might object that the Kulturnation was not forced upon non-European peoples, but taken up by the spokesmen of these peoples as a political tool in the process of liberation from colonial rule. It can, nevertheless, hardly be contested that the principle of nationality (that is of connecting states with culture) has played a dominant role in the creation, recognition and disruption of states in the world.

A closed universalisation eliminates or disguises the gap between perspectives. It is taken for granted that one perspective, the European or Western, immediately can be lifted up to a universal level thereby incorporating two perspectives in one. In its classical form this incorporation of perspectives is found in the European imperialism with its idea of a civilisational mission (or in a racial form as the white man's burden) in the non-European world. Imperialism melted together a national, a European and a universal perspective. Today this form survives in eurocentrist interpretations of development, welfare, human rights etc.

The escape from closed universalisation is not, however, a politically tinged cultural relativism à la Huntington or other forms of relativism such as the one found in a tiersmondist discourse (which, in a way, is only Huntington turned upside down). Cultural relativism does not leave any place for a universal discourse. What is needed is, in my view, an open universalisation, which focuses on the discursive and institutional processes involved in universalisation. I shall make two claims concerning this form of universalisation. The first is that not all values in a specific culture are universalisable, which does not mean, though, that they will not be exported to other cultures. Let us take the example of Christianity, which has played a prevalent role in the forming of European culture. Christianity is in principle universal, formed as it is in a universal language (speaking on behalf of the whole mankind). But precisely because it creates a fundamental split between

Christians and non-Christians its concept of mankind is not open. Only the Christian is the true man. Any negotiation of that term can only be understood in the form of conversion. The history of European colonisation shows abundantly how this process of conversion went hand in hand with perceptions of inferior people.[24] I will not deny that there are elements in Christian ethics that are universalisable, but how this can take place needs, precisely, to be demonstrated, which leads me to my second claim.

Open universalisation is a negotiation between perspectives. Universalisation can be seen as a *relativisation* of more limited perspectives. Only the universal perspective is unlimited and is, consequently, the one that can eliminate differences. In modern Europe this perspective is signified by the concepts of mankind and humanity. There are, of course, numerous limited perspectives referring to individuals, to groups, to societies, and to civilisations. Everyone of these perspectives can be transcended by referring to mankind. As a category mankind primarily belongs to a moral discourse whereas the other perspectives have historical, social and psychological meanings as well. It is possible, however, to match mankind with at least political categories of a *global* scale.[25] Here I am thinking of such categories as world order or world system. Even though the universal and the global is not the same we might say that both concepts have the capacity of transcending the limited perspectives.[26]

On the highest level we thus have two categories, mankind and the world order both of which have to be confronted with more limited perspectives. Mankind is traditionally related to the individual, world order to the states that make up this order. But individuals are, of course, citizens in states and thereby connected to the world order. And states, at least national states, have a strong cultural orientation which makes the citizen part of a culture. Let us try to make

---

[24] Conversion is not to be mistaken for modern assimilation which is based on the idea of formal equality. As we know from European history, Christianity could easily function together with concepts of hierarchical differences.

[25] It could also be argued, as it is done by the many analysts of globalisation, that we have today a global culture, see Mike Featherstone, *Undoing Culture. Globalisation, Postmodernism and Identity* (London: Sage, 1995). The problem with this concept is, though, that it can only be defined negatively as the opposite of the non-global, that is the local.

[26] Whereas the universal is transcending time and space the global is a purely spatial concept, and a limited one insofar as it delineates the limits of the world. In order to add a temporal perspective globalisation analysts often recur to some variant of postmodernity.

some order in the relations between these perspectives by appointing three different levels, the individual, the national/social and the universal/global, and three different types of discourses, the political centred around states, the social-cultural and the moral. In combination this gives the following scheme:

PERSPECTIVE

Discourse type	Individual	National	Universal/global
Political			
Cultural			
Moral			

I do not intend to fill out all the blanks. In some cases this would be very difficult and demand a lot of quarrelsome effort. Whereas there is no great theoretical problem with the individual and the universal perspective in moral discourse the idea of a national moral discourse either points to a simple cultural relativism which incorporates the moral discourse in a cultural one or to a more sophisticated Aristotelian communitarianism focused on the ethical perception of friendship. Another complicated case is made up by the question of global culture which seem to demand quite equilibristic conceptual manoeuvres.

The combination of perspectives and discourse types must be seen as the first step in our clarification of universalism. The second step containing the process of relativisation involves a criss-crossing of discourse types. The general move of relativisation is to transcend the limited perspective by confronting it with a less limited one. Such shifts in perspective can take place by confronting one type of discourse with another. An example of this is the conflict between a national cultural discourse and an individual moral one. The national-cultural discourse would produce arguments stressing the cultural determination of the individuals, whereas the individual moral discourse can circumvent these arguments by pointing to a universal right to freedom. You could imagine a similar situation where a national perception of citizenship formulated in a national-political discourse is challenged by a perception of universal individual rights.

I shall not go through all the possible arguments that can be formulated in a process of relativisation. Below I try to systematise the most interesting forms of relativisation:[27]

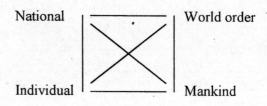

National — World order

Individual — Mankind

As it appears from my figure the two highest perspectives, world order and mankind, can confront each other. This confrontation is only possible in two different discourse types, a political discourse centred on a state reason among states and a moral discourse centred on universal justice. The world order can thus be relativised by references to a universal justice, which in European language would take the form of human rights. And human rights, on the other hand can be relativised by state reason arguments about the impossibility of intervening in another state or the high costs involved in such an intervention.

The other vertical axis of relativisation points to a range of problems around the status of the individual in society, which involves questions such as citizens rights and individual obligations towards the state. The diagonal axis from the national perspective to mankind points to the possibility of relativising the national state (for example its perception of citizenship) from a universal perspective. The other diagonal axis marks a cosmopolitan idea of individuals seeing themselves as members of a world society.[28] The horizontal axis between individual and mankind indicates the general moral form of universalisation which can be transferred to other discourse types; the other horizontal axis points to the political aspects in the relations between national states in a world order.

---

[27] This figure owes a lot to Roland Robertson, *Social Theory and Global Culture* (London: Sage, 1992). But whereas he is mainly interested in describing global discourses my focal point is universalism.

[28] In Europe cosmopolitan ideas have played a certain role in the formulation of a universal political perspective and in developing concepts of international law, see F. H. Hinsley, *Power and the pursuit of peace*. Theory and practice in the history of relations between states (Cambridge University Press, 1963).

OPEN UNIVERSALISATION

Up till now I have only given examples of closed universalisation in Europe. In the following section I will present an example of open universalisation and discuss in what way it is open. The most evident example to discuss is the subject of human rights, which rank higher in all Europeans' estimations of their values. The idea and the institution of human right are products of a European culture and history. The formulation of universal moral rules as (natural) rights has its roots in European political philosophy. The strong weight on individual rights and the crystallisation of these rights in "the right to life, liberty and estate" (John Locke) can be explained by the specific class structure in the European societies with the development of an independent urban class, and by the dominant role individualism played in the formation of a secularised epistemology and anthropology. The French declaration of the rights of the man and the citizen also has its European history, placed as it was in the new elites' attack on the absolutist state and aristocratic society. But the fact that human rights stem from a certain cultural and historical context do not invalidate them per se. The point I discuss is whether the idea of human rights can relativise this context. From a temporal point of view it is evident that the idea has transgressed the historical situation of 1789 since it is still very important in the democratic design of the European states today. The problem to solve is whether the idea is based on exclusively *European* values. Here we have to differentiate between form and substance. The form is no doubt European. The whole liberal language within which human rights are formulated is strongly influenced by a European perception of individualism. It is possible, however, to separate the substance from the form, and, furthermore to spot the most important, substantial elements. The substance of the human rights is the formulation of an abstract perspective, mankind, there allowed universalisation. The man who has rights is not determined by culture. 'Man' is an empty category. Who man is can, of course, be filled out through all sorts of determinations, which, however, do not give the ultimate answer. The category of man is precisely there to remind us that s/he is more than the cultural, economic or political determinations by which s/he is interpreted. Another substantial part of human rights is the claim that man has *rights*. This indicates that man is defined by a set of rights, which must be based on some working principles.

It makes no sense to perceive the concepts of rights as completely empty. They have to be related to basic moral values such as freedom and equality without which it becomes impossible to create other more specific right. A third substantial dimension is indicated by the fact that human rights are *declared*. I do not have the particular legal form in mind in which they were formulated, but the dynamic aspect contained in the process of declaring. Human rights do not exist as abstract rules only, which would make them mainly a case for moral philosophers. They are designed to be interpreted, that is translated from basic principles to a large range of specific rights. In this sense human rights can be seen as containing a general *right to have or demand right* which can be boiled down to a right to relativise limited perspectives. It is clear that this general right must be dependent on a system and a culture of debate. In Europe such a system was formulated through the ideas and practices of popular sovereignty and public opinion.

Let me summarise my argument. The European idea of human rights offers an example of what I have called open universalism. The reason for its universability is due to the substantial elements that can be deduced form its European form. These are first of all the abstract concept of man which points out a universal perspective free of cultural determinations; secondly, the relation between rights and basic moral values that can define man as a moral being; and thirdly the essential relation between moral values and the process of declaration.

The idea of universalisation can be viewed both internally and externally. Internal universalisation is about the efforts within the different states of forming and making universal discourses work. External universalisation means the efforts to establish a universal discourse among the different states of the world. In principle the United Nations has been the most important forum for such a debate. In practice the universal discourses presented here have been embedded in a political discourse of state reason which has checked efforts of engaging in a global debate on universalism. For human rights to get rid of their European dress (which also means its disconnection from European state reason) a debate that takes its starting point in the substantial elements is needed. Such a debate must begin by abstracting the different universal discourses from their cultural roots in order to find a common ground from which the debate on basic moral values can proceed. Subsequently, this debate must examine the different formulations of basic moral values in order to see whether some sort of common moral values can be formulated. There is no doubt that, on a general level, common values exist. As far as I know, no society accepts formal slavery, which means that there is a basis for approaching equality. And in all societies we find ideas of the value of life as such which could be the starting point for a definition of freedom.

The fundamental problem for cross-cultural debates on universalism lies in the participants' unwillingness to separate themselves from their culture or their state reason. Not only the Europeans have to relativise their human rights ideas all other participants must relativise their universal ideas too. I don't think the formulation of Asian values goes in this direction. On the contrary, it confuses universalism and modernisation and draws the former into a cultural discourse leaving no openings for the formulation of a universal agenda. In that sense it works precisely in the same way as the Huntingtonian building of a Western fort in defence of authentic Western values. In stead of blurring the discussion by summarising European discourses in an overall individualistic mentality and contrasting it with an Asian group or family mentality it would be of interest to confront different moral definitions of the individual.

Open universalisation does not exclude the possibility of disagreement. Participants in the debate might, at some point, reach a limit to what they can accept morally and stand firmly on their position. From a European point of view such limits would often be related to individual freedom. It is a delusion to expect that debates on universal values would lead to general agreements. But even though this will not be the result it is still important to know what we disagree upon. And both the efforts of universalisation and the debate on universal values have the effect of moving us and of creating a distance to our own cultural discourse. Let me end by quoting the French philosopher Claude Lefort who, in my view, has a very beautiful formulation of the effect of transcultural debate, such as the one we are engaging in today:

(Les êtres humains) se lient et s'interpellent, chacun ne voulant saisir dans les paroles des autres que ce qui fait écho à ses croyances, dans lesquelles s'est investie son historie propre, mais chacun, au contact des autres, devant faire mouvement, se trouvant affecté par cela même qu'il rejette, déporté, sans souvent qu'il le sache, de la place où il tentait de se tenir. Les hommes (...) se comprennent pour autant qu'ils s'entendent, mais s'entendre ne signifie pas s'accorder: s'entendre, c'est tenir ensemble par la parole qui va et vient, non abolir l'écart du parler et de l'entendre, mais le laisser se refaire, se prêter ainsi à la venue du nouveau.[29]

---

[29] Claude Lefort, *Écrire. À l'épreuve du politique* (Paris: Calman-Lévy 1992), p.50.

The Idea of Europe —
Europe and its Others

Peter Bugge
Department of Slavonic Studies, University of Aarhus

*L*et me confess at once that Asian values, the theme of our conference, will not be the focus of the present paper. Its subject is Europe, or more precisely the role and function of Asia in the evolution of a European self-perception, of an idea of 'European values'. This is defensible, I think, because the Asian values debate is intrinsically linked to its European counterpart. For each of the two, the other serves as a symbolic counter against and through which one's own values stand out, as what we might call a constituting 'Other'.

For centuries the dichotomies of Europe and Asia, West and East, or Occident and Orient have played a great role in European thought, and the significance of a European or Western 'Other' in the present Asian values debate is patent. When Tommy Koh, director of the Singapore Policy Research Institute, listed ten values as typical of the East Asian countries, in four of the ten points he explicitly contrasted these values to 'Western' ones (Le Huu Tang 1999). Also, the values help up by Roh as typically Asian - respect for hard work, thrift, and simplicity, and an emphasis on education and on family values etc. - have a familiar ring to many Europeans. As Eric Hobsbawm points out,

> *we are continuing the old debate, launched by Marx and developed by Max Weber, on the influence of particular religions and ideologies on economic development. It used to be Protestantism which fuelled the engine of capitalism. Today Calvin is out and Confucius is in...* (Hobsbawm 1997: 218)

Many of the same values now presented as inherently (East) Asian ones thus have a long tradition of being associated with (Protestant) Europe.

Two observations can be made from this. First that collective identities are constituted at least as much by their borders, by how the members of the 'we-group' define what or who they are *not*, as by any substance or internal characteristics. And secondly, that the attributes of 'Asian' and 'European' refer to something more than and different from geography. This is already suggested by the fact that the border between the two continents, as conventionally established, runs right through two countries, Russia and Turkey, and also within geographical Europe it has often been held that some parts are more 'European' than others. Even today, the wish to reserve the concept as a whole for a select part of the continent is tangible in the frequent demands that the East Europeans must 'Europeanise' to gain access to 'Europe', i.e. to the European Union. And also the idea of 'Asia' has its centre and its peripheries. The Asian values debate does not refer equally to the Turks, the Eskimo peoples of eastern Siberia, and the peoples of South East Asia, in Hobsbawm's pointed terms it is *"not concerned with Asia as a whole, but with the economic effects of the geographically localised heritage of Confucius"* (*ibid.*).

Thus, the concepts of 'Asian' and 'European' are not neutral, denotative semantic markers. Both invoke - as self-designations and in the perception of 'the Other' - a rich set of connotations, they are themselves value-laden before being associated with any specific values. In the following a brief, and necessarily simplified, discussion will be offered of how, in Europe, the idea emerged that Europe was the home of a particular community with particular values, and how in this context 'Asia' (or the 'Orient'/the 'East') has functioned as Europe's 'significant Other'. I shall argue that in this 'idea of Europe' a tension exists between claims to the universal validity of 'European' values or qualities, and attempts to make them a uniquely European possession. Needless to say, neither the 'Asia' constructed as a mirror for 'Europe', nor the 'Europe' itself emerging from this juxtaposition must be understood in essentialist terms as reified entities. Both are perceived as discursive constructs, relational and subject to constant negotiations and change.

THE HERITAGE FROM ANCIENT GREECE

The very idea of continental divisions, and the names of 'Europe', 'Asia', and 'Libya' (later named 'Africa' by the Romans), stems from ancient Greece. Its origin is unknown, and already Herodotus wondered why what was obviously a single landmass should be split up and given women's names (den Boer 1995: 14). The British historian Arnold Toynbee has offered a plausible explanation. He suggests that the divide is a mariner's concept, a Hellenic piece of nautical nomenclature: as one sailed the Aegean Sea towards the Bosporus, Asia was to starboard, Europe to port. As the Greeks so sailed though the Black Sea to the Sea of Azov they came to the river Don, which marked the end of the then known world and also the border of Europe and Asia. Perhaps for symmetry's sake the Nile was added at the other end as the border between Africa and Asia. But it is worth noticing that nowhere did this border separate distinct cultures or civilisations - waterways united, they did not set apart (Toynbee 1954: 712). Also, these concepts referred only to limited parts of what is today known as Europe or Asia, and the Greek geographical knowledge of Asia was higher than that of Europe.

So, significantly, there was not and could not be any Greek 'Euro-consciousness' at that time. The Greeks lived at both sides of the Aegean Sea, and if distinguishing between self and other it was between Hellenes and barbarians, not Europeans and Asians. Only for a brief, exceptional period of time, during the wars between the Greeks and the Persians in the fifth century BC, the conflict was presented in political terms as a strife between free 'Europe' and despotic 'Asia'. Climatic and behavioural oppositions were added to this, but mostly - as in Aristotle's writings - the Greeks placed themselves *above* both Europeans (the barbarians to the north) and Asians (Persians). And soon, with the empires of Alexander the Great and later of Rome, the Europe-Asia divide lost any significance as a political or cultural divide (den Boer: 16-19; Schlumberger 1994).

THE EMERGENCE OF A EUROPEAN SELF-PERCEPTION

The continents do not appear in the Bible, and in the Christian cosmology Jerusalem was the centre of the world, and Paradise placed in Asia. The opposition that mattered in those days was between Christians and non-believers, not between Europeans and non-Europeans (Hay, 1968: 1-15; den Boer: 19-26).

Only in the fifteenth century a systematic association of Christendom with Europe took place. This happened as all of Europe had been christened, and former Christian lands in Asia and Africa conquered by the Moslem Ottomans. One could say that in this process the Christian community, although potentially universal, began to appear as a territorially rooted entity, living in Europe. The fall of Constantinople in 1453 strengthened this association, since it much reduced the significance of the Schism between Orthodox and Catholic Christendom. But still, crusaders went to fight for Christendom, not for Europe (Hay: Chapters 2-5).

The reformation put a rapid end to this Christian unity in Europe, but instead in the sixteenth century a community of densely communicating territorial states emerged. They shared a set of norms, habits, and institutions,

66

religious and secular, and were tied together politically in a 'balance of power' that recognised the interdependence of these states. So, a European community or 'system' emerged, which also - in particular when meeting other communities - described itself as 'European'. Here, finally, a real identification with Europe can be found, and we also meet the adjective 'European' suggesting that certain qualities or things (places, peoples) could meaningfully be labelled in this way. A rapidly growing cartographic knowledge also enabled the Europeans to rationally perceive the geographical space in which they lived, and thus to develop a more concrete, secular concept and image of Europe (Hale, 1994: 14-27).

The discoveries and the following colonial expansion only added to this European self-awareness. Samuel Purchas, an Englishman, argued in 1625 that *'Jesus... hath long sincè given a Bill of Divorce to ingratefull Asia where hee was borne, and Africa the place of his flight and refuge, and is become almost wholly and onely Europaean.'* And so, with divine blessing, Europe has taken possesion of the world:

> *The Qualitie of Europe exceeds her Quantitie, in this the least, in that the best of the world... Nature has yeelded her selfe to Europaean Industry... Asia yeerely sends us her Spices, Silkes and Gemmes; Africa her Gold and Ivory; America* [is] *almost everywhere admitting Europaean Colonies* (quoted in Hay: 110, 121-22).

The 'us', one notices, clearly refers to 'us Europeans'.[1]

Yet, in all their pride, the Europeans granted to Asia a status very different from the one ascribed to Africa or America. This can be seen in many iconographic allegories of the continents. Europe is here the crowned continent, a queen endowed with symbols of wealth, wisdom, technical skills, art and music, etc., but whereas Africa and America appear barbarian, with semi-naked people and wild animals, Asia is also associated with symbols of civility (den Boer: 44-58).

---

1 Purchas, it must be added, did not explain the superiority of the Europeans in racist or similar terms. To him, the diversity of humankind had to do mostly with lack of religion and civility, and with Christendom, mankind could be united: *'The tawney Morre, black Negro, duskie Libyan, ash-coloured Indian, olive-coloured American should with the whiter Euroepan become one sheepe-fold, under one great shepheard... Without any more distinction of colour, Nation, language, sexe, condition al may bee One in him that is ONE, and only blessed forever'* (quoted from Hannaford 1996: 171).

The European attitude to the nearest 'Asian' Other, the Turks, was profoundly ambiguous: politically, the European states half accepted, half excluded the Ottoman Empire from their state system, and the conventional image of Turkish infidel inhuman cruelty was countered by the observation that the Turks appreciated learning, the arts and civilised comforts. Comparisons with Turks, and also with the Chinese, the Japanese and other Asian cultures, did not always end favourably for the Europeans (Hale: 38-43). Curiously, the term 'Asiatic' was mobilised with pronounced negative connotations from around 1500 in connection with Muscovite Russia, which by the Poles was described as barbarian, Asiatic, and a threat to Christian Europe (Klug 1987).

In sum then, we can say that whereas the Atlantic Ocean and Sahara created a sharp border between a cultivated, a skilled Europe here, and a barbarian, savage non-Europe there, the border to Asia was more complex. Not only was it difficult to separate Asia geographically from Europe, even culturally it was not so clear where Europe stopped to give way to something really different, to Asia.

THE IDEA OF EUROPEAN CIVILISATION

With the Enlightenment these reflections on the nature of Europe and its borders, on how to interpret cultural encounters with other peoples and societies, were summed up in a new, complex concept, *civilisation*, associated again with Europe. Roughly speaking, the idea of civilisation had three key dimensions:

- a *universal* dimension, seeing civilisation as a universal quality or process in which man moves towards a virtuous society (civilisation is a potential in man as man)

- a *spatial* dimension, probably more influential, which sees civilisation as a cultural entity or phenomenon located in Europe. Here, civilisation is at least partly serving as a secular substitute for the earlier association of Europe with Christendom.

- a *temporal* dimension, which located this spatial configuration in time in a process of development. If a community was said not be able to move historically from barbarism to civilisation, this also, at least potentially, opened up for the recognition of the existence of several civilisations (Ifversen, 1998: 24-34).

The universal aspect was predominant in the discourse of Mirabeau the Elder, who coined the concept in 1756. According to him, societies are upheld

68

by the principle of virtue, and civilisation is the process in which virtue is produced and secured as a civilised society develops. The alternative was corruption, which Mirabeau associated with manners, and these again with what was particular in a people. Their predominance may corrupt society. From this point of view civilisation is the victory of the universal pole (humanity) over the particular or cultural pole.

But mostly, civilisation was perceived as located in Europe and discussed in connection with encounters with non-European others. In 1721, in his *Persian Letters,* Montesquieu used fictituous Persian travellers to discuss European manners and customs with an outsider's eye, and in 1748 in his *The Spirit of the Laws,* he compared the political systems of Asia and Europe, explaining the despotism of the former and the freedom of the latter with climatic factors, thus using the old motif of Antiquity (den Boer: 58-59). Also, the first linking of the two concepts 'European' and 'civilisation' stems from 1766 in a discussion of the French colonies in North America (*ibid*: 64).

In 1767 the Scot Adam Ferguson added a temporal perspective to the spatial idea by introducing a stage model, according to which rude nations could move toward civil society with progress in civilisation. Ferguson defined the driving forces in this process as *arts* (skills or knowledge) and *virtue*, which equalled the spirit of the given community. While every nation knew of virtue, there was in the rude nations (as in America, which so became a model of Europe's past) a lack of arts, whereas the Orient displayed the danger of resting upon arts, while forgetting virtue: Society succumbed to 'effimination', or to despotism (Ifversen: 32-34).

This was an elegant model, where America was virtue without art, and Asia art without virtue, while Europe throned in the middle in possession of both. Naturally, these Enlightenment ideas very much bolstered European self-confidence or self-complacency, but the comparisons with other communities also created a platform for critique of the vices of European society, and for praise of civilisational virtues in other societies. At times, a feeling of collective guilt was expressed, both when civilisation's pernicious influence on the Arcadian life of innocent natives was condemned, and in relationship to Asia. In the last three hundred years, the German historian Johann Eichhorn wrote:

> ... the Europeans have run through all corners of Asia that they have found access to. Not to bring better opinions and laws, better customs and habits, but to bring their bad habits and vices, their diseases and sufferings there. Not to relieve the yoke of the unhappy, but to make

69

their old yoke even heavier through a new one, not to help them to a sensible enjoyment of life through education and the enlightenment of the intellect, but to disgrace their human nature even more, to extort, plunder, oppress and kill them (quoted from Gollwitzer, 1964: 61-62).

On the one hand, Eichhorn and the Europeans were certain that they were most advanced in civilisation - that they had the *potential* to enlighten others - but on the other hand actual European behaviour was at times seen as the negation of this potential. So one could talk of a European self-critical self-confidence taking shape in the Enlightenment (Harbsmeier 1988: 88-97).

Still, Enlightenment Europe had - or acknowledged - no equal partner in dialogue. In principle, the enlightened public was potentially universal, and as in earlier centuries the civilised qualities of Asia were recognised. But in reality only a European public was addressed, and even within Europe the attitude was exclusivist. The collective addressed by philosophers like Voltaire transgressed national and state boundaries in western Europe, but stopped before the peoples of Poland, Russia, Hungary, or the Ottoman Empire (Wolff, 1995). A 'semi-orientalised' Eastern Europe was being constructed, which gradually gave way to an 'Orient' beginning somewhere in Russia and the Ottoman Empire and stretching almost infinitely to the East (Wolff 1994, Ifversen).

The Enlightenment idea of civilisation was a great step towards a theory of man in society, transcending religious or ethnic limitations. But with civilisation becoming both the precondition and the result or goal of history (Fisch, 1992: 680), the perceived civilisational superiority of Europe invited explanations (supported by the development of scientific anthropology, and by philosophers like Herder) that sought the key to these differences not *in* history (in variations in the social or political organisation of different societies), but *outside* or *beyond* history in the psychological or physical qualities inherent to different peoples or races. This 'naturalisation' of civilisation or culture (the two words being used nearly as synonyms at that time) was not only a break with the universalist anthropology of the Enlightenment, but also with the old 'cultivating' meaning of culture (as cultivation of mind and manners), and it paved the way for more coherent racial explanations of the history of mankind in the nineteenth century (Hannaford: 233).

EUROPE SUPREME

In the nineteenth century the contradictions in the Enlightenment idea of European civilisation became more pronounced. In the American and French

70

revolutions the universalist perspective paved the way for an idea of *human rights* and of *democracy*, which again potentially - although realised by citizens in states - embraced all mankind. But simultaneously, with the rapid advances of scientific and technological developments at home, and the colonisation of most of the world abroad, the century up to the First World War witnessed the culmination of European self-complacency. Civilisation and Europe became one, and increasingly European superiority vis-à-vis non-Europeans was explained racially, in terms of white and coloured.

The division of Europe after the Napoleonic wars in a liberal 'West' (England, France) and an autocratic 'East' (Prussia, Austria, Russia) allowed for a linking of the paradigm of civilisation to a discourse of political difference. In 1822 a French observer, Abbé de Pradt, explained this split as the outcome of '*the division of Europe into two zones of sociability, which fight each other and which make any common language between its two parts impossible.*' De Pradt drew this dividing line from Stockholm to Cadiz and called it a '*degrading line of liberty as you move closer to Asia*' (quoted from Gollwitzer 1964: 183, 182). One sees a radicalisation of the perspective: now difference is not merely gradual, a question of more or less civilisation, now any communication between *zones* of civilisation is impossible, and hence universalism. And again, although Eastern Europe was discussed, the loss of liberty was identified with Asia.

From the 1820s, Ferguson's idea of a human progress in stages towards civilisation was taken up and applied specifically to (Western) Europe, so that the *history* of European civilisation became an idea in its own right. Ferguson had placed Europe on the top of the universal scale of human progress, but his 'motors' of development were still the universal principles of arts and virtue. - Now, the French historian Francois Guizot in his *The History of Civilisation in Europe* from 1828 used specific traits in European history - i.e. first of all in French and English history - to explain the superiority of European civilisation: the diversity of its institutions, the competition of rival principles and forms, etc. Guizot did not abandon the idea of civilisation in general, but it served him only as a background norm against which to measure the historical advance of European civilisation, Europe's historical quest for universal meaning (Ifversen: 34-35).

The German historian Leopold von Ranke added to this 'nationalisation' of the agents of European civilisational development. In the preface to his *History of the Romance and Germanic peoples* from 1824 he declared his conviction

71

> *... that the complex of Christian peoples of Europe is to be considered as a whole, as one state, otherwise one could not properly understand the enormous difference that exists between the Occidental and the Oriental world, and the great similarity that exists between the Romance and the Germanic peoples* (quoted from Ludat, 1969: 285).

Ranke here reduced the carriers of European progress, civilisation and culture to the Romance and the Germanic peoples, and so he excluded the Slavs of Eastern Europe from any share in Europe's development and opened up for a racial interpretation of what separates Europe from non-Europe. We *are* a certain people, Romance or Germanic, unlike them, the rest.

Also, Ranke's opposition between Occident and Orient was very strong, and in the nineteenth century an historical scheme was developed, most overwhelmingly so in Hegel's philosophy of history with its march of the World Spirit toward human freedom (Gollwitzer: 212-14; Groh, 1988: 175-185). The Orient was seen as the original contributor to the forming of the world of culture, but only as a thing of the past, since with the advance of history this torch of light, of culture, was passed over to the Occident, to Europe, in the now familiar stages of Greece, Rome, renaissance Italy, France and England (and later even to America, cf. the statue of Liberty and the idea of Western civilisation (Davies, 1996: 19-31; Gress 1998; Larsen)).[2] We thus have the idea that history, real history, since Ancient Greece has developed only in Europe or by Europeans, indicating that, as a German historian later summed up Ranke's position, *'world historical dignity was acquired according to one's share in European culture'* (Gollwitzer: 221).

Marx turned Hegel's idealistic dialectics upside down, but his materialistic historical dialectic preserved the opposition of East and West, past and present, as indicated in his notion of an *Asiatic mode of production*. In Marx's perspective there was only one real civilisation, the Western one (Marx

---

2 One relatively recent example from the British Marxist archeologist Gordon Childe: *'If our own culture may claim to be the main current, it is only because our cultural tradition has taken in a greater number of once parallel traditions and made them subordinate rivers. While the main stream in historic times flows from Mesopotamia and Egypt, through Greece and Rome, Byzantium and Islam, to Atlantic Europe and America, it has at several occasions swelled when streams from Indian, Chinese, Mexican, and Peruvian high cultures and from numerous lower societies and wild tribes have been led into it. The Chinese and the Indian cultures have certainly not abstained from taking in streams from each other and further from the West. But by and large they have so far given outflow to these in still, unchangeable backwaters.'* (quoted from Larsen: 11-12).

included North America), which with the right of progress swept aside everything that came in its way. Unlike in the eighteenth century there was no room for a recognition of the civilisational virtues of Asian cultures, the image of these was unequivocally negative. As Marx wrote on China:

> *Faced with British arms the authority of the Manchu dynasty collapsed; the superstitious faith in the indestructibility of the Celestial Empire was shattered; the barbaric and hermetic isolation from the civilised world was broken.*

and on India:

> *... these idyllic village communities, how harmless they may look, have since ancient times been the firm foundation of oriental despotism, they have narrowed the horizon of the human spirit as much as possible, making it a defenceless object of superstition, a slave of traditional habits, and deprived it of all greatness and historic energy* (quotes from Marx, 1972 ed.: 14, 17).

Marx's goal was universalistic, the emancipation of man as man. But this is a universalism that recognises only one binding model, hence Marx's embrace of European colonialist expansion.

Civilisation was thus again thought in the singular, but now unlike in the Enlightenment its positive, universally valid values were not considered accessible to all through reason and virtue, they were reified as European property, a product of uniquely European historical and racial qualities. This segregation was also projected back in time, as nineteenth century historicism met with Hellenomania. So, racist arguments were increasingly used to detach the Ancient 'Arian' or 'European' Greeks from any ties to their 'Asian' or 'African' neighbours around the eastern Mediterranean in order to secure the purity of European culture from its very beginning (Bernal 1987, Larsen 1988: 18-29).[3]

---

3 The idea of Ancient Greece as the 'cradle of Europe', and of the profound civilisational opposition of Greece and the Orient in antiquity has, as hinted at above, little historical justification. But it was and is profoundly influential in perceptions of Europe and Asia, West and East, and of why the two shall never meet. Larsen again offers an instructive example. In his *The Ancient Economy* from 1973 Moses Finley, historian and classical philologist, studied only Greek and Roman societies since, he argued, these cultures were too profoundly different from the cultures of the Near East to allow even for a common treatment: '*It is almost enough to point out that it is impossible to translate the word "freedom", eleutheria in Greek, libertas in Latin, or "free man" into any ancient Near Eastern language, including Hebrew, or into any Far Eastern language either, for that matter*' (quoted from from Larsen:21-22). This simply is not true,

America's entering the stage as an independent political actor led in a way to a reversal of the old way of defining the borders of Europe. If before, there had been a sharp border between Europe and the savages in the Americas, and an unclear border to the East, where Europe's superiority was not so indisputable, then in the nineteenth century the border to the West became blurred. Some - of course especially in the English speaking countries at both sides of the Atlantic - even preferred to talk of Western civilisation, while others included America as the extension of European civilisation. This civilisational space was expanding, whereas, as in the quotation by Ranke, the border to the East was ever increasingly being perceived as a sharp one, separating a superior white Europe from an inferior, coloured Asia.

So, the Enlightenment admiration of China almost disappeared as China was instead associated with opium, stagnation, cruelty, primitivism, etc. With the firm separation of 'the East' from Europe romanticising stereotypes of the exotic could occur, as in the Orientalism discourse (whether or not one accepts the full Saidian scheme), which created an image of the Orient as the very opposite of contemporary European civilisation - female, seductive, irrational and luxurious, cruel. One may, perhaps, suggest that whereas the term 'Oriental' had exotic connotations, granting it a measure of subversive attractiveness, 'Asiatic' had a purely negative ring. But it seems that the closer 'the Orient' got to home, the more it was perceived in non-romantic terms as simply menacing. A separate discourse on the Balkans (Europe's 'Near East') evolved, portraying it not as an exotic escape from civilisation, but as male, poor, filthy, and crude - not an anti-world of the West, but a transitional zone where civilisation runs out (Todorova, 1997: 17).

CIVILISATION'S DISCOMFORT, CULTURE AND RACE

Europe's superiority went hand in hand with Europe's imperialism and granted it legitimacy and meaning. And increasingly (and mostly inspired by Darwinian evolutionism) racialism became the standard mode of explanation of these developments. The biological discourse on human society also allowed for a social Darwinism linking race and class, so that the inferiority of the lower

---

Larsen adds (ibid.), but as shown by Bernal, the impossibility of cultural 'cross-fertilisation' between Greeks and Orientals became a *premise* for Ancient studies, not their result. The value of Bernal's study - in spite of his one-sidedness and factographic errors brought up by his critics (as in Lefkowitz & Rogers 1996) - lies in this illumination of the racial background for such assumptions.

74

races or classes could be explained with the laws of natural selection (Hannaford: Chapters 9 & 10).

If need be, one could 'eradicate the brutes', but mostly Europe's right to rule was explained as a civilising mission on behalf of mankind, the *'white man's burden'* of Kipling, which obliged Europeans to spread modern civilisation to the ungrateful natives. So, while Europe stood for the white man - in the singular, an individual, and male - superior racial qualities, civilisational progress, and values such as honesty, rationality, will, industriousness, etc., Asia was identified with the coloured masses - in the plural, a collective, often portrayed with feminine traits even when men were mentioned - inferior racial material, stagnation, and values like cunningness, irrationality, fatalism, a propensity for idle luxury rather than hard work etc.

These views are well represented in the pre-war writings of Johannes V. Jensen, Danish author and Nobel Prize winner. Inspired by Darwin and Kipling Jensen fully embraced modernity with its machine culture, and he believed that 'Gothic man' was chosen by nature to lead all mankind. Within Europe, he looked down on the Romance peoples, seeing in them representatives of a degenerate Christendom, but in the Orient, all such differences disappeared. He wrote at the beginning of the twentieth century, after some travel in the Orient: *'The lowest stoker may ... go ashore anywhere in the East and take up his privilege as a white man and inviolable... an inferior European is and remains an inferior European; but I find his class sovereignty in the East in its order'*(quoted from Andersen, 1998: 4). One notices the typical confusion of race and class: though inferior in Europe, the lower classes are natural masters in Asia, since through their race they have a share in the virtues of the upper classes from back home. Jensen also described Asia as a passive object, without history or development, incarnating the past that Europe had done right in leaving behind, and he accepted the 'ladder' model of civilisation, seeing in the peoples of the East a human material in which civilisation must find its reserves.

Still, this whole construction had a problem if its civilising project succeeded, i.e. if the coloured masses actually did learn from the white man and got out of their alleged lethargy. An early warning came with the Russo-Japanese war (1904-05), when for the first time in modern history an Asian power defeated a European country. The impact was only lessened by Russia's at best marginally European status, which made the country's defeat bearable and explicable by the corruption of its political system or the inferiority of the Slavs. To Jensen again, the universality of European civilisation was so self-evident that he in 1905 could side with Japan against Russia, since Japan represented modernity, and Russia 'semi-Asiatic' stagnation. Like the USA, Japan thus became 'non-eastern', a Europe outside Europe, proof of the triumph of the technical age (Andersen: 10). 'Asia', then, was a negative principle more than a geographical entity, and Jensen raged against the Asians *within* us (as in the 'semi-Asiatic' Swedish playwright August Strindberg), or, with another linking of race and class, *among* us, in the socially degenerate riffraff of Europe.

THE SHOCK OF THE GREAT WAR

The First World War was a profound shock to European self-perception. Now, in all its ruthlessness, European civilisation turned against itself. More than before, this war called for interpretation and location of guilt, and again, the Asian stereotype was used to label the enemy. In Germany and Austria the war was seen as a racial conflict with the Asiatic Slavs, in which the Germans defended a European cultural heritage also betrayed by England and France, while in the British and French propaganda the Germans played the role of the barbarian 'Huns' (Bugge, 1995: 88-89, 113-116; Heffernan 1998: 86-88, 97-98).

In the end, the pattern of expansion so far associated with Europe was reversed, as the non-European world had to intervene in Europe to bring an end to the war: the USA and Japan entered the war on allied side, and 'coloured' troops from the colonies were brought in to fill the ranks. And meanwhile, Russia jumped from autocracy to revolution in the name of the radical European political doctrines. In all respects, Europe's monopoly on the role of civilisation's avant-garde was shaken, and the impact on the idea of Europe was tangible.

So, conservatives increasingly defined Europe and its borders not in terms of civilisational avant-gardism (the USA and the USSR could claim these positions), but in terms of traditions and cultural heritage. The Americans might have bigger houses, but they could never have the medieval cathedrals of Europe, the popular argument went. Even in liberal circles, the unease created by the collapse of the identification of Europe with civilisation, and the rest of the world with a lack of it, made itself felt. So, the Spanish philosopher Ortega y Gasset remarked that '*in Central Africa the Negroes also ride in motor-cars and dose themselves with aspirin*', but that did not give them Europe's cultural heritage (Bugge, 1995: 123-25).

Also Jensen had to revise his opinions. He called the war a fratricide and was disturbed by Britain's alliance with 'semi-Asiatic' Russia, but most of all he blamed England for *'letting the Japanese loose on a Christian state'*. And after a journey to the Far East (*'what a difference it makes to see the East from Europe and Europe from the East'*) Jensen had to change his mind on Russia. One should have understood, he wrote, *'that Russia was after all Europe and acted as Europe's outpost, and that Japan was the East'*. To Jensen, 'Asia' ceased to a negative principle and became instead a concrete threat to Europe's right to rule, and so to Europe's very being. Also, Jensen's earlier linking of European identity to civilisational universalism was shattered by Japan's success: *'How deep is our culture, since whole peoples can rise and adopt it in one day?'*, he lamented. Now 'Europe' - with its Christendom, its history and dignity, its non-material traditions despised before - became a value to him in its own right (not as the incarnation of racial and civilisational virtues), and the USA and Japan enemies, no matter how modern they might be (Andersen: 9-11).

Though shattered in its pre-war foundations, neither the idea of Western or European supremacy, nor its racialist foundations were, however, abandoned. In Britain and the USA a *'WASP variant'* (White Anglo-Saxon Protestant) of Western civilisation came to fruition, expressed in university curricula as well as in a continued British colonialism, and nor did the French abandon their vision of a *'mission civilisatrice'* in the colonies. And in Germany, Hitler's racist theories and policies may well be called, as the British historian Norman Davies does it, *'the most extreme versions of 'Eurocentrism' and 'Western civilisation' that have ever existed'* (Davies: 38, see also 24-26). In all anti-communist circles, the identification of Bolshevism with Russia, and Russia with Asia was at hand, and again the ultimate conclusion to this logic was expressed by Hitler. The real border between Europe and Asia was, he stated, the one that *'divides the Germanic from the Slavonic world'* and that *'it is our duty to put it where we want to have it'* (quoted from Bugge, 1995: 107). Genocide then became the ultimate solution to the problem of Europe's borders in this meeting of European geo-politics and European racial thinking.

RETREAT, CONSOLIDATION, A EUROPE WITHOUT "OTHERS"?

In 1945 calls for a 'Europeanisation' of the world were not in vogue. The war left Europe exhausted and discredited, a memento more than a paragon, and both laurels and responsibility rested with the two superpowers, the USA and the USSR. A period of retreat - not always voluntary - followed, including a dismantling of the European colonial empires. In Western Europe a remarkable reconstruction began, which based on ideas of democracy, a social market economy, closer co-ordination of national policies, etc., led to the formation of the ECSC, the EC, and now the EU. Its results in terms of securing peace, regional stability, and economic growth have on the whole been impressive.

In this process the 'idea of Europe' for a long time played a very modest role, the scale of its ambitions had changed from the global to the regional, from the ideological to the pragmatic. In Wæver's words now '*the project of Europe is itself - not to launch itself on world history but to prevent another world war starting on European soil*' (Wæver, 1995: 175). Western Europe's success consisted at least as much in its breaking with tradition, as in its living up to it. So, slowly the ground was cleared for the 'rehabilitation' of Europe. The French philosopher Edgar Morin wrote in the 1980's in a celebration of this new Europe:

> *The decolonisation pushed the European nations back to their continent and cleansed Europe from one of its worst sides, whereby it also imperceptibly prepared the cleansing of the concept of Europe itself - namely by removing the tragic ambiguity that made Europe* intra muros *mean freedom, democracy, and human rights, while* extra muros *meaning oppression, exploitation, and unfreedom* (Morin, 1988: 140).

This may be true, but the very mentioning of 'muros', of walls, indicates that 'Europe' still takes shape in a separation of 'ins' and 'outs'. Until 1989 the Iron Curtain functioned as such a physical and mental wall that allowed the old dichotomy of West and East to endure, and although racial arguments largely disappeared, a host of theories were launched to explain why the political division of the continent also reflected a deeper historical or cultural division, which 'naturally' excluded Eastern Europe from Europe proper and associated it with Asia (Davies: 24-29, Wolff 1994).

One may illustrate this with the curious collection of old and new stereotypes in a book from 1950, *Eastern Europe and the Soviet Union*, in which the author, Eugen Lemberg, tried to balance between an *Occident - Orient* dichotomy, using the Catholic - Orthodox divide, and a division into Western and Eastern Europe placing the historical border along the new Iron Curtain. He explained East Central Europe's peculiarity in Rankian terms: '*It is by nature Occidental and yet in important matters different from the original*

Romance-Germanic West', and distinguished so between 'The real East' and 'East Central Europe', which together constituted Eastern Europe.

Lemberg insisted that the Occidental *Menschenbild* (view of man) was relative, not universal, and that unlike us, 'Eastern Man' had not experienced the occidental Middle Ages, the Renaissance and the Enlightenment: *'he is not brought up to causal and rational thinking, not emancipated... The individual is not so important as in the West. Hence Eastern European man's incredible readiness to die'* (Lemberg, 1950: 18). Also - with the motif of Montesquieu and Antiquity - Lemberg claimed that the nature of the homelands of Eastern Man to some extent determined his personality (his wildness and brutality), and he even linked this personality with the mode of rule in Eastern Europe. *'Again and again we can see in Oriental rulers the move towards the big, the monumental. The priest-king, the despot... has become a type since the Babylonian and the Persian empires...'*, Lemberg argued, moving from the Tatar khans, Ivan the Terrible, and Peter the Great to Lenin and Stalin (ibid,: 20 ff.). Present-day USSR was thus directly linked to the ancient Orient!

The ongoing 'rehabilitation' of Europe contains a significant ambiguity. Towards the USA and the USSR a cultural discourse has often been evoked: certain historically given quintessentially European qualities and values are said to be threatened by the two superpowers, who are perceived as alien to Europe. In this essentially conservative, defensive vision of the continent, modern civilisation is not the hallmark of Europe, but a danger to it. As Morin again argued: *'...if European culture has become a civilisation by spreading throughout the world, European cultures have remained cultures henceforth menaced by the civilisation that issued from Europe itself'* (Morin: 71). But within Europe, Western Europe readily assumed its traditional role as a model of civilisation for its more backward peripheries to follow, as has been particularly clear since 1989 in the conception of EC/EU enlargement policies and the treatment of Eastern Europe (Bugge, 1999: 25).

This ambiguity, which may be said to have marked European self-perception since the First World War, affects present discussions of how to bolster a 'European identity' as a corollary to economic and political integration in the EU. Leaving aside the liberal *laissez-faire* argument, one sees a tension between a 'republican' approach, deriving a European 'we-feeling' from a commitment to the political values embedded in the EU project, and a 'culturalist' approach that seeks to distill a uniquely European essence from the history of the European peoples.

It is worth noticing that culturalism has increasingly become an argument of the xenophobic right, where it substitutes for racial arguments in a discourse of segregation and exclusion. From such a culturalist perspective, Europe has obviously identifiable Others in 'the Muslims', or in its 'hordes' of immigrants with an 'alien' background. For those who do not embrace this world view the problem is that any attempt to bolster European identity by conjuring a new post-1989 significant 'Other' - be it the Muslims, Japanese or Chinese, or present-day Russia - ends up undermining the very principles that are said to constitute Europe: its secularism, tolerance, non-discrimination, human rights, etc., since millions of people from these 'othered' communities already live in Europe.

CONCLUSION

The aim of this paper had not been to deny that there are cultural differences between Danes and Vietnamese, or between people in Europe and in Asia. I have just tentatively sought to demonstrate how the concept of 'Asia' or - with slightly different connotations - 'the Orient' has been used in European discourses of identity and difference as a constituting 'Other', embodying the negation of 'European' qualities.

This opposition of 'Europe' and 'Asia' is not, I have argued, a perennial or natural thing. 'Asia' or 'Asiatic' was only used in marked hetero-stereotypes from around 1500, and since then the label has been attached to an immense variety of objects, many of them living outside geographic Asia (like the European proletariat, the Germans, the Jews, or the Russians). Furthermore, the 'Asia' of these discourses has been presented as an object of conquest and exploitation, a threat or a temptation, a different civilisation, or a non-civilisation, the past of modern Europe or its exotic anti-world. Religious arguments have been used to define this 'Asia', then cultural-historical, and often also racial ones. Clearly, the 'Asia' emerging from these discourses is a symbolic counter of identity, not an ontological entity, and - very importantly - nor is the 'Europe' constructed in this opposition.

In the Enlightenment 'discovery' of Europe we met three perspectives on civilisation, the universal, the spatial, and the temporal one. The temporal perspective with its one-dimensional understanding of the advance of civilisation and its 'translation' of differences in space into differences in time, is - though still influential in discourses on 'development countries' or on regional 'backwardness' - of little use today in attempts to define a special European civilisation. It is difficult to claim that Amsterdam or Birmingham are more 'modern' than Tokyo or Shanghai, or Europe more so than the USA or Japan.

The spatial perspective is much stronger, and it is crucial to a culturalist-essentialist argument. But if one perceives cultures as spatially located closed entities with fixed borders, members of foreign cultures can be stigmatised as intruders or threats if they appear on 'your' territory. To define 'European' and 'Asian' civilisation and values in purely spatial terms is to pave the way for ethnic cleansing or strongly assimilationist policies.

The universalist perspective may, however, be useful, once it is freed from the essentialist assumption that certain civilisational values, *because* they are European, reflect the desire of all men (to paraphrase a De Gaulle quotation on French values; see Wæver: 184). A genuine discussion can begin if only we abandon the assumption that a universalist discourse must also be uniform, and that the values discussed (if one takes democracy and human rights), because they were first formulated *in* Europe, must also necessarily be *European* values. Perhaps, we should altogether avoid the whole terminology and idea of inherently 'Asian' or 'European' values and speak instead concretely - and with an eye for change and exchange - of 'values in Asia' and 'values in Europe'.

LITERATURE

1. Andersen, Uffe, *Europa - du moderne, du tålmodige!*, Seminar Paper, European Studies, University of Aarhus, January 1998.

2. Bernal, Martin: *Black Athena - The Afroasiatic Roots of Classical Civilisation, Vol.1* (London: Vintage, 1987, 1991 ed.).

3. Boer, Pim den, Europe to 1914: The Making of an Idea, in Kevin Wilson & Jan van der Dussen (eds.), *The History of the Idea of Europe* (London: Routledge, 1995) pp. 13-82.

4. Bugge, Peter, The Nation Supreme: The Idea of Europe 1914-1945, in Kevin Wilson & Jan van der Dussen (eds.), *The History of the Idea of Europe*, London Routledge, 1995) pp. 83-149.

5. Bugge, Peter, The Use of the Middle: Mitteleuropa vs. Stredni Evropa, in *European Review of History*, Vol.6, No.1, 1999.

6. Davies, Norman, *Europe: A History* (Oxford University Press, 1996).

7. Fisch, Jörg, Zivilisation, Kultur, in Otto Brunner, Werner Conze & Reinhart Koselleck (Hrsg), *Geschichtliche Grundbegriffe Band 7* (Stuttgart: Klett Cotta, 1992) pp. 679-772.

8. Gollwitzer, Heinz, *Europabild und Europagedanke - Beiträge zur deutschen Geistesgeschichte des 18. und 19. Jahrhunderts* (München: C.H. Beck, 1964).

9. Gress, David, *From Plato to NATO: The Idea of the West and Its Opponents* (New York: The Free Press,1998).

10. Groh, Dieter, *Rußland im Blick Europas* (Frankfurt am Main: Suhrkamp, 1961; 1988 ed.).

11. Hale, John, *The Civilisation of Europe in the Renaissance* (London: Harper-Collins, 1993).

12. Hannaford, Ivan, *Race: The History of an Idea in the West* (Washington D.C./Baltimore & London Woodrow Wilson Center Press, 1996).

13. Harbsmeier, Michael, Europas opdagelse, in Hans Boll-Johansen & Michael Harbsmeier (red.), *Europas opdagelse - Historien om en idé* (København: Christian Ejlers Forlag, 1988) pp. 82-114.

14. Hay, Denys, *Europe - The Emergence of an Idea*, Edinburgh University Press, 1968.

15. Heffernan, Michael, *The Meaning of Europe: Geography and Geopolitics* (London: Arnold, 1998).

16. Hobsbawm, Eric, *On History* (London: Weidenfeld & Nicolson, 1997).

17. Ifversen, Jan, The Meaning of European Civilisation - a Historical-Conceptual Approach, *European Studies Newsletter*, Vol.1, No.2, 1998, pp.20-38.

18. Klug, Ekkehard, Das "asiatische" Rußland. Über die Entstehung eines europäisches Vorurteils, in *Historische Zeitschrift* 245, 1987, pp. 265-289.

19. Larsen, Mogens Trolle, Europas lys, in Hans Boll-Johansen & Michael Harbsmeier (red.), *Europas opdagelse - Historien om en idé* (København: Christian Ejlers Forlag, 1988) pp. 9-37.

20. Le Huu Tang, Research on Asian Values - Problems set forth, *Papers from the International Workshop 'The Asian Values and Vietnam's Development in Comparative Perspective'*, Hanoi, 24-26 March 1999, pp. 9-11.

21. Lefkowitz, Mary A. & Rogers, Guy MacLean (eds.), *Black Athena Revisited* (Chapel: Hill University of North Carolina Press, 1996).

22. Lemberg, Eugen, *Osteuropa und die Sowjetunion - Geschichte und Probleme der Welt hinter dem Eisernen Vorhang* (Stuttgart: Curt E. Schwab, 1950).

23. Lemberg, Hans, Zur Entstehung des Osteuropabegriffs im 19. Jahrhundert – Vom "Norden" zum "Osten" Europas, *Jahrbücher für Geschichte Osteuropas*, Vol. 33, No.1, 1985, pp. 48-91.

24. Ludat, Herbert, *Deutsch-Slawische Frühzeit und modernes polnisches Geschichtsbewusstsein - Ausgewählte Aufsätze* (Köln – Wien: Böhlau Verlag 1969).

25. Marx, Karl & Engels, Friedrich, *Om kolonier, industrimonopol og arbejderbevægelse* (København: Futura, 1972 ed.).

26. Morin, Edgar, *Europæisk kultur* (København: Gyldendal, 1988).

27. Schlumberger, Jörg A. (1994): Europas antikes Erbe, in Jörg A. Schlumberger & Peter Segl (Hrsg.): *Europa - aber was ist es?*, Böhlau Verlag, Köln, 1-19

28. Todorova, Maria, *Imagining the Balkans* (Oxford: Oxford University Press, 1997).

29. Toynbee, Arnold, 'Asia' and 'Europe': Facts and Fantasies, Chapter IX. C (i), Annex in: *A Study of History*, Vol.VIII, (Oxford University Press, 1954) pp. 708-729.

30. Wolff, Larry, *Inventing Eastern Europe: The Map of Civilisation on the Mind of the Enlightenment* (Stanford: Stanford University Press, 1994).

31. Wolff, Larry, "Voltaire's Public and the Idea of Eastern Europe: Toward a Literary Sociology of Continental Division", in *Slavic Review*, Vol.54, No.4, 1995, pp. 932-942.

32. Wæver, Ole, "Europe since 1945: Crisis to Renewal", in Kevin Wilson & Jan van der Dussen (eds.), *The History of the Idea of Europe* (London: Routledge, 1995) pp. 151-214.

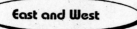

The Iwakura Mission within the Framework of the Modernisation of Japan

Li Narangoa
Nordic Institute of Asian Studies

*T*he rising economic power of Japan awakened increasing interest in the country and the reasons behind its astonishing success within the general public as well as the mass media. The academic world responded by organising a series of conferences assembling scholars from the fields of history, politics and economics. These conferences became famous for their focus on what was to be labelled the "modernisation" of Japan, preceding its impressive appearance in the markets of the world. [1]

This phenomenon was, in fact, not entirely new to students of history. Japan had first captured world-wide attention with its unexpected victory over Russia in the war of 1904-05. Western powers began to accept Japan as an equal, at least in military terms. Japan was a newcomer but had adapted with amazing speed to the production and utilisation of Western technology. Certainly, the Second World War caused a harsh and discouraging setback, but from the sixties onwards one easily gained the impression of Japan as a phoenix rising from the ashes. The aforementioned conferences – organised in the United States and summed up in useful and convincing publications – did not

---

[1] For example, there is a series of six volumes, published by Princeton University Press for the Conference of Modern Japan on the Association for Asian Studies:
Changing Japanese Attitudes Toward Modernization, edited by Marius B. Jansen (1965)
The State and Economic Enterprise in Japan, edited by William W. Lockwood (1965)
Aspects of Social Change in Modern Japan, edited by R. P. Dore (1967)
Political Development in Modern Japan, edited by Robert E. Ward (1968)
Dilemmas of Growth in Prewar Japan, edited by James William Morley (1971)
Tradition and Modernization in Japanese Culture, edited by Donald H. Shively (1971)

lead to a temptation to solve the "secret" of Japan's success once and for all, and to provide an easy answer to the questions raised.

Still, the fact that a nation that was bogged down in feudalism, primarily agrarian and had a pre-modern social order until the second half of the 19th century, headed straight towards such rapid industrialisation elicited enough fascination to be looked upon as a possible model for other nations confronted with similar circumstances. Studies exist comparing Japan with India and Turkey, and these take the standpoint gaining from Japan's experience.[2] One author even attempts to discuss the modernisation of Nigeria alongside Japan's successful past. Nor did the People's Republic of China hesitate to direct its attention to the mechanisms of the Meiji Restoration and its results. However, I do not think it is reasonable to suggest that Vietnam may also have to look toward Japan for possible fruitful decisions. It is extremely difficult to directly compare the development of nations, since each has its own particular history, traditions and characteristic cultural attributes. Nevertheless, impetus and motivation, attitude and studiousness deserve to be seen transgressing borders, and for this purpose I have chosen to talk about and to introduce to you the so-called Iwakura Mission, which is much more than merely an anecdote in Japan's modern history. Its successes and, to be frank, at times its failures provide a wonderful mirror of Japan's metamorphosis into a modern society.

DOMESTIC AND FOREIGN CRISIS

By the mid-nineteenth century Japan had to cope with domestic problems, as well as with foreign affairs. A Chinese phrase, rendered in Japanese as *Naiyu gaikan* (troubles at home and dangers from outside), was used at the time. Today we would say domestic and foreign crises. Like most social crises in the world, it also manifested itself in economic conflicts. To meet financial difficulties, the domains were forced to reduce the stipends of samurai retainers and to levy additional taxes on peasants. These added economic burdens on the large number of samurai retainers and the peasantry fostered antagonism between them and the domain governments and created serious social crises.[3]

Moreover, the Western powers were just beginning to encroach on Asia. China was defeated in the Opium War (1840-42) and England was increasing its influence on the Asian continent. There would have been nothing to fear from the intrusion of Western powers if Japan had provided itself with an

---

[2] For example, *Political Modernization in Japan and Turkey*, edited by Ward, R. E. & D. A. Rustow (1964).
[3] See, for example, Beasley 1972:42–54.

adequate means of defence, but the country totally lacked the military means to resist outside aggression. The over 200-year-old seculationist policy of the Tokugawa Shogunate was challenged. Finally, the expeditions of American Commander Perry in 1853-54 forced the Bakufu to open up the Japanese ports of Hakodate and Shimoda to American ships for supplies and trade, subject to local regulations. In 1855, the signing of a treaty gave the Kurile Islands south of and including Etorofu to Japan, and other islands north of these to Russia. Three ports - Nagasaki, Shimoda, and Hakodate - were opened to Russian shipping. In the same year Japan signed a similar agreement with the Netherlands (Kato 1986: 43-46). In 1858 Japan signed treaties with the United States, Russia, Great Britain, France and the Netherlands. These treaties contained three main aspects. Firstly, Yedo and certain ports were opened to foreigners. Secondly, a very low scale of import duties was imposed upon Japan and lastly nationals of these and 14 other countries with which such treaties were signed were exempt from the jurisdiction of Japanese courts of law. The colony of Cochin China was annexed by France in 1862, after which the protectorate of Cambodia was established in 1867. This was soon followed by French penetration, admittedly with little initial success, in the region of Haiphong and Hanoi. Russia took over the coastal area between the Amur and the Korean frontier from China, and founded Vladivostock, which means 'Ruler of the East', close to this frontier (Storry 1968: 96; 106).

Finally, in 1868 Emperor Meiji issued the proclamation: "Restoration of Imperial Government". The name Edo was changed to Tokyo. In the spring of 1869 the Meiji Tenno moved to the new capital from Kyoto.

FROM OLD TO NEW

Discussing the complexities of Japanese "modernisation" is a difficult task. Certainly, the story already begins in the Edo-period. A researcher would be compelled to study early technological development, which in many ways was related to: 1) the need for enhancing agricultural productivity; 2) the growing importance of trade and manufacture throughout the country; 3) the coming into existence of an increasingly well-to-do and self-reliant township population in competition with the gentry of warriors (*samurai*) – who were losing more and more of their inherited dominance; 4) the Japanese experience in dealing with foreigners; 5) an astonishingly sophisticated educational system. At the end the scholar would have to investigate the problem of the unequal treaties and their impact on Japan. However, I will not dwell on these factors further now but turn directly to the Iwakura Mission and its fate.

The unequal treaties - the first of them concluded with five of the Western powers in 1858 - provided extreme difficulties for every Japanese government. Though officially called treaties of friendship, navigation and commerce, they deprived Japan of its full sovereignty and the right to control its trade. A revision of these treaties was therefore a top priority of Japan's foreign policy. This was, or rather should have been, the main aim of the Iwakura Mission, which we shall now accompany on its tour to the Western treaty powers. The mission left by ship from Yokohama harbour in December 1871 in order to cross the Pacific, heading first for the United States, and was full of energy and optimistic about its aims.

The Japanese government spared no cost or pain in the attempt to achieve these long-cherished treaty revisions and despatched a mission as high ranking as never before or since. The first minister, acting as a pleni-potentiary and extraordinary ambassador, was Iwakura Tomomi (1825-83), a man close to the royal court who had played an important role during the Meiji Restoration and who had been invested with the position of "chancellor to the right" - today we might call his position that of prime minister. Four vice-ambassadors had been allocated to him, three of them with the rank of government ministers - Okubo Toshimichi (1830-78), Kido Koin (1833-77) and Ito Hirobumi (1841-1909). Thus, half of the government left Japan, trusting that the other half would faithfully fulfil its responsibilities at home, just as the mission would try to reach its objectives abroad on this important journey. To ensure the continuance of their policies during their absence, Iwakura and the key members of his Mission had obtained assurances from the "caretaker government" who remained at home. The latter had promised that no important appointments or policy changes would be made during the absence of the Iwakura Mission (Borton 1970:100).

THE MISSION'S TRIALS AND JOYS

The Iwakura Mission consisted of more than a hundred administrators, scholars of various disciplines, and students. They sailed on 23 December 1871 from Yokohama and returned to Nagasaki on 13 September 1873, to Nagasaki. According to their original plans, the mission should have spent about ten and a half months on the entire journey. But since negotiations on the revision of treaties with the United States and the other Western powers turned out to be one-sided affairs and took much longer than expected, the time spent on the journey had to be continuously extended, and in the end an extra year went by.

87

Thus the duration of the excursion covered a total of almost two years (Tanaka 1997:8).

Among the 42 students who joined the mission in order to study in America and Europe were five girls, the first ever to study abroad. They were in fact "guinea pigs" for Japan's new education system.[4] The idea here was that women should also learn from the West to improve their intellectual abilities, with special regard to methods of child rearing and education. It was recognised that, for the development of Japanese civilisation, improved education of forthcoming generations was essential. For this purpose, well-educated and enlightened mothers were needed. The youngest member of the group, Tsuda Umeko (1865-1929), was only seven (!) years old. She grew up in Washington D.C., raised by an American host family, and studied at private schools. Many years later, after her return to Japan she founded an English School for Women, later named Tsuda College. It has remained one of the bastions of women's higher education in Japan to this day. Umeko met, in fact, a lucky fate. Two of her slightly older companions (the eldest being sixteen!), became ill almost immediately when transplanted into the completely unfamiliar surroundings, and had to be sent back to their native land without starting, let alone completing, their studies in America. This experiment of separating children from their families at such an early age for duties in the service of the nation has, understandably, never been repeated.[5]

Besides aiming to find a way of revising the "unequal treaties", the Mission intended to achieve recognition for the new imperial regime and to study and be informed about modern western achievements, with a view to seeking a model for the new Meiji government, in power for only a couple of years, to follow (Tanaka 1997: 8). However, the negotiations failed. They failed in the United States, and they failed all the more in England, as both powers had considerable imperialistic interests in Asia, and were determined to protect their advantages over Japan. Iwakura and other members of the Mission made the painful realisation that Japan had not yet made sufficient progress with its internal reforms to be able to negotiate successfully with the Western nations, and recognised the necessity of modernisation in order to deal with Western countries as an equal. Consequently, the mission was instructed to gain as much

---

[4] The Ministry of Education had been established in the summer of 1871, and a team of experts with Western advisers was beginning to work on the draft of a compulsory education scheme when the embassy left (See, for example, Nagai 1971:35–76).

[5] See, for example, Furuki 1991:xi-xiv.

practical knowledge as possible of foreign governments, industries, and public works. They therefore spent the majority of the tour travelling in 15 countries, all respective treaty powers. They did so realistically, without great political expectations, visiting public institutions, various factories, schools, military installations, dockyards, prisons, museums and so forth.

In order to encourage the public in Japan to begin the process of modernisation and to gain its understanding for the Mission's journey, the Mission decided to publish a comprehensive account of the information and data they would collect during their journey. A Confucian scholar, Kume Kunitake (1839-1931) was appointed as official diarist to compile a record of the mission's activities. Kume, under personal instructions from Iwakura, kept a daily account of all of the embassy's tours and excursions, receptions and discussions, explaining new inventions or describing scenic spots, omitting only very confidential business, for example the question of treaty revision. The work was financed by the government and published in 1878 as *Tokumei Zenken Taishi Bei-O Kairan Jikki* (A True Account of the Tour in America and Europe of the Special Embassy) in five impressive volumes, richly illustrated with depictions of places of interest throughout this diplomatic ramble around the world. The mission's account contains its observations and analyses of Western politics, economics, society, military systems, education, culture, history, religion and philosophy, among many other things. Kume used the classical Japanese and Chinese literary style and made frequent references to Chinese philosophy, history, and poetry. It is a comparative study of Western and Eastern culture and is, as one of our leading contemporary scholars on Japan's modern history concludes, a kind of an "Encyclopaedia of the West" (Tanaka 1997:10).

Visits to Museums and exhibitions were some of the most pleasant undertakings of the Mission's members. They were especially impressed by the World Exhibition in Vienna. They stayed in Vienna for a couple of weeks altogether and used four days in all in visiting the exhibition. It was certainly the best opportunity the Mission had to observe the "world" as a whole in a very short time and to compare the cultures, art and industrial progress of the different countries of Europe as well as of the Orient. The exhibition appeared as a microcosm of the planet for them. As Kume wrote: "It seems to me as if the planet is so miniaturised that it can fit into this park" (*Jikki* V: 35). He described the aims, meanings and history of various World Exhibitions as well as that of several museums. In the Mission's account there were many detailed notes about industrial products, from machines for agriculture and the weaving industry to medical instruments and handicrafts, as well as the fine arts of every country. The differences in the products of the various countries were compared, for example French and Italian art were considered the best in Europe, but the Italians had more sense for natural and classical beauty. The Belgians had a character similar to that of the French, their technology and art resembled each other. The products of Austria and Prussia shared a similar style and were of good quality, but those of Austria seemed more luxurious. The Dutch had a great number of abilities. Among their products there were a lot of excellent diamond and lacquer goods. Russia produced great numbers of scientific instruments, but its other wares were not as good as those of France, Germany, Italy and Austria. Denmark exhibited a very small number of wares and they were quite uninteresting. The Persians wove excellent carpets. The products of China at the exhibition were not particularly special. Kume appreciated the European oil paintings very much and was deeply disappointed at the Japanese oil paintings exhibited. In his own words, "they are not even as good as the painting of European children". The Japanese traditional paintings of flowers and birds were extremely pleasant, but the portraits looked so awful "that one sweated" in shame and fear. Kume was very pleased that the visitors were so fond of the Japanese souvenirs sold at the exhibition. He concluded that free (liberal) minds were the most important sources of creative works in every discipline (*Jikki* V:32-50).

Every part of the account contains comments on what might be useful for Japan's modernisation. But the most essential tendency of the mission's account with regard to reform or modernisation is the perfect combination of tradition and modernity.

HARMONY BETWEEN TRADITION AND MODERNISATION?

The mission's members paid considerable attention to political and social structures, industries, military affairs, infrastructures, education (particularly elementary education for the masses) and so on. They soon realised how much domestic reform was necessary before the Western Powers would begin to consider Japan as an equal. They did not, however, lose their critical sense while observing and learning from the West, and concluded that reforms should occur gradually, with regard for Japan's own particular circumstances and traditions. They were, of course, also aware of the fact that continued reliance upon tradition was as risky as radical change. The phrase *wakon yousai* (Japanese spirit, Western sciences) suggests a harmonious solution.

The Mission intended to add to its existing knowledge of Western political practices and theories. In the course of the journey it realised that no Western country individually could provide an ideal model for Japan, but rather that Europe on the whole had produced a higher form of civilisation than that of East Asia. In the Mission's account, Kume made a probing analysis of German culture and society. It was often pointed out that the German example could be most relevant for Japan, since both nations shared similarities in their recent problems and present aims: restoration of the monarchy, political centralisation and unification, popular education, the security of its frontiers, recognition abroad, and the development of commerce and industry. England was said to enjoy both freedom and order because reformers had moved carefully and gradually, building upon tradition and avoiding the destructive revolutionary tendencies of the French. Kume referred back to the Eastern classics to illustrate the best approach to reform and the basic responsibilities of government and education. To achieve wealth and power, a people must work hard, be self-reliant, trustworthy and obedient. Abroad, national dignity must be upheld; at home, there must be peace throughout the land.[6] Rulers should adopt policies, which conform to the manners and customs of the people. In Germany, for example, Bismarck and the Kaiser were undertaking many reforms, but their policies were in accord with the customs and traditions of the German people (*Jikki* IV: 220).

The Mission's members were greatly impressed by the way which the Western countries preserved and cherished their history, culture and arts. Kume linked the recent spurt in Western material civilisation to a longer historical preparation. The progress did not really occur overnight. It was not the destruction of the old order by the new, but the perfection of tradition by degrees. "No matter how much we grow and change, we remain products of the past." The people of the West were assisted by their love of history. They kept a careful record of it and built upon it. They probed the past for secrets, visited ruins, collected documents, recorded tales, and made excavations of ancient sites. They revered the study of new things as well. Japan should do these things too, stressed Kume, and "we must not lose any old pieces of paper, not even a part of a letter" (*Jikki*, IV: 56, 217-21). He seemed so convinced by his own words that he began work on editing Japanese history and criticising Japanese historiography following the publication of this account in 1878.[7]

---

[6] See Mayo 1973:33.
[7] See Sugiya 1997:16-17.

The concerts and operas sponsored by the several European Royal families and governments inspired Iwakura considerably and he began to patronise the traditional Japanese theatres, *No* and *Kabuki*, on his return from the journey. Kume was deeply impressed by the Bible-reading, church-going habits of the Americans and the English. It amazed him that the city streets were so quiet on Sundays and that shops and offices shut while people worshipped. In Scotland he discovered that tourists who stayed in their hotels and did not go to church on Sundays were scolded. This kind of religion, he had to admit, motivated people to undertake projects and get things done. But he also stated that the upper classes in Europe made an outward show of honouring religion, while in actuality they used it as a tool to gain the people's support of particular policies and to ensure obedience to authority (*Jikki* I: 39).

During the journey Christians often said that Japan was hostile to Christianity. Iwakura therefore promised them that Japan would not issue any further anti-Christian legislation. The restrictions on those Japanese professing to be Christians were removed on 24 February 1873, before the mission's return home.[8]

THE IWAKURA MISSION IN SAIGON

The return trip took the mission from Marseilles to Alexandria, then on to Aden, Bombay, Calcutta, the Malacca Straits, Singapore, Saigon, Hong Kong, Canton, Shanghai, and finally home to Nagasaki. Kume was just as indefatigable in collecting information during their short trips ashore in these countries as in Europe, but his descriptions are condescending. He contrasted the prosperous, clean foreign sections of these port cities with the impoverished, dirty indigenous areas.

The mission arrived in Saigon on 22 August 1873 and stayed for only one day. Kume wrote a short report about the city, its people, history and climate in the embassy's account. It was a day with temperatures of up to 86°F, so that Kume came to think of Aden. He was not pleased with the roads in Saigon. "The roads are quite broad, but they are not in good condition. There are many trees, and plenty of wild grass on the roadside" (*Jikki* V:315). Throughout the whole journey, wherever the mission found itself, Kume paid a lot of attention to roads and infrastructures. He measured the modernisation and civilisation of a country by the condition of its roads. It said in the *Jikki*: "From the condition of a country's roads, you can easily learn how the country is progressing, and

---

[8] See, for example, Anesaki 1963:337-38.

whether its inhabitants are hardworking or not" (*Jikki*V: 172). He was not as much impressed by Saigon itself as by the sweet and sour mangosteen served at dinner in their hotel. He gave a very detailed description of this fruit. According to the mission's account Saigon at that time had 180,000 inhabitants, and most businesses and shops were owned and run by the Chinese. There were lovely Buddhist temples decorated with engravings of dragons, and Catholic churches in the city. He noted that the common people chewed the leaves of the betelnut tree so that their teeth became terribly blackened, and that the Chams and Malays were brave and impatient: "They easily became annoyed and shouted. It was then difficult to cool them down. Even small matters made them angry and gnash their teeth and bellow" (*Jikki*V: 317). Observing the characters of different nations seemed to be one of Kume's hobbies. He often mentioned the characters of different nations. For example, at that time the Germans were considered slow and disciplined, and Kume even wrote down a joke he was told on his journey:

In Europe, they say that if an Englishman, Frenchman, German, and American are assigned a task and given six hours to complete it, the American will finish in four hours and spend the rest of his time taking a stroll or wandering around. The Frenchman will finish in four hours and then dine and sing songs. The Englishman will take five hours and then work on something else for another hour. But the German will not be finished even in six hours and will resume the task in the evening, continuing to work even in his spare time (*Jikki* II: 43).[9]

Kume was not so ignorant that he would have forgotten to point out the French colonisation of Vietnam. France occupied this land and made it its "Eastern storeroom", exporting all manner of commodities. The buildings in the French settlement were a combination of Asian and European styles and looked clean and pleasant compared to those of the natives. The French government had invested 8,000,000 francs per year in a French Shipping company in order to improve the transport to Saigon and had benefited from this (*Jikki* V:315;320).

Whilst staying in Saigon they visited the outlying area of Cholon (now the China-town of Saigon) where they enjoyed the natural beauty of the area. On the way there they passed by a coffee plantation which lay next to a French military barracks. There they happened to meet a group of prisoners who were

---

[9] Cited in Mayo 1973:46.

being taken to be executed. "There were tens of prisoners, led by native Cham solders. They were put into huts made of coco leaves. Some of them even wore handcuffs" (*Jikki* V:317). Kume did not mention why the prisoners were to be executed.

The mission's stay in Saigon (now Ho Chi Minh City) seems to have been little more than a break for the members to rest. But here already they felt at home to some extent, because the natives were physically small, like the Japanese, and the shop signs were written in Chinese. In the Mission's diary it said: "Almost every house had wall posters made of red paper on which were written wise and happy maxims. They were so prominent that I felt, I had returned home and forgot about being abroad in a place with a different language" (*Jikki* V:316;318).

The Mission sailed to Hong Kong from Saigon on 23 August and then via Canton and Shanghai to Nagasaki.

CONCLUSION

The journey of the Iwakura Mission is one of the most intriguing events in Japan's recent history, and can undoubtedly be seen as an important step within the framework of understanding the modernisation of Japan. It could not achieve its original aim of revising the unequal treaties, but the members of the Mission were sobered by what they had observed abroad and were more convinced than ever that Japan's primary task was to strengthen its internal economy and military power. The first major decision that the Mission influenced strongly upon its return was that of calling off the planned expansion into Korea.[10] Its voice soon initiated reforms in every aspect of education, the military and industry. One of the vice-ambassadors, Ito Hirobumi, later returned to Europe to study political philosophy in Berlin and Vienna in preparation for the drafting of Japan's future Constitution. This constitution, proclaimed by the Meiji Government in February 1889, was the last and most crucial step in furthering Japan's progress.

---

[10] In the early months of 1872, Japan had sent official envoys to Korea to negotiate a treaty and to open up the country from its seclusion. Saigon, who had great confidence in the newly established conscript army, recommended an aggressive policy. In October 1873, the Emperor ordered the government to concentrate on internal improvements and to forget about a military expedition to Korea (Borton 1970:101).

In conclusion, the awfully long and laborious dealings with the Western powers for their consent to revise the unequal treaties forced the Japanese government to make greater efforts to hasten the process of modernisation. Japan hurried its modernisation because it had to protect itself from possible colonisation by Western countries, and in order to amend the unequal treaties with foreign nations. Finally, in 1894, after a quarter century of painstaking efforts from every Japanese government consequently in office, the problem of revision of the unequal treaties had been largely resolved. The end of the fight for equality with the West was in sight.

If the political form of a nation shapes its development and history, the history and culture of a nation effect the form of its politics. The Japanese ambassadors were most impressed by the standard of industrialisation in England and America, but also inspired to a great extent by Germany, a young and rising nation among the other European empires. The Prussian type of constitution, eventually to be introduced in Japan, is rooted somehow in this experience.

The journey of the Iwakura Mission took place almost a hundred and thirty years ago. It was a time when Japan found itself in crisis in domestic as well as in foreign matters, as well as in a period of transition. From that time on until today more than a century has passed. Many things have changed since then, with problems solved or made insignificant. Still, both the diary left to us by Kume and the efforts of Iwakura Tomomi and his mission to cope with new developments and to accept the challenge of the West despite the heavy emotional and financial burdens of carrying out their task, are as convincing today as then. The Mission's vivid accounts and recordings provide valuable reading to help us in understanding the problems of a country forced to balance her traditional society and culture with the needs of accepting new methods of modern development.

LITERATURE

1. Anesaki, Masaharu, *History of Japanese Religion* (Charles E. Tuttle Company of Rutland, Vermont & Tokyo, 1963).

2. Beasley, W.G., *The Meiji Restoration* (Standford University Press, 1972).

3. Borton, Hugh, *Japan's Modern Centrury* (The Ronald Press Company, 1970).

4. Furuki, Yoshiko, *The White Plum. A Biography of Ume Tsuda* (New York-Weatherhill-Tokyo, 1991).

5. Jikki (Tokumei Zenken Taishi Bei-O Kairan Jikki I–V*), edited by Kume Kunitake (Tokyo: Iwanami, 1997).*

6. Kato, Yuzo, "Kaikoku no seikai-shi", in *Kaikoku he no uzushio. Kaigai shiten. Nihon no rekishi no. 12* (Tokyo: Gyosei, 1986).

7. Mayo, Marlene J., "The Western Education of Kume Kunitake, 1871-6", in *Monumenta Nipponica. Studies in Japanese Culture.* Volume XXVIII no.1, (Tokyo: Sophia University, 1973).

8. Nagai, Micho, "Westernizaton and Japanization: The Early Meiji Transformation of Education", in *Tradition and Modernization in Japanese Culture*, edited by Donald H. Shivelly (Princeton, New Jersey: Princeton University Press, 1971).

9. Storry, Richard, *A History of Modern Japan* (Harmondsworth, Middlesex: Penguin Books Ltd., 1968).

10. Sugiya, Akira, "Rekishika toshite no Kume Kunitake", in *Rekishika Kume Kunitake* (Tokyo: Kume Museum of Art, 1997).

11. Tanaka, Akira, "Kume Kunitake to O-Bei kairan jikki", in *Rekishika Kume Kunitake* (Tokyo: Kume Museum of Art, 1997).

12. Ward, R. E. & D. A. Rustow, *Political Modernization in Japan and Turkey*, (Princeton, 1964).

Asian Values and EU-ASEAN Relations

Bui Huy Khoat
Center for European Studies, NCSSH

J mmediately after its foundations in 1967, the Association of South
East Asian Nations (ASEAN) was recognised by the European Union
(then known as the European Economic Community, EEC). In March 1980,
both parties signed the EEC-ASEAN Cooperation Agreement to speed up
cooperation. EEC-ASEAN relations after that witnessed encouraging steps of
development. Since the end of the 80s, these relations have qualitatively
evolved, gradually shifting from a donor-recipient relationship to partnership.
The subsequent intention of the European Union (EU) to upgrade its
relationship with Asia, including ASEAN, and increase its presence in this
region, has been expressed in the document *"Towards a New Asia Strategy"*.

So far, the path to the development of EU-ASEAN relations has led to
good results. But the relationship has not always been smooth; particularly,
differences in the perception of Asian values are complicated and sensitive
issues found at every step along this path.

There seems to be a common view that Asian values are not in
concordance with Western liberal democracy. Proponents of this view hold
that, contrary to people in the West, Asian people tend to prefer power,
authority and hierarchy. Therefore, Asian values promote high collective rights
over individual ones, stressing unity, social harmony, consensus and order.
Also from this point of view, the Asian people think that the family, not the
individual, is the fundamental social entity, and whence, as an inseparable part
of the collectivity, each individual has not only his or her rights but also
obligations and duties which are given greater weight, especially when a
common stability and interest is needed. Human rights should therefore be
understood in the context of the culture, history and economy of each specific

nation. For example, in a country where poverty has not yet been eradicated, socio-economic rights are placed higher than political rights in the priority list.

. This viewpoint seems to totally oppose Asian values to Western liberal democracy, thus indicating that what Asian societies need is not liberal democracy but good governance. And good governance in turn is understood as to bring about economic well-being, political stability, social order, communal harmony and effective and honest administrative management.

Though differences and even disagreements are available in the perception of Asian values, it does not mean that the EU is pursuing a totally value-based policy in its relationship with Asia. In practice, EU-ASEAN relations were not seriously affected by disagreements before the early the 1990's. It was only the collapse of socialism in East Europe that made many people in the West believe in the eventual victory of Western type liberal democracy that has strongly revived the idea of associating value perceptions to EU policies in regard to ASEAN. With their conviction on the ultimate triumph of Western liberal democracy in the former Soviet Union and East Europe, Europeans think that it is their obligation to assist in the success of this democracy elsewhere as well. In this background, almost all EU members have envisaged a policy of linking aid with human rights, democratisation, market economy and so on.

As a response to the policy of EU, which they considered as interference in their internal affairs, Asian countries seem to stand for the view that highlights Asian values as a self-defence reaction to the intention of the United States to impose the so-called "*a new Pax Americana*" for the formation of an unipolar world on the basis of the hegemony and uniqueness of Western values. Meanwhile, with the deep-reaching economic recession of the West in the early 1990's and economic achievements made by Asian countries, Asian values seemed then to have the "upper hand" as compared against "signs" of such "degradation" in the West as unemployment, drug addiction, huge increase in crime, the family in crisis and so on. It was then that Asian economic achievements were considered as a proof for the universality of a purely indigenous, non-Western hybrid type of socio-economic development and management. Proponents of Asian values made use of this opportunity to claim those values to be efficient tools for the maintenance of the political status quo in Asian countries, countries that had been increasingly confronted with pressure for political reform.

Faced with an economic recession more serious than expected, and about losing their position and reduced influence in a region considered then to be the scene of the most dynamic economic development in the world, West European countries and the EU have gradually returned to a more pragmatic relationship with ASEAN and Asia in general. However, at the outset, EU by no means achieved absolute consensus. Compromise has been obviously seen in the different attitudes adopted by greater and smaller EU member countries in regard to Asian partners. For example, France, Great Britain, Germany and Italy, owing to their export demand and global economic competition, have tended to give priority to economic relations, thus wishing to implement a more pragmatist policy while others in EU, The Netherlands, Scandinavian countries and Portugal, are less anxious to make their foreign policies dependent on their economic objectives. So, it may be realised that since 1993 the Asia policy of the EU has oscillated between realpolitik and moralism. However, it seems that pragmatism has led the EU side to avoid reference to such delicate issues as human rights at various summits and to lesser their criticism against ASEAN behaviour regarding Myanmar.

At present and also in the immediately coming years, probably the most efficient approach for a closer Europe-Asia relationship would be to accept a policy of realism and pragmatism as the "rule of the game", to imply in it both dimensions of values and economic essentials. In so doing, this does not mean implementing a policy in which such fundamental values as human rights, democracy and governance by the rule of law would be sacrificed for economic interests. This is a multi-layered policy that should be carefully considered so that both parties, the EU and ASEAN, may share together a variety of economic and political interests and security to secure the maximum benefits of both sides. In short, it is arguable that the policy to be pursued for the development of EU-ASEAN relationship in the first decades of the 21st century at least should be one based on fundamental values, but implemented in a manner that its economic costs are bearable. This is because the unbridled pursuit of certain values regardless of vital economic interests will undermine the very foundations of economic prosperity and social security. As disagreement on the views of values between the two sides may be unavoidable, possibly it may be necessary to establish an early warning mechanism so that such disagreements do not threaten fruitful traditional relations between the EU and ASEAN.

LITERATURE

1. *Human rights: Important documents* (Hanoi: Social Science Information Institute, 1998).

2. Pham Nguyen Long, *ASEAN: Problems and tendencies* (Hanoi Social Science Publishing House, 1997).

3. Douglas C. North, *Institutions, institutional changes and economic activities* (Hanoi: Social Science Publishing House, 1998).

4. Kim Dae Jung, "Is culture destiny? The myth of Asia's anti-democratic values", *Foreign Affairs*, Vol. 73, No. 6, pp. 189-194.

5. Hadi Soesastro and Jusuf Wanady, "Towards an Asia Europe Partnership - A Perspective from Asia", *The Indonesian Quarterly*. Vol. XXIV, No.1.

6. Fareed Zakaria, "Culture is destiny. A conversation with Lee Kuan Yew". *Foreign Affairs*, Vol. 73, pp. 109-126.

7. Khub Chand, "German Foreign Policy in the 1990: Dilemmas and directions in Germany in the nineties", (ed.) by Rajendra K. Jain.

8. Carl-Andreas F. Von Steglin, "Germany's New Asia Policy, in Germany in the nineties", (ed.) by Rajendra K. Jain.

Nordic and East Asian Values Compared - In Search of a Balance between Isolation and Globalisation

Geir Helgesen
Nordic Institute of Asian Studies

*T*oday more than at any other time since the World War II the social sciences are preoccupied with debates over values and politics, and values in politics. The ideologically based dividing lines between what we Europeans called East and West (encompassing only Europe and the US, since the rest of the world is seen as more or less dependent areas and countries) are gradually being replaced by culturally based dividing lines on a global scale.

This paper is not going to discuss globalisation as such. The phenomenon is taken for granted as a point of departure. However, a few words are needed to state my position toward the globalisation. It seems evident, whether we like it or not, that major economic agents operate on a world scale. No barriers seem effective to withstand this economic globalisation. Self-proclaimed independent (or so called self-reliant) economies heads for disaster. North Korea is a point in case. Markets are global, and globalisation is furthermore strengthened by a true revolution in our means of information, communication, and transportation. The seminar in Hanoi is a very good example. It seems as if we have, in a positive way, utilised all these means of international relations to realise this event.

Talking about a positive way indicates that there might be a negative way as well. I think there is, and following scholars who have dealt with this problem in the early 1990s I will term these negative aspects the process of MacDonaldisation.[1] It has been called Westernisation or Americanisation, and even if these geographical terms so far have been adequate, this will not

---

[1] Ritzer, G., *The MacDonaldization of Society* (Thousand Oaks: Pine Forge, 1993).

necessarily be so in the future. The globalisation process of markets, information, communication and transportation promote global convergence. Norms and standards are increasingly sought after that smooth economic and technical cooperation and thereby promote the general convergence. In his book *Globalisation,* Malcolm Waters (1995) describes the fully globalised world, where "there will be a single society and culture occupying the planet" (p. 3). Defining the topic he deals with, he says that globalisation is "A social process in which the constraints of geography on social and cultural arrangements recede and in which people become increasingly aware that they are receding." (*ibid.*) This process is challenging humankind and the way we have known social life from time immemorial.

Thus we are currently confronting a world where a country's absolute independence presupposes isolation, which in turn inevitably seems to cause economic and human disaster. The opposite option, to fully engage in globalisation and accept convergence as the ultimate result (and prepare for MacDonaldisation) is not particularly tempting. MacDonaldisation not only includes the American national menu 'Burger and Cola' from a fast-food stand. As the aforementioned author of *Globalisation* writes, the principle of fast-food restaurants is coming to dominate more and more sectors of society all over the world (p.1). This can be interpreted in different ways, undoubtedly also in positive ways. But my interpretation is not a positive one. To me, convergence based on MacDonaldisation means (and we are already observing this process) that we are increasingly being bombarded with products of all sorts with the common feature, that they are pre-chewed, easily digested, and with standardised tastes. If you don't like it in the beginning, you better get used to it, because it will not easily disappear. The entertainment industry operates with similar recipes; for movies and music to be easily digested, they appeal to basic instincts, the least possible common denominator. Main ingredients are simplified human relations and desires focusing on sex and violence, often in a peculiar mix. The older generations may find it cheap and immoral. But who cares? The target group is the younger generations. They are the future, and they consume it in great quantity.

But how will the future be, if culturally rooted values are replaced by converging norms based on universally applicable market principles? The ideal seems to be a free-floating individual, not restricted by the burden of tradition or culturally related moral obligations, but free in time and space, free to follow his own desire, to realise his needs, preferably those he can purchase. This person - he or she - is the ideal globalised individual, because he is the ideal

102

consumer.

He is probably not the ideal citizen, however. The end of the cold war and the beginning of a new world-dis-order has revealed that, when ideological beliefs are replaced by more or less convincing ideas about the glory of freedom of the individual, there is no longer a demand for the 'glue' that keep society together, intact and united. This 'glue' or 'cement' or whatever one prefers to call it, which used to function as the common ground (allowing for all sorts of differences), is now increasingly seen as a negative, past-oriented and conservative force. It is something that hinders development, modernisation, and globalisation, all three perceived as beyond doubt positive phenomena. The question is whether human beings are ready for total freedom? From the perspective of the human mind and human emotional needs is the ongoing globalisation process to be perceived as progress or does globalisation operate with such perspectives at all?

What if the disappearance of traditionally derived values and norms actually leaves the human being with some sort of empty space, where his life compass used to point out the direction for his actions? Global values and norms are not, as far as I know, replacing traditional ones. Among critics of the culture perspective it is a popular saying, that man has no roots, but feet. So trees have roots and need soil to grow, while man is a mover, he's independent of any soil and can decide where to live and grow. This metaphor seems immediately convincing, but it can hardly survive a more thorough scrutiny. While it is a correct observation that feet and roots are designed to perform rather opposite functions, the problem with this comparison is that trees have neither heads nor hearts, or, a culture telling them how to grow. Meanwhile no community of human beings has ever existed without a culture in the form of basic guidelines for social coexistence. It is because human beings have feet and move, that we need culture to avoid unnecessary social friction and conflicts. And in this era of globalisation we need to be cultured and to be culturally literate. In other words while thinking and acting within our own cultural sphere we have to be aware of and respect other cultures.

Although preferable, a middle path between absolute isolation and total globalisation might be a difficult political strategy to pursue. It is, however, a serious question whether there are alternatives to ethnocentrism, parochialism, and nationalism on the one hand, versus the total abandoning of indigenous ways in favour of global convergence, in effect full 'MacDonaldisation' on the other. From a political point of view, we can obviously just state our preference and fight for the one or the other alternative. We don't really have to motivate our position. In this paper, however, my ambition is to substantiate my argument by referring to data from surveys conducted in six different countries in East Asia and in the Nordic countries.[2] In other words, I will present attitudes of relevance for the question we are addressing here, in an effort to seek the link between culture and politics, the link without which politics may degenerate and alienate people instead of activating them.

Space does not allow for a more detailed account of the two cultural regions we are dealing with. It is common knowledge, however, that East Asian political culture is heavily indebted to Confucianism, with a strong social morality based on an idealised hierarchical and patriarchal family institution, moreover with a strong desire for excellence through education. In treatises on the Confucian political discourse this familism is often accentuated, and a latent conflict between the private and the public is implied. This might be a central misconception of Confucianism. In Chaibong Hahm's words, "Confucianism is the effort to regard family not as the repository of the private but rather as the training ground for public spiritedness".[3] This interconnectedness between the private and the public sphere is an important aspect of East Asian cultural roots to bear in mind when looking at empirical data from that region.

The cultural traditions of the Nordic region, in particular Denmark and Norway, shall also just briefly be mentioned here. The first and most important aspect to mention is that the Nordic region belongs to the protestant wing of the Christian tradition, more specifically as this tradition has been interpreted and communicated by the Danish clergyman, philosopher and poet, N.F.S. Grundtvig (1783-1872), who developed his Christian thinking into a sort of emancipating and educating force for the peasantry. Grundtvig became 'the Confucius' of the Nordic region. He developed an idealistic nationalism by revitalising and reconstructing the past to make up a model for the present. Other aspects of his teaching was a strong belief in the capacity of the

---

[2] I refer to a pilot study conducted in China, Taiwan, South Korea, Japan, Denmark, and Norway in 1998. All the research teams were local and associated with EPCReN, the Eurasia Political Culture Research Network. Each study had between 200 and 300 respondents, of whom half were university students, half from the adult population, preferably highly educated people. The pilot surveys were conducted in preparation of nation-wide studies to be carried out in 1999 and 2000.

[3] Personal communication with Professor Hahm, June 1998.

104

individual, the importance of education, and of dialogue as the basic mode of conflict resolution. His philosophy has imbued generations of individuals, as well as the State Church, the school system and the organisations regulating the Nordic labour markets.

With this brief and incomplete sketch of important cultural traits of East Asia and the Nordic countries, we will now turn to the surveys and in doing so, aim to shed some light on three basic questions:

- Do the people we approached harbour general attitudes and opinions which might be of importance to their social and political preferences?

- If so, do these general attitudes and opinions differ from one cultural region to another?

- And finally, if the first and the second question receive affirmative response, is it meaningful to interpret the attitudes revealed within the context of the cultures described above as Confucian and Grundtvigian Christian?

Results from six pilot surveys

The data presented are basically descriptive findings, and to some extent they are even simplified by being reduced from four to two categories, one positive, accepting a given statement, and one negative, rejecting the same statement. I have not conducted any kind of sophisticated statistical analyses, but will report the marginal distribution of the data gathered in China, Taiwan, South Korea, Japan, Denmark, and Norway during early autumn 1998.[4]

Before presenting the data, there are two pieces of information I would like to share. The first one concerns the respondents' interests in political matters. Since we are asking rather political questions, it might be relevant to know that 55 percent of the Chinese sample expressed interests in politics, while 70 to 80 percent of the Japanese, Korean and Taiwanese respondents said they had little interest in such matters. In the case of the Nordic countries, 90 percent of the Danish and 96 percent of the Norwegian sample expressed an interest in political matters. The other relevant information is how the respondents judged the questionnaire. The question was formulated as follows: "How well do you think that the questionnaire covers your political and social attitudes." There were four alternative answers: Not at all; Not so well; Adequately; Very well.

---

[4] The number of respondents to the pilot survey in each of the seven countries: China: 240, Japan: 197, South Korea: 216, Taiwan: 298, Denmark: 354, Norway: 100.

Combining adequately and very well to one positive category, all except the Japanese sample responded positively (Chinese: 67%, Korean: 74%, Taiwanese: 84%, and Danish: 86%).[5] In the case of the Japanese respondents only 39 percent found that the questionnaire covered their perceptions adequately or very well.[6]

In the following I shall address eleven questions[7] that were presented to respondents in six countries, mostly as statements they were asked to relate to. It was stressed that there were no correct answers or preferable attitudes, and that respondents would remain anonymous. In East Asia, primarily in South Korea, I have conducted several similar studies, where the response patterns have been close to those presented in the following.[8] It is nevertheless hazardous to draw strong conclusions based on survey data alone. I find it

---

[5] The question was not included in the survey in Norway.

[6] The Japanese research group said that they had urged the students among the respondents, probably around 59 percent of the group, to be critical in relation to the questionnaire. Whether this affected their response concerning the quality of the questionnaire is difficult to say, but there is at least a possible relation.

[7] The total number of main questions was 48, several of them with a number of sub-questions. In total 185 questions, including statistical information, were asked. The multiple choice questionnaire generally had four response alternatives. The research network agreed to omit a neutral category, since several East Asian researchers had experienced extraordinary high percentages of response in the neutral category, when it was available. By omitting that possibility we hoped to exert a mild pressure toward the respondent to make a stand in each and every case. Judged by the low number of blank spots in the questionnaire, our effort was successful.

[8] Geir Helgesen and Soren Risbjerg Thomsen, *Measuring Political Attitudes in East Asia. The Case of South Korean Democratization*, NIAS Reports, No.27 (Copenhagen: Nordic Institute of Asian Studies, 1995); Geir Helgesen and Li Xing, 1996, "A Democracy or Minzu: The Challenge of Western Versus East Asian Notions of Good Government", *Asian Perspective*, Vol. 20, No. 1; Geir Helgesen, *Democracy and Authority in Korea. The Cultural Dimension in Korean Politics* (New York: St.Martins Press and Richmond, Surrey: Curzon Press, 1998). Geir Helgesen, *Korea and the Asian Values Debate. Observations and Findings Concerning Democracy*. Paper delivered at the conference on Current Political and Economic Issues in Korea, Swedish Institute of International Affairs, January 28, 1999.

reasonable to assume, however, that there is some kind of link between the opinions presented here, and respondents' values and norms. A causal link between attitudes and action is a much more doubtful claim which will not be forwarded here.

The eleven questions covers four spheres of relevance to a given political culture. These spheres are:

1. Interpersonal trust.

2. Perceptions of power.

3. Trust in the system.

4. Political efficacy.

These themes obviously overlap. Interpersonal trust and trust in the system for example cover different dimensions of trust, but it is also quite clear that trust and power are linked, and the way people relate to these three dimensions cannot but influence their perceptions of political efficacy.

Interpersonal trust

The trust we are dealing with here is the one that may or may not exist between strangers. People without family or friendship connections, who have not attended the same school or do not come from the same village. It is the relationship between people that seldom meet, and if they do, it usually happens in formal settings and because of events like elections, or because an individual is approaching some part of the political system.

This statement was not included in the Chinese questionnaire.[9] Comparing the response pattern in the five remaining countries, the Taiwanese sample differs from the two other East Asian countries, where a majority reveals no trust in elected representatives. The Danish and Norwegian data reveal the opposite, with strong confidence in those elected. There are many possible reasons for this difference. An obvious one is that we are witnessing a difference between old and new democracies. I will not totally reject this explanation, but in that case Taiwan is an anomaly. Since we find anomalies in all aspects of social research, I'm ready to accept the suggested explanation as

---

[9] In agreement with our Chinese colleague in the EPCReN we decided to omit some questions and statements from the Chinese questionnaire. In some cases because we found them to be too politically controversial, in other cases because we deemed them irrelevant to the Chinese situation.

one that is possible. Another explanation that is closer to a political culture approach is that representation based on political party affiliation and elected on this basis is a difficult phenomenon to relate to when people are used to more personalised relations, even in politics.

Table 1. Question 2a, response in percentage.

"The people we elect stop thinking about the interests of the people after taking office"

	Disagree	Agree
Japan	14	86
Korea	16	83
Taiwan	43	57
Denmark	80	20
Norway	73	27

The next statement focuses on opinions about the most numerous and visible of the people populating the administrative and political institutions. They are called bureaucrats, civil servants or, as in the table below, public officials. This group is probably the one that most people come into contact with, when they deal with the system, or when the system deals with them. Everywhere their reputation is easily strained, and the statement below is probably an often heard complaint (Table 2).

The pattern is clearly divided between East and West. The Korean respondents are the most negative, while the Danish respondents are the most positive in their perceptions of public officials. Again old and emerging democracies might be a reason for this difference. While Taiwan differed in Table 1, the Taiwanese respondents follow the general East Asian pattern in this case. No matter what the reason is, the response pattern reveals distrust in East Asia, and trust in the Nordic countries.

Having covered perceptions of politicians and public officials, the third table deals with interpersonal trust in general. The two alternatives reflect the basic attitudes to other people: Either we harbour some suspicion, or we meet them with trust.

Table 2. Question 12d, response in percentage.

"Public officials don't care much what people like me think"

	Disagree	Agree
China	30	70
Japan	30	70
Korea	18	82
Taiwan	28	72
Denmark	82	18
Norway	69	31

In Table 3 China differs from the other East Asian samples. The Chinese response might reflect the 'politically correct' attitude or Chinese respondents might be more trustful in interpersonal relations. The Taiwanese respondents are almost equally divided between the two positions, while in Japan and Korea a majority expresses distrust. The Nordic response pattern is again quite opposite, with a large majority expressing trust in people in general.

Table 3. Question 31a, response in percentage.

	"You can't be too careful in dealing with people"	"Most people can be trusted"
China	35	65
Japan	60	40
Korea	59	40
Taiwan	51	49
Denmark	18	81
Norway	28	72

Perceptions of power

There are many ways of explaining the differences we can observe in the three tables above. There seems to be a general difference between East and

West, although political correctness might disturb this picture to some extent. Related to perceptions of interpersonal relations are perceptions of power. This concept is probably the most central of all the concepts used in dealing with politics. It has long been taken for granted that power is a universal concept, denoting the same phenomenon always and everywhere. One of the founding fathers of the political culture approach, Lucian W. Pye observed, however, that power is extraordinarily sensitive to cultural nuances. We try to test an assumption holding that a Western audience mainly will perceive power as a privilege, while an Eastern audience will lean towards the opinion that power is more of a burden (Table 4).

It is difficult to maintain the either-or assumption, as a clear difference is not easily observed. A majority of the respondents in Japan, and a slight majority in Korea and Taiwan see power as a privilege, while only the Chinese respondents find power to be more of a burden. This might reflect the current political reality in these countries, or it might be due to the influence of Western thinking. In this case we have the advantage of comparing with the response pattern in the two Nordic countries, where a convincing majority of more than 80 percent find power to be a privilege. In this light we may still maintain our initial assumption. Or, more in line with the figures in Table 4, we may conclude that Nordic respondents perceive power mainly as a privilege, while East Asian respondents are divided in this case, which reflects that power in East Asia is perceived as a burden as well as a privilege.

Table 4. Question 21, response in percentage.

"Power can be perceived as a privilege or as a burden. What is your opinion?"

	It is a burden	It is a privilege
China	59	41
Japan	37	63
Korea	47	53
Taiwan	45	55
Denmark	14	86
Norway	16	84

One aspect concerning the East Asian notion of power as both a privilege and a burden is that there is a caring perspective included in the East Asian concept of power. Stemming from Confucianism and other patriarchal traditions, a political leader is seen as a father figure. In classical Confucian texts the family is used as the model entity for social life, and in moral education textbooks this ideology is developed further in great detail. In leader-follower relations in daily life situations the clear hierarchy often seems 'softened' by exactly this caring attitude. With the following statement we seek to test whether this extension of a 'familistic' attitude is recognised by our respondents.

Table 5. Question 23j, response in percentage.

"A leader should care for people like parents care for their children"

	Disagree	Agree
China	15	85
Japan	29	71
Korea	30	70
Taiwan	4	96
Denmark	44	56
Norway	69	31

The results presented in Table 5 substantiate the above mentioned assumption, that power is perceived as a privilege and a burden. All East Asian respondents, with the Taiwanese as the most enthusiastic, accept the sentence claiming that a leader should care for people like parents for their children. It is more surprising that a majority of the Danish respondents (56%) accept this claim. Concerning the Norwegian respondents who are the only group to reject the statement, it should be mentioned that this is a group a fairly young people, 89 percent are below 29 years of age, when there is an expected feeling of opposition to the more conservative notions such as this leader-father idea.

It seems quite clear that East Asian respondents feel comfortable with the leader-father analogy. That a majority of the Danish respondents feel likewise is surprising, but it might reveal that Denmark is more of a consensus society than we are aware of in daily life. Even more so, it may be than we like to acknowledge in a political system that ideologically is based on acceptance of conflicting interests and organised according to that ideology.

Trust in the system

We have now considered interpersonal trust and perceptions of power. We will now focus on how much people trust the political system in terms of the institutions that represent the system in relation to the individual.

Table 6. Question 18, response in percentage.

"How much do you trust the government to do what is right?"

	No trust at all	Some degree of trust	Basically trust	Trust completely
Japan	19	51·	30	0
Korea	18	62	20	0
Taiwan	14	66	20	0
Denmark	2	34	60	5
Norway	2	27	69	2

The question focuses on the respondents' level of trust in the government (Table 6). Even though in party political systems a government comes to power due to the support of those who voted for them, it is important that they act as the whole country's government, and thus all people should ideally express a certain amount of trust in any legally elected national government. This may not be written down in the rules of the system, but from a practical point of view it is difficult to see how the political process can work without this basic trust.

Once again we decided to leave out this question in the Chinese questionnaire. The three remaining groups of East Asian respondents express a hesitant trust in their government, while the Nordic respondents have the opposite attitude. Although trust is important for the political process to work, a critical sense is also a necessary ingredient in a dynamic political process. One could argue that any government must be prepared to accept criticism, as they are responsible for decisions affecting people's daily life. If we want to test the legitimacy of the political system therefore, we have to shift focus from government to a more neutral political institution.

The next question shifts the focus from the government to the parliament. Responses will indicate whether respondents have confidence in the system as such, regardless of political preferences. One aspect that such a question obviously touches upon, without mentioning it specifically, is whether the highest political institution has legitimacy, i.e. whether it is seen as the uncontested body for national legislation. Another aspect is whether this institution acts according to respondents' expectations.

From the results in Table 7 one can see that the Korean respondents are highly critical, but also the Japanese and Taiwanese respondents seem to have limited confidence in their parliament. The Chinese respondents are divided, with a small majority on the critical side, while the Nordic respondents express strong confidence in their parliament.

Table 7. Question 19a, response in percentage.

"How much confidence do you have in the parliament?"

	None at all	Some	A good deal	Very much
China	22	36	37	5
Japan	20	72	8	0
Korea	69	31	0	0
Taiwan	16	74	9	1
Denmark	1	21	61	17
Norway	0	14	74	12

Having surveyed aspects of social and political trust, perceptions of power, confidence or lack of confidence in the given system, the next question deals with the outcome of politics. Do the respondents see government actions as something affecting their daily life situation?

Only the Japanese respondents, but a strong majority of these, seem to disregard the effects of government actions, which comply with the 'common knowledge' about the Japanese political system having weak governments (and leaders) but strong and very powerful bureaucratic institutions. The Taiwanese and Korean respondents are divided, while a majority among the Chinese respondents think that government actions do make a difference. The Danish and Norwegian majority response, of more than 90 percent, is a convincing illustration of polities where the national decision making institution is perceived as having direct influence on people's daily life.

Table 8. Question 7, response in percentage.

"How much effect do you think that the activities and laws passed by the government have on your day-to-day life?"

	Little effect	Much effect
China	36	65
Japan	75	25
Korea	44	56
Taiwan	51	49
Denmark	7	93
Norway	9	91

The response pattern in Table 8 above may in itself be difficult to interpret. The main problem is that it is not evident whether the effects of government actions are perceived as negative or positive. We tried to shed some light on this issue in two other questions where we asked for opinions on government intervention. The alternatives were: "The less government the better", versus: "There are more things the government should be doing." A majority in all surveys favoured 'more government', strongest in Taiwan (77%) and China (69%), while in the other cases between 55 and 60 percent favored 'more government'. When we formulated the question in a more specific way, the response pattern became more clear. The next two alternative statements presented were: "We need a strong government to handle today's complex economic problems", versus: "The free market can handle these problems without government involvement." In the Chinese case 83 percent favored strong government, 59 percent in all the three other East Asian countries shared that opinion, while 62 percent both in Norway and in Denmark preferred the strong government alternative. It seems safe to conclude that a majority of those we have approached in all the countries surveyed expect their government to take care of certain societal affairs, in contrast to a belief in the free market. This might be taken as an indication of a rather infertile soil for the globalisation process.

Political Efficacy

From dealing with trust and power we are now moving to the aspect of political efficacy. This aspect concerns people's view of themselves in politics, whether they see themselves as actors and participants, and to what extent political influence can be exercised. Political parties are well known institutions in all the countries surveyed. What we ask then is whether the respondents perceive the political party as a useful tool to exercise influence on political decisions.

In Norway, Denmark and China, it makes good sense for the majority of the respondents to work through a (the) political party, in Taiwan the respondents are almost equally divided on this issue, while in Japan and Korea a majority rejects that this kind of political work should be effective. In the following section we will add the aspect of trust to that of efficacy with regard to political parties, to see if this somehow can explain the attitudes presented above.

Table 9. Question 13f, response in percentage.

"How effective do you think it is to work through a political party in order to influence a government decision?"

	Not effective	Effective
China	40	60
Japan	72	28
Korea	53	47
Taiwan	49	51
Denmark	32	69
Norway	17	83

Different or not, trusted or not, the political parties are the bases for the group of political activists from where the leaders of the country are recruited. Because of this simple reason it seems important that there is a certain level of confidence in these organisations.

Table 10 shows a somewhat problematic pattern. While the first, the third and the fourth alternatives are all rather clear, the second alternative 'some' is neither positive nor negative. 'Some' might be how people feel about this matter, but it is inexact, to say the least. It was not thought of as a middle category, as we operate with a four point scale, two negative and two positive alternatives. If we leave 'some' as a negative category, Japan, Korea, and Taiwan have very critical respondents. The Chinese respondents are leaning more in the positive direction, more so the Norwegian respondents and only the Danish respondents have strong confidence in the political parties (again the young age of the Norwegian sample is probably a reason for the more critical stand toward political parties compared to the Danish sample). With such general critical stances towards political actors, one may wonder whether party politics make sense in East Asia at all? This is the next and the final question in this brief outline of our survey.

Table 10. Question 19b, response in percentage.

"How much confidence do you have in the political parties?"

	None at all	Some	A good deal	Very much
China	13	30	47	10
Japan	40	56	4	1
Korea	63	36	1	0
Taiwan	18	70	12	0
Denmark	1	21	61	17
Norway	0	40	59	1

In response to the statement in Table 11, Korea and Taiwan stand out, Japanese respondents are equally divided, while Chinese respondents are more close to the Nordic pattern. The Chinese respondents are situated in a different political setting, however, and may thus relate to the statement from a totally different point of view. Danish and Norwegian respondents clearly stand out by strongly disagreeing with the statement claiming that party differences do not really matter.

Table 11. Question 12c, response in percentage.

"I can see no difference between the political parties."

	Disagree	Agree
China	73	26
Japan	50	50
Korea	34	66
Taiwan	36	64
Denmark	91	9
Norway	84	16

Implications of the findings

As already mentioned, pilot surveys are not the best possible basis upon which to conclude on matters as complex as those we are dealing with here. The following is therefore to be seen as preliminary thoughts for further consideration in an ongoing research process aiming at developing a cross-cultural study of political cultures and their impact on political attitudes and opinions in East Asia and in the Nordic countries.

The question we set out to investigate was whether the people we approached harbour basic cultural attitudes and opinions that might be of importance for their social and political preferences. If this could be established, the second question was whether these basic attitudes and opinions differ from one cultural region to another? The third question was then to consider the usefulness of interpreting these attitudes as reflections of cultures defined as Confucian and Grundtvigian Christian. And finally: What are the implications in a globalised world?

Having presented a small fraction of the material we have gathered in six different countries, there seems to be reasons for upholding a claim that the respondents express attitudes that characterise a fundamental political culture in their country, and that these basic attitudes (although with some clear exceptions) differ between the two regions we have dealt with. Whether the recognisable basic attitudes affect social and political preferences is a complicated question, especially because there seems to be an effect from the political to the cultural sphere as well, notably in the case of China, but also the Japanese respondents expressed opinions hardly expected. This brings us to the third question: Is it meaningful to interpret the majority response pattern within the context of the dominant political cultures in the two regions? With the exceptions in mind, I will, nevertheless, maintain that a culturally-based dividing line seems to exist, hence why it is meaningful to interpret differences within a relevant cultural context. In the following section, I shall sum up the findings.

With regard to inter-personal trust, the confidence in impersonal relations, such as those between ordinary citizens and different kinds of leaders, are particularly strong in the two Nordic countries. This underpins the idea and practicality of political representation. Basic distrust in impersonal relations, on the other hand, as it seems to characterise a majority of the East Asian respondents, undermines the same idea and promotes the idea of personalised politics. This idea is meaningful where the distinction between private and public is absent or at least more blurred, as is the case in Confucian cultures.

Different attitudes towards power are also recognisable between different cultures. The East Asian respondents are more or less equally divided between perceiving power as a privilege and a burden, while a strong majority of the Nordic respondents think of power mainly in terms of privilege. The East Asian response pattern reflects the ideal Confucian attitude, where leadership implies a strong sense of responsibility, where loyalty from the led presupposes care from the leader. This is made quite explicit in the response to the statement comparing the leader with a father, a statement that strong majorities among the East Asian respondents accept. Interestingly, this idea is not alien to the Nordic respondents either, but the difference between the regions is still clear.

Trust also divides the two regions. Taking the government as a point in case, nobody among the East Asian respondents completely trusts their government, while about one sixth of respondents expressed total distrust. In the Nordic case the picture was almost entirely opposite. In general a majority among East Asian respondents expressed *some* trust, while the Nordic respondents expressed *basic* trust. From a cultural point of view, it is important to bear in mind that the expectations towards government in East Asia might be stronger than in the Nordic countries, which paradoxically explained the more critical attitude. If the leader and the institutions 'that leaders populate are expected to perform the role of the father in the family, one might easily become disappointed. This pattern of trust or lack of trust in the system is repeated when we replace the government with the parliament, with the exception of China. When it comes to the governments' impact on people's daily life, a majority of all the different countries' respondents, except the Japanese, actually think that what governments do influences their life. But only in the Nordic countries is this majority almost total.

Finally, concerning political efficacy, we have focused on political parties and whether they are conceived as effective means of· exercising political influence. Again Japan differs from the other East Asian samples by rejecting the importance of political parties. The Chinese respondents are almost as positive as their Nordic counterparts, while Korean and Taiwanese respondents are nearly equally divided in this matter. The Chinese 'dissent' is also clear when testing the respondents' confidence in the political parties. The Danish and Norwegian samples express strong confidence, but as many as 57 percent of the Chinese respondents do the same. On the opposite pole we find Korea with 99 percent distrust, Japan with 96 percent and Taiwan with 88 percent respondents answering in the negative. In effect the one-party system of China mobilises more trust than emerging and even stable multi-party democracies in the rest of East Asia. As illustrated by the very last table, the political parties through which individuals are expected to channel their political activities are perceived by the Nordic and the Chinese respondents as real political alternatives, in that the respondents perceive parties as different entities (the Chinese response might have to be explained more in detail). The Japanese respondents are equally divided on this issue, while a majority of the Korean and the Taiwanese respondents "see no differences between the political parties".

118

How can all this be summed up in a just way, in a way where we always consider the results within a relevant cultural context while at the same time performing the comparative study we aim at? The data we have presented suggests that culture divides the respondents in two regions: A Nordic, where respondents express more interpersonal trust, more confidence in the political institutions, and stronger efficacy, and an East Asian, where less of this is apparent. This pattern is not just apparent, it is a fact. The difference is clear for all to see. There could be several reasons for this state of affairs. Among these, the fact that my post of observation is located in the Western hemisphere is an obvious one to start with. As I see it, the reasons are more problematic than this. It is not the observer's position, but that the whole political system observed being originally came from the Western hemisphere, has been transplanted to East Asian soil, but has only partly become rooted. This is clear when the traditions, first and foremost Confucianism, are introduced in the questionnaire. A leader like a father seems acceptable to all East Asian respondents, who also generally see power both as a privilege and as a burden. This is very much as leadership is taught in textbooks inspired by Confucian moralism, and very much also as it is experienced in daily life.

The consequences of this in a larger, international or even global perspective might be the following: The Western oriented modernisation of East Asia has been a process of trial and error for more than 50 years. Several of the basic aspects of the political process, as well as the fundamental institutions in a representative political system, are not yet fully accepted in East Asia. Nevertheless the globalisation process is pushing for further modernisation, more distant institutions to regulate our daily life, more economic rationality in politics and trade, but also as regulating mechanisms in social relations. It has been suggested that politics has been removed from the local and the national political scenes, where politicians has become managers, administering a development that is seen as a necessary consequence of technological possibilities and non-political economic development patterns.

When suggesting that an impersonal (party-based) representative political system is *not yet* rooted in East Asia, it follows that it is an ongoing process that will succeed one day. One could as well consider the possibility that this process, after the end of the cold war, and as a reaction against globalisation, might transform into a search for more indigenous ways. There are at least good reasons to do so. One such reason is that, as long as the East Asian political systems are measured against a Western model, because of different cultural traditions they will always come out as the second best. Another reason may be that, as long as the cultural traditions are perceived from a modernisation perspective, which is a Western perspective as well, East Asian cultural traits will turn out as problematic in relation to the preferred direction of development, which more often than not is towards realisation of liberal democracy and respect for human rights. In both cases the rights of the individual are the most central and seldom-contested aspects.

Individualism and liberal democracy is no panacea for good government, however. Even in the most individualised of the liberal democracies there is currently a search for communal values. "Too many rights and too few obligations" has for years been the complaint forwarded by Amitai Etzioni and a group of communalist intellectuals in the USA, feeling that their country is falling apart. In less individualised societies such as the Nordic countries there is a growing interest in the role of values in the modern society. In Norway they have established a commission to promote a national public debate over this topic. This is a reaction towards a growing uncertainty concerning the direction and the speed of development in our times, a process that by many are seen as out of human control. What is felt missing is a general clarity in life, a more manageable social and political environment, space for emotions in human relations, time to reflect upon the meaning of life. As one Danish politician expressed it recently, "We have more than enough to live by on, but not so much to live for." Will we automatically get more to live for if development means globalisation and with it MacDonaldisation?

Realising that ideologies are in deep crisis, and that many people in the modern world are experiencing some kind of a value vacuum, sometimes causing social and mental alienation, it is about time to question if the market qualifies as the basic measurement of progress in this not yet established new world order. From data presented in this paper it appears that real progress might be to perform some kind of conscious retrogression. More, higher and faster may not be the answer to our yearnings. The most precious thing for a human being is another human being. How we relate to each other both on the personal level and globally are the most important political question of our times. Our data suggests that cultural traditions make a difference. To establish a well functioning political system we believe that it is crucial to seriously consider the links between politics and culture. From this perspective, globalisation may be an inhumane process making good government a very difficult goal to accomplish.

Citizen or Subject, Right or Duty? A Comparison of Social Policy Principles in China and Denmark

Hatla Helweg Thelle
The Danish Centre for Human Rights

O ur topic at this workshop contains two concepts and their mutual relation: Development and values, and the overall question is, how do the latter influence the first? I will begin by stating my understanding of these two concepts as the framework I am proceeding from.

DEVELOPMENT

Development is here defined as in the UN "Declaration on the Right to Development". This declaration was contested from many angles even at the time of drafting. In the end (1986) it was adopted by the UN General Assembly with an overwhelming majority. Only US voted against, while eight Western states (among them all Nordic countries except Norway) abstained. All developing countries, the communist bloc and the rest of the Western countries constituted the majority in favour.

Important for my purpose is the definition of development in the preamble:

..a comprehensive economic, social, cultural and political process, which aims at the constant improvement of the well-being of the entire population and of all individuals on the basis of their active, free and meaningful participation in development and in the fair distribution of benefits resulting therefrom (Declaration on the Right to Development, resolution 41/128 of 4 December 1986: preamble, 2nd paragraph.).

Everyone agrees that economic growth is an important factor in development; in fact the issue is often treated as if the two are synonymous entities. But the political question of distribution of resources is more and more seen as just as important an element in securing sustainable development in the long run.[1] Too many poor or otherwise deprived people constitute a grave threat to stability, which in turn is itself seen as a prerequisite for economic growth. Not only security but also humanistic reasons are prominent in the debate:

Economic growth matters a great deal, for without it very little can be done to achieve development. But development itself means improvement in the quality of life of people - in health, education, employment, equality and participation (MacPherson 1995: 223).

VALUES

Values will be addressed with due regard to the ongoing debate on 'Asian Values' initiated by the Vienna Conference on Human Rights in 1993. This debate touches on how different world outlooks and ideas about man influences the conditions for personal freedom, economic growth and the distribution of resources.

The ideas or values that are especially relevant to my presentation are the relation between the individual and the state, and between right and duty in the Eastern and the Western traditions. Since 1993 cultural values has been suggested as an impediment to a common understanding of methods to reach the good life in a steadily more globalised environment. The head of the Indonesian delegation phrased it like this in Vienna:

...many developing countries, some endowed with ancient and highly developed cultures have not gone through the same history and experience as the Western nations in developing their ideas.... In fact they often developed different perceptions based on different experiences regarding the relations between man and society, man and his fellow man and regarding the rights of the community as against the rights of the individual (Tang 1995: 230).

INTRODUCTION

Keeping in mind the two definitions - development as growth *coupled* with fair distribution of resources and values as ideas about the relations between the person and the state - I shall discuss how distributional mechanisms as expressed in social policy are both reflecting and influenced by traditional values in Eastern and Western cultures. All social security systems are made to

---

[1]. See Leftwich 1994: 381-382, about the need to bring politics more into the development debate.

redistribute income from more to less privileged parts of the population. As such the establishment of some kind of social security is a precondition for sustainable development, and the responsible actor is the state apparatus. The principles behind the institutional set-up of a given government reflects deeper-lying value systems, understood as ideas about the rights and duties of man and state, respectively, and the relationship between the two.

Two kinds of principles or values underlying social security systems are at stake here: First, the inherent principle, i.e. that every person by virtue of being born have a right to protection from the community. The individual is at the centre as a priori deserving her right, regardless of her contribution to the community. This is the value underlying the social democratic ideology and the human rights regime, as enshrined in the Universal Declaration of Human Rights. Second, entitlements, i.e. rights acquired through some accomplishment in the form of work efforts, correct behaviour or some other contribution.[2] The community is at the centre, and the individual earns the right to protection by doing her duty. This principle is part of the roots of Confucianism as political ideology.[3]

In the Western concept of statehood the citizen's right to enjoy basic livelihood and personal freedom is guaranteed by the state, i.e. provided by government intervention to a degree that the citizen is not able to provide for herself. Qua the international conventions and national legislation this right is a legal matter, even though it is not always justifiable. Everyone has the right by virtue of being born human: The first principle of the two mentioned above. In the Eastern tradition the ruler has the duty to care for his subjects. He is morally obliged to take care of the people and provide them with the means by which to sustain themselves. This duty is a moral one, not based on law, but on a transcendent idea of 'goodness' expressed through the personal virtue of the ruler. The individual, on the other hand, has the duty to contribute to society by

---

[2]. Entitlements can also be acquired at birth by belonging to a special group, an aristocracy, a caste or just a rich family. This type is not particularly relevant in a Danish context, but important in the case of China, where your possibilities are closely connected to your birth place, see Popper & Potter 1990: 296-313.

[3]. For the distinction of the different uses of the word 'Confucianism': As philosophical thought, political ideology, state policy and practices, or way of life see Chan, J. (1996): 2. or Loden 1997: 125.

behaving correctly, in order to enjoy the protection of the ruler. The fulfilment of needs is based on performance: The second principle.

The above stereotyped statements will be examined in this paper, using the development of social policy in China and Scandinavia in the 1980's and 90's as the testing ground. Both places are undergoing great changes in relation to institutional systems and value-based attitudes towards social security. My assumption is that in both kinds of societies we should see a movement of the actual and perceived responsibility for basic livelihood from the state to other levels like the market, the family or the individual. From the outset, the two different systems seems to be converging. First a short presentation of the social systems in Denmark and in China.

DENMARK

The social system

Denmark is a social democratic country, with deep roots in an ideology built up around social welfare. That means the final social guarantee rests with the state, not with the family. The inherent rights principle is especially expressed in the areas of health and old age care. Every citizen is entitled to free access to doctors and hospitals and subsidised medicine, and to a basic pension allowance at the age of 70 – at the latest. However, other areas of social security, like pay during sick leave, depends on one's affiliation with the labour market. With regard to daily living, every person, who can work, is legally obliged to support herself, her children and her spouse (but not her ageing parents). Most Danish families, of course, care for themselves, but where they cannot, the state has an obligation to provide them with means of livelihood. It is stated in the law that all population groups should enjoy decent living conditions and all citizens be guaranteed certain fundamental rights in the case of social events like unemployment, sickness or old age.

The main elements of the Danish model are thus, that every citizen is entitled to some basic services, regardless of degree of affiliation to the labour market. Nearly all social welfare are financed by direct and indirect taxation (the tax rate is about 50 percent of personal income). The social obligations are decentralised and controlled through framework laws. Responsibilities for important elements of social policy rests with municipal and county authorities, while the central government sets up the relevant statutory and economic framework.

124

The Ministry of Social Affairs is the highest body dealing with social policy. It serves as a secretariat for the Minister for Social Affairs and formulates guidelines and principles as well as prepares laws in the social area to be passed by the parliament (*Folketinget*). The Ministry has the authority over service and care functions, measures for special groups, and the majority of transfer payments. These functions are mostly implemented by the municipalities under supervision by local boards of appeal and ultimately by the Ministry. Service and care refers to responsibility for the elderly, family policy, activation of unemployed and young people, and preventive social measures. The special groups taken care of are the physically and mentally disabled, the socially disadvantaged and part of the commitment to psychiatric patients and substance abusers. Transfer payments are for old age and health pensions, sickness benefits, cash assistance for immediate need, and special benefits like housing subsidies for single parents and others.

Three functions, which in an international context are often considered part of social policy, are in Denmark omitted from the social sector. These are:

- The health care and hospitals, which are under the Ministry of Health;

- Transfer payments for insured unemployed people, which mostly are administered by the Ministry of Labour through (mainly publicly financed) unemployment funds and job centres outside the purview of local authorities;

- Housing policy, which is mainly regulated by the market.

Municipal and county authorities are independent, politically governed, integral units with their own tax base. The decentralised structure means that coverage may vary from place to place, depending on local conditions. The maintenance area, like pensions, family allowance and sickness benefits, are paid by the state and governed by uniform, central rules about amount paid and personal entitlements. In other services, like care for the elderly, child day-care facilities and rehabilitation as well as support for non-insured unemployed people, the localities can distribute resources according to their own judgement, still within frames laid down by national laws.

Denmark has a long history of public participation in cooperative production (*Andelsbevægelsen*) and folk high school movements (*Folkehøjskolebevægelsen*) in the educational field. Today both employees and consumers are engaged in carrying out social policy objectives. This may involve membership of parents' boards in day-care centres, participation of citizen's groups in the development of local policy and delegation of competence to institutions in local communities. Voluntary social work was important until the beginning of the 1970s, but plays now a smaller part than is the case in many other countries. The declining popular engagement in social work is seen as a problem by the present Minister of Social Affairs, who has established a fund meant to support and strengthen social activism.

Even so, family life in Denmark is generally characterised by the fact that everybody is busy. Parents are working and the children participate in different activities in the late afternoon or evening, besides going to school or kindergarten. Sports or music activities organised by local communities are very popular. The only people having time to spare are the elderly, who live alone. They, on the other hand, feel lonely, as nobody else takes the time to visit them and have a chat. Lack of time, then, is an important element in modern family life.

Another important feature is the many divorces, which means that many households have only one parent. This has created new ways of living, especially for children, where a common solution to the question of custody of the children is that both parents have the responsibility and the pleasure of daily life with the child, who must accordingly move from one home to another on a regular basis. The many divorces gives many new relationships, in which children from different families are brought together and live in the same home for shorter or longer periods of time.

Problems

Social policy in Denmark is subject to a wide range of debates and conflicting proposals from the political right and the political left. The traditional cleavage is between the socialist parties, who want the strengthening of state support to vulnerable groups, and the liberal parties, who want the state to withdraw from direct responsibility and support schemes that enable people to care for themselves via market mechanisms and private insurance. The former stresses collective state-organised redistribution, while the latter advocates the individual's own responsibility as most important. At the same time socialist parties do put less stress on the role of the family and traditional values, like religion, which is the prerogative of the liberal parties.

A big problem in our social policy is seen by researchers and practitioners alike, to be the 'professionalisation' of emotional ties, and the fear that too much

126

help makes people passive and unable to care for themselves.[4] The 'professionalisation' or 'victimisation' problem has been addressed through measures enabling family members to care for old or sick people. It is now possible to get leave from your job and a subsidy from the local authorities to nurse a dying family member. Parents are encouraged to live with their hospitalised children, and there has been suggestions from the political right, that parents should be paid to quit their job and take care of pre-school children.[5] The solutions are not satisfactory and do not change the over-all situation, as social norms work against substituting a job career with family life.

The 'pacification' problem has been addressed by a new social law, the Social Service Act from 1997. The new law strengthens the already existing obligation to work by instituting an 'activation' scheme. If you are jobless and not entitled to unemployment benefits, the municipality will give you some kind of job or activity, you have to attend based on the premise that a life without duties is unhealthy and enhances the marginalisation of already socially weak persons. The problem with the scheme is, that the activity mostly are either meaningless or else compete with the regular job market, as the 'activated' work force is much cheaper for the employer than a worker hired in the market place.

Even though Denmark in these years has a socialist democratic government, trends seem to suggest that the disassociation of the state from social responsibilities is on the agenda. The solutions to the two above-mentioned problems express on the one hand a concern for betterment of life quality, by changing the values and principles behind social assistance. On the other hand, they fit remarkably well with a wish to curb high public spending. They help the state save money. Recently, the issue of privatisation of some

---

[4]. A so-called 'victimisation' concept has been introduced, arguing that in a welfare system like the Danish, people confuses rights and needs. They increasingly feel that they have a right to everything they need, for instance, artificial insemination in case of barrenness or any new medical treatment. See Henrik Jensen (1998), *Ofrets århundrede (the Century of the Victim)*.

[5]. "In recent years it has become evident that a one-sided emphasis on professional, public solutions to social policy problems may have reached its limits"(Ministry of Social Affairs 1995: 12), "In future, however, the strengthening of the business community's role and involvement in welfare matters will be debated and tested as part of the overall revamping of the welfare model" (Ibid.: 29).

social services has been hotly debated. Some municipalities have tried to privatise home help to the elderly; even kindergartens run by private companies have been suggested. As formulated in the presentation from the Ministry of Social affairs: *"The strategy of experimentation and development [during the 1980's] was also targeted at seeking new ways of involving private sector resources in the solution of social problems"* (Ministry of Social Affairs 1995: 13).

Another way of saving on the public budget has been mentioned. To graduate more social allowances according to income. The issue of subsidies independent of income, for instance in relation to family allowance or old age pensions, has been debated heatedly at times, as critics feel that rich people do not need the child allowance or other benefits from the state. Many services in the Danish system are dependent on taxable income, so the principle is well ingrained. It constitutes a break, though, with the deep-rooted social democratic principle: Everybody is entitled to a basic support from the state.

All in all the social policy in Denmark shows a mixture of inherent and acquired rights. It provides a fair degree of protection against want, while it weakens the role of family ties and collective responsibilities, that the state has the ultimate responsibility. There is currently a trend further away from a principle of inherent rights to entitlements based in performance. The whole welfare idea is under debate, and voices are heard demanding a more duty oriented value system.

CHINA

The social system

Built into communist ideology in its Chinese form is the idea of sacrifice of the individual for the common goal. Translated into our present context, this manifests a strong commitment to the duty principle; by contributing to the collective you earn your right from society for protection. China's social security system was established in the early 1950's immediately after the communist takeover, when it covered retirement, industrial injury, birth, illness and death, but only for a limited part of the population. From its inception the system was to a large extent built on the principle of acquired rights or entitlements.

There is little doubt that the labour insurance program was intended to protect only those workers and staff, who had satisfactory family antecedents

128

and political attitudes and who were making a positive and continuing contribution to economic reconstruction (Dixon 1981: 37).

This principle, however, was modified by its opposite value of an inherent right: The system that developed during the 1950's and 60's, secured most people a work unit (*danwei*) in the cities and an agricultural collective in the countryside, responsible for social needs. The units were of different status with different resources, so there was little that was 'egalitarian' about it, but most of the time[6] there was an access to a minimal living standard for most of the people. Up till 1979 pensions, health care, work injury, maternity leave and housing were in the cities covered by the work units, while the rural population was basically covered by the lowest level of the people's commune: The production team. Social security was closely connected to the workplace. The workplace was in the cities allocated by a state organ and could not be chosen freely. In the countryside you was born into it. The urban workplaces seem mostly to have been distributed in accordance with family background or political affiliation and, to a lesser degree, on academic performance. So, acquired rights ruled on a basis of an inherent rights principle.

Substantive reforms have been initiated since the beginning of the economic reform policy in 1979. The new system consists again of two different parts: One for the urban and one for the rural population. Following the reform agenda, agricultural production was 'privatised'[7] and the work units in the cities were supposed to shed the social obligations, they had before. Social security should be separated from your employment situation, and the burden should be shared between the state, the work place and the individual. The new systems under construction for health care and pensions - the two most expensive areas of social security - are based on a savings principle, that means your direct dependence on your specific work place is meant to be overtaken by government funds, paid jointly by the employee and the employer, and administered through personal accounts. By far the greatest proportion is at the outset to be paid by the workplace, which proportion will gradually decline relative to the individual share, so the two are aimed ultimately to be the same.

---

[6]. Disregarding the times of violent social upheavals like the Great Leap Forward and the Cultural Revolution.

[7]. In reality, though not on paper. Land is still not privately owned; user rights are contracted by the village to households on a long-term basis.

If this system turns out to be the final outcome of the process, individual social coverage will still depend on relation to the labour market.

In the countryside public social systems are virtually non-existent any more. Less then 10 percent of peasants are covered by any kind of social guarantee, and these are dominantly in the affluent south-eastern part of the country, already in many ways benefiting from the new open economy. In the cities the transformation process has created a chaotic situation. Pensions and salaries are not being paid; health care reimbursements are subject to endless negotiations; jobs are bought and sold; anything can be obtained by money and good connections, and nothing without. Rules are unclear to people and central attempts to build a national system is slowed down by local inertia.

Based on preliminary results from my own research[8] in China, I will discuss two prevalent myths about East and West with the aim of confusing the clear picture of unrelated processes and substantiate the view of convergence.

Myth 1: The collective Asians and the individualistic Westerners

The way out of a socially unacceptable situation is most often individual, or based in a family choice. Because of the breakdown of the work-unit system of protection many families are suffering great social insecurity. Unpaid salaries and pensions are used by enterprise directors for private luxury or commercial speculation. A lot of energy is spent on bureaucratic matters. Reacting to the socio-economic changes is a creative process, as there are no strictly enforced rules or generally accepted procedures to follow. Actually there are rules, but they are not implemented, so people do not see them as guarantees; they can count on them. Most people do not know or know very little about their formally guaranteed rights, like health care insurance or free schooling. But they ostensibly do not care about it, either. The attitude is that rules are not that important, "they are not useful to ordinary people". Laws and regulations are used not as basis for rights claims, but as something distant, you can read about in the papers or hear on TV. The information does not affect expectations or alleviates worries about when to get your next salary or how to pay your medical bill.

---

[8]. Research project on social and economic rights for urban people in China under reform, conducted at the Danish Center for Human Rights in Copenhagen and financed by the Carlsberg Foundation, Denmark.

130

Two types of reactions are the most common: The wait-and-see attitude and the taking-matter-in-your-own-hand attitude. The first type is mostly seen with all the retired people. When they feel wronged, they do not believe in their own ability to change the situation, so they tend to wait patiently, and hope their money will turn up one day. It is seen as reasonable that old people get different treatment from the young ones. Some place great hope on their children and expect that they will take care of them, if they become ill or frail in old age. Younger people tend more to invent strategies to cope with the upcoming problems. These strategies are often based on the use of personal connections and mobilising individual resources. It is repeatedly stated with great certainty that without money and connections nothing can be achieved at all. Connections are pulled by giving gifts - often money - by visiting people and offering them help or explain one's own situation. Actually, everybody talks about gifts; the ones they have given, or they will not give, or they have to give in the future; even the ones they did not have to give.

The 'collectivism' in this particular context does not include the community at large. Colleagues and neighbours are seldom referred to as assets and, if they are, they are used for solutions to individual family problems. Bad social conditions are not treated as collective problems, demanding collective actions higher up in the system. An interesting phenomenon compared with the strong European tradition of a collectivism based on professional ties. The labour movements in the end of the 19th and the beginning of the 20th centuries constituted the root of both socialism and the present North-European social welfare ideology.

Myth 2: Rights and duties[9]

In the Confucian universe duty occupies a lot of space. It has to be kept in mind that the Confucian idea of duty is not confined to the duty of the subject towards her ruler, the child to the parent or the pupil to the teacher. Duty is reciprocal and is as much the moral obligation of the father to take care of his children as of the children to obey the parent.

Ironically - if we accept the idea that market economy and a rights regime are twins - it seems that the traditional tendency to value duties over rights in

---

[9]. As seen the Asian way: "The Rights and obligations of a citizen are indivisible. While enjoying his legitimate rights and freedom, a citizen must fulfil his social responsibilities and obligations"(Tang 1995: 215).

China was partly weakened in the 'socialist' period (1949-1979) through the incorporation of almost everyone in some kind of protective unit, but has increased in a China on its recent road to a market economy. Or more precisely in socialist China the duty of the ruler (= the CCP-Communist Party of China) was given relatively more weight to effect distribution of resources than is the case now where the economic reforms legitimise the diffusion of the responsibility of the state. This is especially so in the areas of social and economic rights, which are now officially claimed to matter more than individual freedom.[10] The basic social obligations are now increasingly a matter for the family, as reflected in the family-based choice of solutions to economic problems described above. Modernisation has not individualised social lives, but strengthened the family as an economic entity. Martin Whyte concludes likewise from a survey in Hebei province that family obligations has been reinforced rather than eroded during the reform period, contrary to expectations from conventional modernisation theory (Whyte 1997: 21).

The new systems under consideration mostly operates with principles like savings and insurance, as mentioned above, supplemented by charity as ways of providing people with social security. Experiments are conducted whereby the individual and the workplace pays a fixed amount to a common fund for, for instance, pensions and health insurance, allocated to personal bank accounts. That means everyone will know exactly, how much is left for health care or pension at any given time. These principles link protection to performance, and thereby stresses your duty to contribute to society to safeguard your own livelihood. The movement is away from a partly inherent right towards an acquired right or entitlement.

The question of a special Confucian or East Asian welfare model has also been discussed and answered in the negative by a couple of Scandinavian scholars, researching emerging social security schemes in seven Asian countries. They conclude:

...different types of social security schemes have been developed, though not always implemented, in East and Southeast Asia particularly from the mid 1980 onwards. But they can hardly be described in terms of a single Confucian or east Asian model (Hort and Kuhnle 1998: 24) .

---

[10]. "The Progress of Human Rights in China", *Beijing Review*, Special Issue, 1996.

Interestingly they point out that Malaysia and Indonesia - two of the countries most advocating the argument that Asia has a much more collective culture than the West - have the lowest level of social security protection.

CONCLUSION

Returning to my own society in Northern Europe, I have argued that the social democratic notion of equal treatment regardless of social position is eroding. Our new social policy claims that it is against human dignity to receive social relief without working and consequently demands that to receive assistance you have to accept assignments from the local community. In contrast, China's new social system also elaborates on the model of protection dependent on performance, i.e. relation to the labour market.

Certainly, values influence development, but the cultural complexity is much bigger than often seems to be recognised. The convergence, proposed above, suggests that we are not dealing with two different sets of values that unilaterally influence the course of development. Further scrutiny is needed, though, to ascertain whether the idea is sustainable in the first place, and secondly to give food for speculations about the reasons behind it.

LITERATURE

1. Peter Baehr et.al. (eds.), *Human Rights in Developing Countries. Yearbook 1996* (The Hague: Martinus Nijhoff Publishers, 1996).

2. Joseph Chan, "A Confucian Perspective of Human Rights", Paper prepared for the second workshop on "The Growth of East Asia and its Impact on Human Rights", sponsored by the Carnegie Council on Ethics and International affairs and the Faculty of Law, Chulalongkorn University, in Bangkok, Thailand, March 24-27, 1996.

3. Deborah Davis, "Chinese Social Welfare: Policies and Outcomes", *China Quarterly*, no. 119, 1989, pp. 577-597.

4. John Dixon, *The Chinese Welfare System 1949-1979* (New York: Praeger, 1981).

5. Adrian Leftwich, "Governance, the State and the Politics of Development", *Development and Change,* Vol. 125, no. 2, 1994, pp. 363-386.

6. Gao, Shangquan and Chi Fulin, *China's Social Security System* (Beijing: Foreign Languages Press, 1996).

7. Sven Hort and Stein Kuhnle, "The Coming of East and South East Asian Welfare States?" Paper presented at Roundtable on "Comparative Modernization: Scandinivia and China", Center for Nordic Studies, Fudan University, Shanghai, 27-29 November 1998.

8. Stewart MacPherson, "Social policy in China in contemporary perspective", in Wong and Macpherson (1995) pp. 216-250.

9. Torbjörn Lodén, "Från Mao till mammon: Religion och social utveckling i Kina". *Den Ny Verden*, no. 1, 30. Årgang, 1997.

10. Lu, Xueyi and Li Peilin (eds.), *Zhongguo Xin Shiqi Shehui Fazhan Baogao (1991-1995), Social Development 1991-1995* (Shenyang: Liaoning Renmin Chubanshe, 1997).

11. Ministry of Social Affairs, *Social Policy in Denmark* (Copenhagen: The Ministry of Social Affairs, 1995).

12. Sulamith Heins & Jack M. Potter, *China's Peasants. The Anthropology of a Revolution* (Cambridge: Cambridge University Press, 1990).

13. James Tang (ed.), *Human Rights and International Relations in the Asia Pacific* (London: Pinter, 1995).

14. Martin King Whyte, "The Fate of Filial Obligations in Urban China", *The China Journal,* ho. 38, 1997, pp. 1- 31.

15. Linda Wong and Stewart MacPherson (eds.), *Social Change and Social Policy in Contemporary China* (HongKong: Avebury, 1995).

16. Stephen Philion, "Chinese Welfare State Regimes", *Journal of Contemporary Asia,* 28, no. 4, 1998, pp. 518-536.

National Development and East Asian Values: Cultural Perspective

Uichol Kim
Department of Psychology, Chung-Ang University

CULTURE: WHAT IS IT?[1]

When we as people want to learn about another culture, we usually study cultural products (e.g., art, music, dance, language, dress, food, and customs) and psychological constructs (e.g. values, beliefs, and norms). In order to understand another culture, we typically study its history, language, customs, and folkways. Even if we can understand these aspects of culture, our knowledge would be limited. We would still be an outsider looking in and not an insider capable of thinking, feeling, and behaving like its members and identifying with the culture.

Although people identify culture through visible cultural product and inferred psychological constructs, these entities are not enough to reveal the essence of culture. Since I did not participate in the creation and recreation of these products, I may lack the experience and phenomenology that insiders possess. The creation and recreation of culture represent a continuous process that occurs every moment when a child is born into a cultural community and raised by its members. Behind the external products and inferred entities, there are creators and created, both at the individual and collective level, who share a particular set of intention, values, and goals. It has a special meaning and relevance to the participants and this meaning is communicated and shared by its members.

---

[1] Parts of this paper include revised and updated material from Kim (1994), Kim & Park (1998) and Park & Kim (1998).

For example, if I choose to burn a piece of cloth, it is of no concern to others. However, if I decided to paint the cloth red, white, and blue, pattern it with stars and stripes, and then burnt it in front of Americans from the US, it could be viewed an extremely offensive act to Americans, but of little or no concern to Danes or Vietnamese. Similarly, if I chose to burn pages of collated paper that would be of no concern to others. But it could be highly offensive to the religiously devout if the collated papers were the Bible, Koran or Bhagavagita. Objectively, they may be a piece of cloth or paper, but people have waged war for these symbols and have died as heroes defending these symbols.

Although some cultural symbols and meanings are often arbitrary (e.g. a flag), in most cases they can be linked to adaptation to natural and human-made environment. In Korea, for example, the most popular food is *kimchee*. It is composed of cabbage, radishes, seasoned with a variety of spices (e.g. hot pepper, garlic, onion, ginger), fruit (e.g. pears), salted anchovies, and it is fermented for several days. When Westerners taste *kimchee* for the first time, they are struck by its hot and spicy flavour, pungent smell, and usually people have difficulty enjoying its taste and digesting it. But for *kimchee* lovers, they often remark that it is refreshing and soothing to the stomach. Also, they comment they can digest food better with *kimchee* than without it. This contrasting evaluation of *kimchee* can be bewildering to an outsider: How can a dish that is so pungent, spicy, and hot be deemed as refreshing and soothing to the stomach? Enjoying *kimchee* is an acquired taste and your body needs to adapt to enjoy its taste. Physiologically, it helps with your digestion since it contains a large amount of lactobacillus. Once you acquire the taste, you can become addicted to it.

Historically, *kimchee* was created by Koreans as a way of preserving vegetables over the long winter months. From November to March, it is very difficult to find fresh vegetables in mountainous regions of Korea. Without consuming the necessary vitamins founds in vegetables, many Koreans would have died of malnutrition. Koreans found a way to preserve vegetables by adding spices, salted anchovies, and storing it underground. It served a similar preserving function as the German sauerkraut, the salted anchovies found in Vietnam, and chemical preservatives that are currently used. Thus, the cultivation of *kimchee* represents a cultural adaptation to ecological demands. Koreans themselves are socialised to enjoy it, physiologically and psychologically.

UNDERSTANDING CULTURE: THREE APPROACHES

There are three approaches to understanding variations in culture and values: the universal, comparative, and indigenous approaches. In the universalist approach, a group of scholars, politicians, and lay public believe that there is no such a thing as culture: It is a symbol created by a particular interest group to fuel ethnic or national pride. They instead argue for universal values and basic human rights. However, if we analyse the content of the universal values, they are highly abstract to the extent that they explain everything and thus end up explaining nothing. For example, they point to basic requirement for maintenance of human life (such as the need to eat, sleep and breathe) and to psychological requirements (such as need for security, happiness, expression, and freedom). Everyone agrees that these needs are fundamental. But the universalists cannot explain the variations of how these needs are met within a particular ecological and national context without falling into an ethnocentric stance.

People who argue for universal values do often recognise or understand that the values that they are espousing reflect their own implicit and deep-seated cultural values. The universal values that they are referring to are their own cultural values, disguised in abstract terminology. Other cultural values are simply added as appendages, or reinterpreted to fit their framework. They often resort to tautological and rhetorical arguments, but lack empirical evidence to support their claim. Historically, these arguments emerged during colonial periods where politicians and scholars attempted to justify imperialism and colonialism. Most often they are blind to their own cultural influences and their ideas are culture-bound rather than representing universal values.

In the comparative approach, a group of scholars recognises the existence of cultural variations and that culture affects the way we think, feel, and behave. In cross-cultural psychology and anthropology, more than 100 years of research examined how culture affects psychology and behaviour of individuals. In this approach, culture is treated as an independent variable and individuals' psychology and behaviours are treated as dependent variables. This dichotomy between culture and individuals is unnecessary and fraught with tautology. Also, many scholars adopted the evolutionary approach creating a dichotomy between traditional and modern, primitive and advanced, non-Western and Western. Many scholars believed that with modernisation, industrialisation, and urbanisation most cultural differences would disappear. However, even with modernisation, cultural differences still persist. Thus, the evolutionary perspective is biased and ethnocentric, rather than being based on scientific evidence.

The approach that I would like to propose is the indigenous approach (Kim, 1999; Kim & Berry, 1993). In this approach, culture is not something that lies outside the individual. It is natural and basic. Culture *is* the way we think, feel, and behave. Since we think, feel, and behave *through* culture, it is difficult to recognise its existence. To use a metaphor, culture is like our eyes. We see through our eyes, we often forget that it exists, and we do not know how we perceive reality. Culture is basic and fundamental. Without culture, we are reduced to basic instincts and we cannot think, feel, and behave as we do. Culture allows us to define who we are, communicate with others, and manage our physical and social environment.

In psychology, medicine, biology, and anthropology, scholars have attempted to explain human psychology, behaviour, and culture wholly in terms of physiology. Explanation of culture or individuals cannot be reduced to physiological level. Physiology is the tool that we use to interact with our world. Physiology is similar to the hardware of a computer and culture is similar to the software. Depending on which software is used, very different tasks can be performed using the same hardware. One central difference between computer software and culture is that computer software lack agency and intentionality that culture possesses.

Culture needs to be understood both as an entity and as a process. As an entity, culture is defined as *the rubric of pattern variables*. Culture is not a variable as cross-cultural psychologists and anthropologists have assumed. Culture is a superordinate construct that provides meaning, direction, efficacy, coherence to its members. To use an analogy, painters use different colours to create their art work. The different colours that they use can be compared to different variables that operate within a culture. These colours are used to create certain forms and pattern (such as the face, apple, or a house). These forms are combined to provide a particular ethos, such as joy, sadness, and mystery (providing coherence, or a rubric). Artists use colours as a tool for creating a desired painting. The explanation of these paintings cannot be reduced to wavelengths of light. Like different coloured paints, people use available natural and human resources to achieve desired outcomes (such as solving subsistence and psychological need). This is the process definition of culture: *It is the collective utilisation of natural and human resources to achieved desired outcomes*. To understand culture, we need to examine the context in which cultures have developed.

138

RENAISSANCE AND WESTERN CIVILISATION

Recently, I visited the Louvre Museum in Paris. I noticed that in most medieval paintings, Jesus, Virgin Mary, or some other holy person occupied the centre and human beings were on the periphery. I believe that these paintings represent the-Christian belief and value system. God, as the Creator of the universe, represents the Truth, light, beauty, and goodness. Human beings are in the periphery since we were created by God.

People in the medieval paintings do not have any particular expression, except for showing reverence for Jesus and Virgin Mary. Individuality is not important or valued in medieval Christian culture. In order to know the Truth, you have to know the Will of God, and the Truth is revealed through Him, priests, or the Bible. Even music was created for God to hear: It was monotonic and directed toward the Heaven.

The Renaissance period in Western Europe represented a different way of thinking, feeling, and behaving: it represented a cultural revolution. What happened was a change in the perception of reality: The relationship between figure and ground became reversed. Human beings were no longer on the periphery, but occupied the centre stage. With the changed perception, people began to take more active control of the environment and began more effectively utilising the natural resources for their own benefit.

At the Louvre Museum, one piece of artwork attracted enormous attention. Throughout the day, people encircled the picture of Mona Lisa and they were busy taking pictures. The question is why does the painting attract so much attention even after 500 years. She is not a saint or a gentry, but a commoner. There is a striking difference between Mona Lisa and other medieval paintings. She appears to have an expression, which displays her individuality. Also, behind her is a landscape, which provides the context for the picture. She is at the centre of attention and the landscape is in the background. Compared to the traditional medieval painting, context and the figure has been reversed: Human beings now occupy the centre.

During the renaissance, people discovered that individuals had the potential to discover the Truth without the aid of religious leaders, Bible, or through Divine revelation. In stead of viewing human beings as sinful and the world as a forsaken place, human beings were considered to be beautiful, and they had the capabilities to discover the Truth first-hand. In the medieval Christian period, the human body was considered sinful and covered. In contrast, the sculpture of David by Michelangelo is an example of celebration of the beauty of human body.

RELIGION, CULTURE, AND SCIENCE

Descartes was living in a period where many conflicting ideas emerged and new discoveries were being made. He was in turmoil due the conflicting ideas, doctrines, and beliefs. He decided to adopt a method of critical doubt in which he rejected all ideas, doctrines, and beliefs, unless its truth was self-evident. He could doubt virtually everything: traditions, customs, beliefs, and even his own perception. There was, however, one thing he could not doubt - his existence. The fundamental question was how did he know that he existed? He concluded that it is through his rationality and reason that he knew with certainty that he existed. Descartes concluded: *"Cognitio, ergo sums"* ("I think therefore I am"). Through his rationality and reason, he discovered himself.

Through rationality and reason, he could understand natural scientific laws. This was considered impossible in medieval period, because only God can know the Truth. Through rationality you can discover and understand mathematical truth. Through rationality you can know God exists, since rationality is a special gift from God. This is the basis of Western individualism: Other people, authorities, cannot tell you what is right and wrong, only you can know with absolute certainty what is true.

Descartes influenced and modified the Christian world view. His view created a dichotomy between mind and body, good and bad, light and darkness, justice and deceit, heaven and earth. Life is viewed as a struggle between truth and light on one hand and evil and darkness on the other. Western movies, TV dramas, and novels depict a struggle between good and bad and the triumph of human capacity to overcome evil for good (e.g., Star Wars, police dramas). Emotions, on the other hand, were considered unreliable as they were linked with the desires of the flesh, the body.

Western Liberalism

Descartes' discovery was purely an individualistic enterprise: He alone could determine what is the Truth and not some arbitrary body. Western individualistic societies emphasise individual uniqueness and the pursuit for his or her own identity and truth. Liberal education is a training of this rationality with the belief that there is just one Truth. Through democratic discussion you can arrive at this Truth. Democracy and social institution represent the development of collective rationality.

In the West, the liberal tradition focuses on a rational individual's rights to freely choose, define, and search for self-fulfilment. The content of self-fulfilment depends the goal that an individual freely chooses. The nature of the goal can vary from one individual to another and can range from hedonistic fulfilment to self-actualisation. This freedom of choice is collectively guaranteed by individual human rights. At the interpersonal level, individuals are considered to be discrete, autonomous, and self-sufficient, and respectful of the rights of others.

From a societal point of view, individuals are considered as abstract and universal entities. Their status and roles are not ascribed or predetermined, but defined by their personal achievements (i.e. by their educational, occupational, and economic achievements). They interact with others utilising mutually agreed upon principles (such as equality, equity, non-interference, and detachability), or through mutually established contracts. Individuals with similar goals are brought together into a group and they remain with the group as long as it satisfies their needs. Laws and regulations are institutionalised to protect individual rights; everyone is able to assert his or her rights through the legal system. The state is governed by elected officials whose role is to protect individual rights and the viability of public institutions. Individual rights are of prime importance, and collective good and harmony are considered to be supererogatory.

Modernism and universalism are based on this notion that it is just one Truth, reflecting the Christian belief in One God and scientific determinism. However, Western societies are going through a crisis with respect to this idea about one Truth and the maintenance of collective rationality. Post-modernism questions the existence of One Truth, and feminists, gay and lesbians, and others ideologues suggest that there may be several truths. In some Western societies, collective rationality is being threatened by excessive individualism and hedonism.

EAST ASIAN PERSPECTIVE: THE CONFUCIAN INFLUENCE

Descartes grew up in France during the Renaissance. What if Descartes were Chinese, Japanese, Korean, or Vietnamese? How would he answer the fundamental question of his existence? I believe he would have replied: *I feel, therefore I am*. Can we verify your existence through your feeling? I think we can. East Asian cultures have been developed believing that emotions are reliable and provide the fundamental basis for harmonious familial and societal relationships.

Rather than individualism and rationality, which is viewed as unstable in East Asia, collectivism and emotional relatedness are emphasised. This is not to say individualism and rationality do not exist, but rather relationship and emotion are emphasised over individualism and rationality. In other words, relationships and emotions are at the centre and individuals and rationality are placed in the background. These values evolved in traditional agricultural communities that adopted rice-planting practices. In rice planting in paddy fields, people have to work together and cooperate with one another.

In East Asian art, human beings are placed in the context of the natural and social environment. The individuality is not emphasised. In traditional landscape painting, we cannot see individuals' expressions as we see them in Western art. Human beings are considered as part of nature in Confucianism and Buddhism. In Confucian and Buddhist philosophy, harmony is the most important value that integrates human beings with nature and with other individuals. Rather than the emphasis on rationality, which is considered the basis of Western democracy, science and society, *jen* (human-heartedness) and compassion are considered basic in East Asia.

Confucianism promotes collective good and harmony as its ultimate goal. Individuals must cultivate themselves to be rid of individualistic and selfish desires in order to become a person of virtue and a respected member of a group. Individuals are conceived to be embedded and situated in a web of particular roles and status. They are bound by ascribed relationships that emphasise common fate. Individuals are encouraged to put other people's and the group's interest before their own.

From a societal point of view, individuals are considered to be interrelated through their ascribed roles and social network. Duties and obligations are prescribed by their roles and they lose 'face' if they fail to fulfil them. Concession and compromise are essential ingredients in promoting role-based and virtue-based conception of justice. Social order is maintained when everyone fulfil their roles and duties. Institutions are seen as an extension of the family and paternalism reign supreme. For example, a leader is typically considered to be a father figure who is paternalistic, moralistic, and wellfaristic.

Although Confucianism emphasises emotions and relationships, Confucian cultures have also evolved in the modern era, from the traditional agricultural communities to rapidly developing industrialised nations. Many people think that East Asian societies have simply Westernised, but the situation is much more complex. Although some aspects of Western cultures have been adopted, the more significant change involves the transformation of Confucian and Buddhist cultures.

National Development: The Korean Example

In modern Korea, the exploitation suffered during the Japanese colonisation (1910-1945) and the ravages of the Korean War (1950-1953) left Korea totally devastated in all strata of society. The transition from a war-torn country to a rapidly developing country was interrupted by numerous social and political upheavals. At the beginning of the 1960's, Korea had all the problems of a resource-poor, low-income developing country. The bulk of its population was dependent on scarce farmland for bare subsistence, adding to the problems of the familial, social, and political disintegration. The literacy rate and the educational level were one of the lowest in the world. Korea's per capita gross product in 1961 stood at a meagre $82, near the bottom of the international economic scale.

During the last three decades, the Korean economy has been drastically transformed with the economy growing at an average annual rate of 8.6%. The per capita GNP increased to $1,640 in 1981. By 1997, the per capita GNP increased to $10,000 and Korea joined the elite circle of developed nations: The Organisation of Economic Cooperation and Development (OECD).

The modern era saw Korea face dramatic changes in all aspects of the society. Koreans had to learn to change from an agrarian to an industrial society, from rural to urban communities, from conservative to progressive ideologies, from being past- to future-oriented, from choosing the middle-path values to achievement values, from sentimentalist and reflective thinking to practical and analytical thinking, from hierarchical to democratic political organisation, from acceptance of nature and harmony to controlling nature and its forces and becoming its master. In brief, Koreans had to adapt to the forced colonial rule of Japan, to the dislocations and to the ravages of the Korean War, to the reality of a divided Korea, and to the harsh realities of bleak economic, political and social crises all in one lifetime. Although the nature of Korean society has significantly changed, their desire to become educated and to obtain financial security remained a top priority. Even in modern Korea, people view education as the most viable way to achieve personal, familial, and national prosperity. Moreover, the spirit of Confucianism and Buddhism, viewing education not only as a means to an end, but as an end itself still persists. It became a moral imperative that all individuals, regardless of sex and social class, acquire higher education.

Korean Educational Aspiration: Historical Context

Korea shares the Confucian heritage with other East Asian societies. Confucianism, however, became indigenised, being modified by the ecological, social, and political conditions in Korea. Confucianism was adopted in Korea about 2,000 years ago. At an early stage, the influence of Confucian philosophy was limited to political and academic spheres. In 1392, when the Yi Dynasty was newly established, neo-Confucianism was chosen as the state's guiding philosophy, influencing not only scholarship and politics, but affecting all aspects of individual and social life, especially the educational system.

Within the adoption of the neo-Confucian political system, individuals of merit were selected through regional and then finally through a nation-wide examination. Successful applicants were given an official position as a government, military, or local official. In return for their services, they were given a tract of land from which they could acquire a stable income. This landed gentry was collectively called the *yangban*. The land grant lasted for three generations. In order for the family members to maintain their gentry status, a descendant of the family must pass another national examination by the third generation.

With the adoption of neo-Confucianism, economic, military, and political power became centralised and success in the national examination became the most viable access to power. Successful applicants were respected for their knowledge, wisdom and self-cultivation, and they had access to social, economic, and political power. Since education was the most viable means for social mobility and recognition, the desire to succeed educationally became deeply ingrained in the Korean people's mind.

The neo-Confucian stronghold on Korean political, educational, and social system was maintained until the late 19th century. With the Western encroachment and colonisation of East Asia, Korea attempted to maintain its independence by curtailing all Western influences and by reifying its staunch support of neo-Confucian ideals. By the end of the 19th century Korea became known as the "hermit kingdom."

The enlightenment movement (*kyehwa undong*, also known as modernisation movement) was initiated in the late 19th century, attempting to reform the economic, political, and educational system. Many leaders saw the entrenchment of neo-Confucian ideals as a major obstacle to national progress and development. They argued for the adoption of Western education, economic, and political system as a viable alternative to remedy the country's backward status. During this time, with the aid of North American missionaries, many Western-style primary and secondary schools were built. These schools educated the general public about the new Western knowledge and the world beyond its borders.

The enlightenment movement was curtailed with the annexation of Korea by Japan in 1910. With the Japanese colonisation, the Japanese style of educational system was forcefully implemented. The goal of the educational system was not to enlighten the general public, but it was used as a vehicle of its colonial dominance. Korean history, geography, and culture were systematically distorted to justify Japanese colonisation of Korea.

Educational Success: The first Transformation

The economic 'miracle' in Korea is closely tied to the educational aspiration and investment. At present, the literacy rate is over 97% in Korea, one of the highest in the world. According to a cross-national survey conducted by Secretariat Ministry, Government of Japan (1979), Korea had the highest percentage of adolescents wishing to obtain a university degree (85%), followed by the United States (81%), Thailand (69%), Japan (62%), England (50%), and France (38%) (Korea Educational and Development Institute, 1983). In 1983, Korean Education and Development Institute conducted a similar study asking Korean parents the desired educational aspiration for their children. The vast majority (90%) of Korean parents wanted their children to at least graduate from high school, 74% from university, and 21% from graduate school. The main reason for educating their children was that it provided access to obtaining a desirable job (37%), followed by cultivating a moral character (35%), improving their natural talent and interests (14%), increasing their chances of finding a good marriage partner (9%), and compensating for their own low educational status (6%) (Korea Educational Development Institute, 1995).

In a cross-national comparison with the United States, England, West Germany, France, and Japan, Korean parents were second only to Japanese parents in the actual amount they contribute financially to their children's college education (Gallup Korea, 1983). In terms of eagerness or willingness to pay for their children's college education, Korean parents exceeded all the other nations. Korean parents were also at the top in their willingness to pay off their children's debts and in paying for their children's wedding expenses (Gallup Korea, 1983).

Educational Attainment: The Role of Family and School

Korean parents are instrumental in motivating their children to achieve a high level of educational success. Through socialisation and enculturation practices, these values are transmitted to their children.

Although the influence of Confucianism has declined with modernisation, researchers (e.g., Azuma, 1986; Ho, 1986; Kim & Choi, 1994) agree that two important features still persist: Devotion and indulgence. Mothers in modern Confucian cultures view unselfish devotion to their children as a critical feature of their personality and motherhood (Azuma, 1986; Ho, 1986; Kim & Choi, 1984). Choi (1990) found that for Korean mothers, their children's accomplishments and failures become their own, and children vicariously fulfil their own dreams and goals. Attaining this vicarious gratification is one of the most important aspects of motherhood, and it is the most valued meaning that Korean mothers have in raising their children (Choi, 1990).

When a child is born, a Korean mother remains close to the child to make the child feel secure, to make the boundary between herself and the child minimal, and to meet all of the child's needs, even if that means a tremendous sacrifice on her own part. Children's strong dependency needs, both emotional and existential, are satisfied by their mother's indulgent devotion. As children mature, they sense that it is through the mother that they obtain gratification, security, and love. As such, children become motivated to maintain a close relationship and they do so by gradually taking a more active role by pleasing their mothers and behaving according to their mothers' wishes. Thus, the feeling of dependence helps children to assimilate their mothers' values and beliefs as their own.

The phenomenal educational attainment, especially in mathematics, in East Asian societies has been systematically documented (e.g. Stevenson & Lee, 1990; Stevenson, Azuma & Hakuta, 1986). In addition to the supportive environment that parents provide, an important aspect of educational success has been attributed to the "social-oriented achievement motivation" (SOAM, a desire to fulfil the expectation of the ingroup (Yu and Yang, 1994)). The SOAM emphasises the following four qualities: (1) interdependence, (2) effort, (3) substantive goals, and (4) compatibility of values.

As children grow up they are expected to extend and transfer their identification and loyalty from their mothers to a wider circle of ingroup members, such as friends and teachers. A mother's job is to use her interdependent relationship with her child to prepare her child for social life.

She becomes a mediator between the home environment and the school environment and she gradually implants appropriate social values to her children (Azuma 1986; Ho, 1986; Kim & Choi, 1994).

In Korea and Japan, the relationship between teachers and their students is seen as an extension of the mother-child relationship. A typical climate of Korean and Japanese schools affirms maternalism, pressures the student to strive for personal excellence, and encourages students to cooperate in a group (Kim & Choi, 1994; Stevenson, Azuma & Hakuta, 1986). Children are motivated to please the teacher and their attention is focused on the teacher. Even in a class size that is as large as 40-60, Korean and Japanese students are more attentive, less disruptive, and more devoted to doing their schoolwork and homework than American students are (Kim & Choi, 1994; Stevenson et al., 1986).

The second important value is the emphasis on effort (an internal and controllable factor). Consistent with Confucian and Buddhist philosophy, individual striving is viewed as a necessary component of the self-cultivation process. Excellence in performance provides evidence that a child has developed a moral character through perseverance and persistence. It is a visible demonstration that a child has deeper abilities to be a virtuous person. Furthermore, Holloway, Kashiwagi and Azuma (1986) point out that "the emphasis on individual effort includes a sense of responsibility to the group to which one belongs" (p. 272). In Confucian societies, individuals are pressured to contribute to the group and success is collectively defined and shared. American parents, in contrast, blame external conditions for their children's failure (such as the school, luck, difficulty of the task), or uncontrollable internal factors (such as ability) (Hess et al., 1986; Holloway et al., 1986).

In East Asian societies, effort is believed to lead to success, especially in education (Kim & Park, 1998; Stevenson & Lee, 1990; Yu & Yang, 1994). Lebra (1976) has found, in a free-association task, that over 70% of Japanese respondents (both young and old, men and women) attribute success to diligence, effort, and endurance, and only 1% attributed it to ability. Kim and Park (1998) similarly found that nearly half of Korean students and adults view effort as the most important factor contributing to both success and failure.

Finally, in East Asia, there is a greater congruence between the values emphasised in the home environment and those learned in the school environment than there is in the United States. In the United States, individualistic values are often in conflict with relatively rigid classroom

147

structure, curriculum, and the teacher-student relationship. In addition, students, parents, teachers, and administrators often hold different views about the meaning of success and factors that lead to success. This diversity of viewpoints is considered to be the strength of individualistic societies. In Korea and Japan, there is greater congruence among all parties about the goals of education and the method of achieving this goal (Kim & Park, 1988; White & LeVine, 1986). For example, Korean adults and adolescents view educational success and self-regulation as one of the most important aspect of their life (Kim & Park, 1998). This collective agreement among family, school, and society is a key factor in motivating students to attain a high level of achievement. White and LeVine (1986) point out that this congruence minimises conflicts and contradictions in the development of a child's character, ability and values.

ORGANISATIONAL CULTURE

According to U. M. Kim (1994), organisations in Japan and Korea are perceived as extensions of a family. In these societies, companies and the government encourage paternalism and communalism. To examine the nature of paternalism and communalism in Korea, surveys were obtained from personnel managers from mining and manufacturing firms with more than 100 employees with 90% response rate (i.e., 985 out of 1,097 personnel managers completed the questionnaire). U. M. Kim (1994) found that the vast majority (over 80%) of the managers strongly endorsed the ideas of paternalism and communalism. He found that many companies provide services to foster paternalism and communalism, which are believed in turn to enhance production, efficiency, solidarity, loyalty, job satisfaction, and social control.

In Japan, Misumi (1988) assumed, along with his colleagues and company executives, that the *authoritarian paternalism* would be the most effective leadership strategy. It was taken for granted that supervisors would unilaterally give orders and subordinates would passively obey them. In reality, this type of leader was the least effective. In contrast, those leaders who emphasised *benevolent paternalism* were much more effective. Misumi (1985, 1988) has found that leaders who demanded high productivity were effective only when they were able to develop a strong sense of group solidarity. In a study of leadership conducted in four nations, Smith, Misumi, Tayeb, Peterson and Bond (1989) found that leaders in individualistic cultures (i.e., Britain and the United States) stressed performance, whereas leaders in collectivist cultures (i.e. Hong Kong and Japan) emphasised both performance and group solidarity.

Sullivan, Suzuki and Kondo (1986) found that in the United States and Japan, the nature and role of a group are conceived very differently. They found that American managers used the equity principle to allocate rewards and provided greater rewards to individuals when the group's influence on individuals was low. In the mind of American managers, the successful person working alone can expect the greatest share of rewards (Sullivan et al., 1986). According to Sullivan et al. (1986), American managers focus on *risk reduction* (i.e. individual members in a well-functioning group help to insure that group members do the assigned and expected work). A well-functioning group ensures the expected outcome by encouraging individual members to monitor the activities of other members and thereby reducing the probability of unexpected and unpleasant outcomes.

The Japanese managers, in contrast, distributed rewards equally and gave greater rewards to individuals who worked in a group and who had been influenced by the group (Sullivan et al., 1986). According to Sullivan et al. (1986), Japanese managers see groups as *productivity enhancers* (i.e. as a facilitating factor). Consistent with this belief, Japanese managers rewarded individuals who worked with their group members in a highly interdependent manner and who were highly influenced by the group's attitudes and advice, regardless of their level of performance. In other words, managers are sending a strong message that "there is much to gain and nothing to lose" when individuals choose to work in a group (Sullivan et al., 1986, p. 393). Consistent with Sullivan et al.'s (1986) study, Gabrenya, Wang and Latane (1985) found that for meaningful, skill-related tasks, American students who worked in a group tended to loaf (called 'social loafing'), while Chinese students tended to work harder in group (called 'social striving').

The Asian Economic Crisis and the Second Transformation

There is currently an economic crisis looming over Asia during the closing years of this millennium. In particular, Korea was able to achieve phenomenal educational and economic achievement, but she is currently experiencing a severe economic crisis. The current financial crisis reflects fundamental structural problems in need of a second transformation. About one hundred years ago, many Koreans believed that the external challenges they faced could be resolved internally, through regulating themselves and supporting ingroup members. Such a belief system enabled Koreans to achieve a phenomenal educational and economic success. Such a pattern of belief still persists in Korea, but they need to be revised. The current economic crisis arose due to a fundamental bias in Korean mentality: The over-emphasis on self-regulation, coupled with an over-emphasis on ingroup loyalty and harmony.

Recently, a study was conducted with a sample of over 1,100 Korean students and adult to examine the what the participants considered as their accomplishments and the factors that led to their success and failure (Kim & Park, 1998). Overall, both Korean students and adults place a prime importance in educational attainment. They view education as the most important life goal to achieve. Once an individual has achieved a high level of educational success, it brings social and economic rewards. In order to succeed in Korea, whether it is academic or occupational, people believe that self-regulation is the most effective strategy. In other words, if they work hard and try their best, they could accomplish their desired objectives. This belief in effort contributed to phenomenal educational and economic achievements.

In contrast, to the importance in self-regulation and social support, ability and environment factors were mentioned infrequently. Personality was mentioned frequently, but it was mainly for maintaining good social relationship. Overall, it appears that Korean respondents believe that success is contingent on self-regulation and support received from significant others, and play down the role of innate ability and environmental factors.

Furthermore, Korean responses focus on affective domains. Similar responses were also found for stressful events. In others words, Koreans utilise more emotion-focused coping styles than problem-focused coping styles (Kim & Park, 1997). Moreover, for most respondents the coping style tends to passive such as self-regulating negative emotions and avoiding the situation (Kim & Park, 1997). These factors are currently limiting Korean people's ability to shape and change their environment.

The major weakness that Korean society face is its limited ability to control the external environment. They have difficulty understanding, predicting, and managing their natural and social environment. They are more adept in adjusting to a given environment rather than changing it. With globalisation and international of national economies, Korea and other East Asian nations are facing severe structural problems. This may be due to the existing coping strategy that focuses on emotions, self-regulation, and social support among close ingroup members not in understanding and participating actively in the global market and environment.

The Korean government and business are attempting to cope with these problems and to find a solution to the financial crisis. The most important aspect of Confucian cultures has been the maintenance of social harmony and collective good. Individuals in Confucian cultures emphasise how an action of an individual or a group could produce greatest amount of good for the greatest amount of people; the emphasis on individual rights and creativity are considered secondary. The maintenance of seniority rule, for example, provides a framework for smooth interpersonal relations and harmonious transition of power. It has, however, impeded individual competition and equitable distribution of resources based on merit. More importantly, the emphasis in the maintenance of harmony has shielded Korean society from self-criticism, objective evaluation, and an atmosphere to stimulate transformative changes.

Secondly, a collective in Korea and East Asia is a small exclusive ingroup and not an inclusive entity (Kim, 1995). In Korea, people maintain harmony within the ingroup and maintain a separate orientation (i.e. that of apathy, exploitation, and neglect) for outgroup members. Such discrimination has historically become the basis of factionalism, regionalism, nepotism, and blocked the creation of a well-functioning civil and democratic society.

Koreans have invested their energy and hopes in people that they know well (i.e. family members, teachers, and colleagues) and have excluded outgroup members. For example, although women are included as ingroup members as wives and mothers, they are not given equal opportunity as colleagues to participate and contribute to the larger society. The challenge that the Korean society faces is to create a system in which everyone could participate on an equal footing and have equal access to various opportunities. In Korea, interpersonal connections through regional networks, familial ties, and school ties, and even gender, have excluded competent individuals from full participation. This exclusive membership and emphasis on harmony created homogeneity of thought and actions that have limited the diversity of ideas that could have been utilised in creatively transforming Korean society.

Although the success of Korean education is based on a system where individuals are objectively evaluated and are given opportunities based on individual merit, this is not the case in the economic and financial sector. In the economic arena, outcomes are often based on personal, social and political favoritism and are not contingent upon performance. For this reason, many employees and investors distrust the system. In this environment, employees did not invest their effort in developing professional skills to improve production, but rather developed political skills to maintain and enhance their social network.

In order to compete in the international arena, Korean society must create a transparent system that people could trust and that could ensure equal opportunity for everyone, including women, people without a college degree, and non-Koreans. This does not, however, mean an equal outcome. Korean society must respect differential outcomes that are based on merit and performance rather than simply dividing the outcome equally to maintain harmony. This must be done while maintaining group cohesiveness and viability rather than at the destruction of the group.

In order to participate fully in the international arena, the mentality of Korean leaders and the general public must change. The solution to the current economic crisis remains largely within. The balance of self-regulation and controlling the environment must be created. Furthermore, Korean society must create a system that is harmonious, but a system that is also fair, just, and open. It must be a system which people can trust, everyone has equal access, and which can incorporate diversity of ideas and lifestyles.

Emerging economies such as Vietnam and China must learn from the mistakes of Japan and Korea. Although these countries have been able to create tightly-knitted functional work groups to produce high quality goods, they have largely failed in the financial sector. Skills that are useful in industrial sectors (tightly-knit ingroups) have shown to have devastating effect on the financial sector (i.e. banks have given loans to tightly-knit ingroups which turned out to be bad or corrupt investments). In the financial sector investments were made based on interpersonal considerations and not on sound financial management. In some instance, the exclusivity of the ingroup and lack of transparency allowed corruption to fester.

I do not believe that Asian societies can resolve the current problems by simply imitating Western practices, since the cultural assets are very different. The United States and Europe experienced economic crisis in 1970's and 1980's. As Western societies learned from East Asia the value of teamwork, commitment, and quality control, East Asian societies must learn from Western to enhance transparency, rationality, and system-based management rather than utilising interpersonal network.

LITERATURE

1.   Azuma, H., "Why Study Child Development in Japan?" in H. Stevenson, H. Azuma, &•K. Hakuta K (eds.), *Child Development and Education in Japan* (New York: W. H. Freeman, 1986) pp. 3-12.

2. Hess, R. et al., "Family Influence on School Readiness and Achievement in Japan and the United States: An overview of a longitudinal study", in H. Azuma, K. Hakuta, & H. W. Stevenson (eds.), *Child Development and Education in Japan* (New York: W. H. Freeman and Company, 1986) pp. 201-216.

3. Ho, D. Y. F., "Chinese Patterns of Socialisation: A critical review", in M.H. Bond (ed.), *The Psychology of the Chinese People* (Oxford: Oxford University Press, 1986).

4. Gabrenya, W. K., Jr., Wang, Y. E., & Latane, B, "Social Loafing on an optimising task: Cross-cultural differences among Chinese and Americans", *Journal of Cross-Cultural Psychology*, 16 (2), 1985, pp. 223-242.

5. Holloway, Kasgiwagi, & Azuma, "Causal Attributions by Japanese and American Mothers and Children about Performance in Mathematics", *International Journal of Psychology*, 21, 1986, pp. 269-286.

6. Kim, U., "After the Crisis in Social Psychology: Development of the transactional model of science", *Asian Journal of Social Psychology*, 2, 1999, pp. 1-19.

7. Kim, U., "Individualism and Collectivism: Conceptual clarification and elaboration", in U. Kim, H. C. Triandis, C. Kagitcibasi, S. C. Choi, & G. Yoon, G. (Eds.), *Individualism and Collectivism: Theory, Method, and Applications*, (Thousand Oaks, CA: Sage, 1994) pp. 19-40.

8. Kim, U., & Berry, J. W., *Indigenous Psychologies: Experience and Research in Cultural Context* (Newbury Park, CA: Sage, 1993).

9. Kim, U., & Choi, S. C., "Individualism, Collectivism, and Child Development: A Korean perspective", in P. M. Greenfield, & R. Cocking (eds.), *Cognitive Socialization of Minority Children: Continuities and discontinuities* (Hillsdale, NJ: Lawrence Erlbaum, 1994).

10. Kim, U., & Park, Y. S., An indigenous and cross-cultural analysis of the perception of success, failure and future aspiration: The case of Korean, Japanese, Canadian and the US students and adults. Research report submitted to the Korean Research Foundation (Seoul, Korea, 1998).

11. Kim, U. M., "Significance of Paternalism and Communalism in the Occupational Welfare System of Korean Firms: A National Survey", in U. Kim, H. C. Triandis, C. Kagitcibasi, S. C. Choi, & G. Yoon (eds.), *Individualism and Collectivism: Theory, Method, and Application* (Thousand Oaks, CA: Sage, 1994).

12. Lebra, T. S., *Japanese Patterns of Behavior* (Honolulu: University of Hawaii Press, 1976).

13. Markus, H. & Kitayama, S., "Culture and Self: Implications for cognition, emotion, and motivation". *Psychological Review, 98,* 1991, pp. 224-253.

14. Misumi, J., *The Behavioral Science of Leadership* (Ann Arbor, MI: The University of Michigan, 1985).

15. Misumi, J., Small group activities in Japanese industrial organizations and behavioral science. Paper presented at the XXIV International Congress of Psychology, Sydney, Australia, 1988.

16. Park, Y. S., & Kim, U., "Attributional Style of Korean Students: Comparative analysis of primary, secondary and university students", *Journal of Educational Psychology, 11,* 1997, pp. 71-97.

17. Park, Y. S., & Kim, U., "Locus of Control, Attributional Style, and Academic Achievement: Comparative analysis of Korean, Korean-Chinese, and Chinese students", *Asian Journal of Social Psychology,* 1, 1998, pp. 191-208.

18. Stevenson, H., Azuma, H & Hakuta. K (eds.), *Child Development and Education in Japan* (New York: W. H. Freeman, 1986).

19. Stevenson, H., & Lee, S. Y., "Context of Achievement: A study of American, Chinese, and Japanese children", *Monographs of the Society for Research in Child Development, 55,* 1990.

20. Sullivan, J. J., Suzuki, T., & Kondo, Y., "Managerial Perceptions of Performance: A comparison of Japanese and American work groups", *Journal of Cross-Cultural Psychology, 17,* 1986, pp. 379-398.

21. White, M. I. & LeVine, R. A., "What is an *Ii ko* (Good child)?" in H. Stevenson, H. Azuma, & K. Hakuta K (eds.), *Child Development and Education in Japan* (New York: W. H. Freeman, 1986) pp. 55-62.

22. Wirth, L. Preface to K. Manheim, *Ideology and Utopia: An Introduction to Sociology of Knowledge,* (New York: Harcourt, Brace and Company, 1946).

23. Yu, A. B., & Yang, K. S., "The Nature of Achievement Motivation in Collectivistic Societies", in U. Kim, H. C. Triandis, C. Kagitcibasi, S. C., Choi, S. C., & Yoon, G. (eds.), *Individualism and Collectivism: Theory, method, and applications* (Thousand Oaks, CA: Sage, 1994).

Filipino Values at the Threshold of the New Millennium

Elena L. Samonte
University of the Philippines

INTRODUCTION

The new millennium is, figuratively speaking, just around the corner. It holds much promise of a highly technologically advanced world. However, despite the repeated attempts and calls of scientists and professionals to develop a technology-oriented culture (Follosco, 1992) by accelerating industrialisation (del Rosario, et.al., n.d.), the technological future of the Philippines is viewed with pessimism (Garcia, 1991) and scepticism (Roque and Posadas, 1987). Scientists decry the "technological dependence" and "lack of self-reliance attitudes on the part of scientists and engineers" (*ibid.*). As a social scientist, specifically a psychologist, I would raise two questions: 1) What kind of future do the 71.5 million Filipinos want? 2) What values influence the attitudes and behaviour of Filipinos so they get what they want? In other words, do the Filipinos want the country to be another "tiger" similar to some of its ASEAN neighbours?

As Rokeach (1973:25) pointed out, values guide and determine our actions, attitudes towards objects and situations, ideology, presentation of ourselves to others, evaluations, judgements, justifications, comparison of ourselves with others and attempts to influence others. "They provide the social framework within which judgements are made" (Windmiller, et. al., 1980: 204). They may be instrumental (means) or terminal (end) values (Rokeach, *op.cit.*: 28).

This paper will review studies that may provide the answers to these two questions of what we want and the values that guide us to attaining what we want in the next millennium.

WHAT DO FILIPINOS CONSIDER IMPORTANT?

A study on the measurement of the well-being of Filipinos was conducted to come up with indices to measure the quality of life of Filipinos, as defined by Filipinos. In the light of the "new paradigm of human development which emphasises the broadening of human choices and access to various options", it was necessary to get the perspective of the beneficiaries of development (SyCip, et. al., 1998).

Table 1. Top 11 items given "very important rating".

Item	% Rating	Domain
Faith in God	78.9	spiritual
Prayer and reflection	74.7	spiritual
Long life	68.4	health
Doing good to others	68.2	spiritual
Going to church activities	67.3	spiritual
Good marital relations	66.7	social relationships
Love of spouse	66.1	social relationships
Love of children	65.2	social relationships
Regular food	61.5	health
House ownership	60.9	savings & wealth
Being with children	60.4	social relationships

The 1997 nationwide survey had 2400 respondents in four major areas (National Capital Region, Pangasinan, Iloilo, and Zamboanga), each with a rural and urban component. In a previous 1993 survey done in Laguna, it was found that the three most important items were in three domains: Spiritual (having faith in God), employment (having a permanent job), and social relationships (good marital relations). Results of the 1997 survey showed that the two top items were from the spiritual domain. Social relationships were, however, also important (Table 1). A comparison of the data across the four areas revealed marked differences in their concerns. For the respondents from the National Capital Region and Pangasinan, the deteriorating peace and order situation highlights their concern about their security (Table 2). For Iloilo respondents, it is their housing situation while for the Zamboanga respondents, it is their family life (having children, a spouse).

Satisfaction ratings show that respondents derived their greatest satisfaction from items in the areas of social relationships and spirituality (Table

156

3).

Table 2. Top three items with a majority rating of "very important" by sample site.

Area	Items	% Rating
National Capital Region	Security from crime	80.3
	Unity of Filipinos	76.0
	Freedom from sickness	75.7
	Land ownership	75.7
Pangasinan	Security from crime	53.7
	Ability to read & write	51.9
	To finish college	49.7
Iloilo	House tenure	66.6
	Clean surroundings	64.7
	Freedom from sickness	64.5
Zamboanga	Having children	66.3
	Having a spouse	64.0
	Being with spouse	56.3

Table 3. Items with a majority indicating that they were "very satisfied".

Item	% Rating	Domain
Faith in God	68.3	Spiritual
Prayer and reflection	64.7	Spiritual
Love of spouse	61.5	social relations
Having children	60.9	social relations
Good marital relations	59.9	social relations
Love of children	59.4	social relations
Going to Church activities	59.0	spiritual
Having spouse	53.8	social relations
Being with children	51.7	social relations
Long life	49.1	physical health

Clearly, the areas which Filipinos find most important are also those with

157

which they are most satisfied. It is little wonder then that, in a survey of happiness conducted by the Survey Research Group, 94% of Filipinos were 'quite happy' or 'very happy'. Another survey in 1991 showed that 84% of Filipinos were either 'very happy' or 'fairly happy'. The survey also found that the proportion who feel happy rises with socio-economic class. Unhappiness was found to rise with age and to differ according to geographical area, with the older ones and those living in Metro Manila having the greatest proportion of unhappy Filipinos (Mangahas, 1994:64-66).

However, A recent SWS survey (Rufo, 1998 as cited in SyCip, 1998) showed that more Filipinos (38%) consider themselves to be worse off today and more consider themselves as poor (65%). But as the study of SyCip et. al. (1998) showed, the Filipinos were optimistic about their future, expecting their lives to get better. What is significant is that majority believed that they could change their quality of life through their own efforts.

Acquisition of Values

But where do Filipinos get this optimism and resilience? Parents play a major role in the acquisition of dominant values (Windmiller, et.al., 1980). Through the socialisation process, individuals learn values, particularly as they are rewarded by their parents for doing good and punished for not doing good. This has been described as the prescriptive value orientation as opposed to a proscriptive value orientation whereby children are rewarded for not doing bad and punished for doing bad (Fig. 1).

Fig. 1.

Reinforcement

Value Orientation	Reward	Punishment
Prescriptive (Thou shall)	For doing good	For not doing good
Proscriptive (Thou shalt not)	For not doing bad	For doing bad

A survey showed that the values to be taught to children are: Good manners, religious faith, hard work, responsibility, and independence (SWS, 1996).

158

Filipino Values

The word 'value' has no exact translation in the Philippine language. The closest word suggested by F. Landa Jocano (Talisayon, 1996) is 'asal' (normative patterns of behaviour). Reviews of the literature on Filipino values (Manalang, 1982; Hennig, 1983; Talisayon, 1996; Cariño, 1997; Miralao, 1997) have different approaches, some with theoretical frameworks, others without. For example, Talisayon in his review of about one hundred academic, journalistic and opinion articles about Filipino values, orientations, attitudes and idiosyncracies found that:

1. The core or central clusters revolve around seven values: family/kinship 0orientation, *makatao/kapwa tao* (personalism), '*loob* complex' (religious/psychic orientation), social acceptance, *pakikiramdam*, *pakikisama* (group-centeredness), and economic security (See Annex A).

2. The strongest macroclusters are, in order of strength, relationship, *loob*, social, livelihood, and optimism

3. Value clusters can be 'lined up' along one principal dimension or axis with two extremes: the indigenous, rural, inward-looking, passive pole and the Westernised, urban, outward-looking, active pole. (Talisayon 1996:105)

He did not, however, describe his methodology nor his theoretical framework.

Hennig (1983), on the other hand, provides an analytical framework which uses three orientations: philosophical (cosmological), sociological (situational), and psychological (personality) to understand Philippine values (Annex B). However, the paradigm is incomplete as it "does not consider the unsystematic evolution of the Philippine social system arising from international contacts, especially those of a colonial nature." Moreover, his interpretation of *Bahala Na* as 'fatalism' lacks the perspective of the culture bearer (Lagmay, 1993).

CONTEMPORARY VALUES OF FILIPINOS

Studies have shown historical changes in value orientation. Values change over time because people respond to needs which are unfulfilled (Inglehart,1977, as cited in Montiel, 1991).

Generational/Ideological variation: Montiel (1991) addressed the question of differences in the central values of student activists across generations and ideological groupings. Respondents were former student leaders of the early 1970's (during the Martial Law era) and youth protesters involved in the EDSA revolution of 1986. Results showed that the first generation of student leaders valued daringness and excitement during their college years while the second generation valued control and personal tranquillity. The findings suggest that the generation's historical context and ideological groupings may affect the student activists' values. The causal direction of the relationship between personal values and social context, however, could not be ascertained.

Cultural variation in values: Hofstede, in his study of 116,000 IBM employees from more than 60 countries, found cultural variation in values. The four dimensions he studied are: *Power distance, uncertainty avoidance, individualism* and *masculinity*.

Power distance is the extent to which members of a culture accept inequality and whether they perceive much distance between those in authority and those who do not have such control over others. The Philippines, Mexico and Venezuela, were found to be top on *power distance*. Hofstede characterises such countries as having parents who emphasise obedience, an acceptance of a paternalistic type of management, status differences and respect for the old (Hofstede, 1982, 1983 as cited in Triandis, 1994).

The Philippines was also found to be masculine in orientation; the highest was Japan. This dimension shows how much a society differentiates according to sex. Countries high on the masculinity index (MAS) have stronger achievement motivation where achievement is defined in terms of recognition and wealth. Thus earnings, recognition, advancement and challenge are relatively more important to employees. Hofstede (1984) found the Philippines to be one of the Asian countries[1] aside from the 'Anglo' cluster that could be described as countries that have the highest nAch or what he labels as 'masculine risk-takers.'

The above-mentioned descriptions are supported by a study of Torres (1990) on work motivation and the productivity of government workers. Government frontline workers when asked to rank ten different potential motivators considered personal goals such as "personal sense of achievement" and "opportunities for growth and promotion" as more important than qualities of the work setting. Factor analysis showed that they were also concerned with maintenance variables such as relationship with peers, a participative management style and close supervision over their work.

A paternalistic type of management is also underscored by Balite (1996)

---

[1]The other Asian countries are India, Hong Kong and (marginally) Singapore.

160

and Jocano (1990) where leaders show concern for the workers and "act like responsible elders: morally upright, responsible and compassionate." A survey of residents in Camarines Norte (Talisayon, 1996) and a nationwide survey revealed that Filipinos value in their leaders and in general the following: Affectional-relational 'motherly' qualities (showing care and concern, being hospitable and friendly, having respect for others), courage and will or 'fatherly' qualities (having high moral values, fairness and justice and being hard-working).

The MAS is negatively correlated with the percentage of all working women who are in professional and technical jobs (Boulding, et. al. in Hofstede, 1984). There is evidence that in more masculine countries, there are less men who are favourably disposed towards women holding high and/or leading positions. A review of the profile of women in public as well as private life shows that women have very little representation in both elective and appointive positions (Samonte, 1990; Torres, 1995). At present, in the Supreme Court, only two of the 15 justices are women while in the Court of Appeals, there are 10 female appellate justices and 34 males. Of the 1488 judges nationwide, only 272 (18%) are females (Porcalla, 1999). These figures, however, are an improvement over those in 1979 (Torres, 1995).

In a study of 545 Filipino respondents consisting of students, farmers, urban poor coordinators, administrative staff and teachers, it was found that two of the four indices, power distance (PDI) and masculinity (MAS), were basically the same as those found by Hofstede (Acuña and Roman, 1994). However, for this sample, respondents rated higher on individualism (41.3) (IDV) and uncertainty avoidance (54.4) (UAI) than Hofstede's estimates of 32 (low individualism) and 44 (weak uncertainty avoidance) respectively. It will be noted that highest (116) on the PDI is the group of public school teachers who must work within a very hierarchical structure. This is in contrast with the PDI of private school teachers (79) who may have more autonomy in their work and some participation in decision-making.

Hofstede (1984) found that respondents in high UAI countries tend to differ from those in low UAI countries in such aspects as resistance against change and pessimism about employers in general. A low UAI means a greater willingness to take risks. This may bode well for Filipinos as far as innovation and entrepreneurship are concerned.

In low individualistic countries, the role of the family in the work setting and harmony are important such that nepotism is acceptable and avoidance is a common mode of dealing with conflict. These underscore the salience of the family and the Filipino's strong attachment to family and kin group (Miralao, 1997) and greater concern for family substitutes in organisations (Salazar,1970). In high power distance/low individualistic countries, self-interest is less valid (Triandis, *op.cit.*:128). This is shown in the IDV of the farmers and rural college students from Bukidnon who prioritised group goals over personal concerns (Acuña and Roman, 1994).

The study also found significant differences in the four dimensions across different research sites (urban and rural). For example, the PDI (87) of the National Capital Region (NCR) is signficantly lower than those found in Pangasinan (111), Bataan (107) and Cebu (102). Results of this study show changes over a span of two decades towards greater individualism. Doronila (1992) also found that in more urbanised communities, there was a growing tendency to perceive a traditionally familistic orientation as a hindrance to development. However, her sample of students and adults still chose the relational values such as *pakikisama* (getting along well with others), *utang na loob* (debt of gratitude), *marunong makiramdam* (sensitive), and *madaling mapahiya* (easily embarrassed).

Miralao (1997) utilises sociological perspectives in discussing the possible role that Philippine values and the family system may play in determining the future of the country. Citing the work of Johan Galtung, the basic socio-cultural change accompany the transformation of societies from a 'primitive' state to a 'traditional' one, then to a 'modern' state and finally a 'post-modern' phase.

As societies move from one stage to another, structures of human interactions shift from those congruent with or promotive of primary, personalistic, personalistic and diffuse relationships (Beta) to those which are secondary and universalistic (Alpha). Societies display mixes of Beta and Alpha. Beta structures thin out and weaken as Alpha structures are required in agricultural villages and become dominant in modern societies. Beta structures are thus relegated to small families which interact only after its members have come home from the bureaucracies that emphasise specificity in social relations and universalism in the treatment of people. In the post-modern stage, the crisis brought about by the 'dehumanisation process' brings about feelings of alienation and social anomie, prompting the reconstruction of Beta structures that would deconstruct the individualism, secularism, rationalism and scientism which accompanied the transformation to modern societies.

In the Philippines, the role of the family remains central and pivotal. Its characteristics are: 1) extended (vertically and horizontally), 2) with members maintaining close relationships with a 3) continuous flow of help, assistance, favors and reciprocal exchanges. The family is thus a very big source of support and protection for the individual. As shown by Hofstede (1984:172), "in stable low IDV societies, members will transfer part of their extended family or clan allegiances to the organisation they belong to". Thus, in Filipino organisations, family relationships are replicated through ritual kinship (as in co-parenthood arrangements in baptisms or marriages) or by using a kin term such as 'kuya/manong' 'ate/manang' (older brother/sister) for a non-relative (boss, supervisor, colleague) (Miralao, 1997).

This continuous flow of assistance is clearly manifested in the literature on migration (Licuanan, 1982; Cruz and Paganoni, 1989; Pertierra, 1992; Tacoli, 1996; Samonte, 1991; 1998a). Financial considerations prompt millions of Filipinos[2] to work abroad, the beneficiaries are really family members (siblings, parents, spouse), whether the end goal is their education, purchase of a property, building a house, or having one's own business. In fact, they are likely to sacrifice for the family and stay longer abroad for as long as these goals are not yet met (Tacoli, 1996; Samonte, 1998a; 1998b). On the other hand, the vicarious migrants (family members left behind) do their share in managing the family. It is not unusual that the extended family (grandparents, aunts, uncles, cousins) act as surrogates in caring for the children (Miralao, 1997; Cruz and Paganoni, 1989).

The earlier literature on Philippine values (Bulatao, 1962 Hollnsteiner, 1970; Lynch, 1970) underscored the values of personalism, social acceptance, smooth interpersonal relations (SIR), emotional closeness, economic and social betterment, and patience, suffering and endurance. Current studies still support the importance of these values in the lives of Filipinos. Economic and social betterment is a terminal value for many women in migration. The remittances of migrant workers are sizeable, US$8-10 billion a year. However, these women have other motivations for going abroad which are less altruistic and more focused on the self, e.g., self-development, curiosity, adventure, and status attached to travelling abroad, dissatisfaction with home life or career (Samonte, 1998; Tacoli, 1996).

Other changes related to the family are such realities as one out of six

---

[2]At present, there are some 6.97 million Filipinos abroad, 2.94 million of whom are overseas Filipino workers (OFW), 2.15 million immigrants and 1.88 million undocumented workers (CFO,1997).

children or 3.7 million children between the ages of 5-17 worked in the *last twelve months* (de los Angeles-Bautista and Arriola, 1997). It is estimated that there are 25 inducated abortions per 1,000 women aged 15-44 each year, which nationally would mean some 400,000 per year (Perez, et. al., 1997). There are changes in sex values, with fairly high levels of premarital sex among young unmarried women, 33.4 and 40.5 for the 15-19 and 20-24 age groups (Asis, 1993 as cited in Medina, 1995:38). There is an increase in the number of women who want to limit their childbearing after having one child (NSO and MI, 1999). Family size has also decreased to four children, about two children less than in 1970 (NDS, 1993 as cited in Miralao, 1997).

However, despite the threats to the stability of the family, social scientists have highlighted its resilience and adaptability to the demands of the time (Medina, 1995; Miralao, 1997). Respondents to surveys on the family underscore values that contribute to ensuring this: Respect and love for one's parents, responsibility for caring for one's children (even at the expense of one's well-being), belief in marriage as an institution and disapproval of a woman having a child as a single parent without having a stable relationship with a man (SWS, 1996).

CONCLUSION

The juxtaposition of values associated with traditional societies and those that are characteristic of modern societies have posed challenges to the Filipinos. The Philippines has seen changes in structures and values, in response to the demands of the time. However, the spiritual and social relationship values which Filipinos have lived by seem not only to have guided behaviour but also enabled Filipinos to weather the storm. Research on resilient individuals shows that faith (in surmounting and faith in human relationships) fuels the resilient spirit. "There is ample evidence that they choose how to *see*, how to *be*, and how *not* to be" (Higgins, 1994). For now and the coming millennium, Filipinos seem to choose values which are still linked with the traditional, although they are open to those that are associated with industrialisation and modernity. However, Filipinos are in no great rush to replace one for the other.

LITERATURE

1. Acuña, Jasmin and Roman, Emerlinda. "Value Orientations in Selected Filipino Work Groups", *The Philippine Management Review*, 5 (1),

1994, pp. 20-40.

2. Balite, Flordelia A., *Satisfaction of Filipino Workers with Japanese Management and Production Practices in Three Japanese Companies in the Mactan Export Processing Zone (MEPZ)*, Unpublished M.A. Thesis. Submitted to the Asian Center, University of the Philippines. 1996.

3. Bulatao, Jaime C., "The Manileño's Mainsprings", in *Four Readings on Philippine Values*. Frank X. Lynch (Comp.) (Quezon City: Ateneo de Manila University Press, 1962) pp. 50-86.

4. CFO (Commission on Filipinos Overseas), *Estimated number of overseas Filipinos* (as of December 1997).

5. Cariño, Ledivina, "The Values We Live By: The Congruence and Distribution of Values in Academe with Filipino Values and Goals of National Development". *Philippine Sociological Review*, 45 (1-4), 1997, 159-188.

6. Costello, Michael A., "The Elderly in Filipino Households: Current Status and Future Prospects", *Philippine Sociological Review*, January-December, 42 (1-4), 1994, pp. 53-77.

7. Cruz, Victoria Paz and Paganoni, Anthony, *Filipinas in Migration*. Big Bills and Small Change (Quezon City: Scalabrini Migration Center, 1989).

8. del Rosario, E. J., Bantilan Jr., F.T., Barril, C.R., Mercado, B.T. and Pacardo, E.P. *Integrated Program in Science and Technology for Accelerated Industrialization*. Assessment paper prepared by an ad hoc committee. n.d.

9. delos Angeles-Bautista, Feny and Arriola, Joanna C., *To Learn and To Earn. Education and Child Labor in the Philippines*, (Manila: International Labour Organisation. 1997).

10. Doronila, Maria Luisa C., *National Identity and Social Change* (Quezon City: University of the Philippines Press and UP Center for Integrative and Development Studies, 1992).

11. Follosco, Ceferino L., "Science and Technology Reforms and Innovations", in J.V. Abueva and E.R. Roman (eds.), *The Aquino Administration: Record and Legacy (1986-1992)* (Quezon City: University of the Philippines Press, 1992) pp. 159-172.

12. Hennig, Obert P., "Philippine Values in Perspective: An Analytical Framework", *Philippine Sociological Review*, 1983, pp. 55-64.

13. Higgins, Gina O'Connell, *Resilient Adults. Overcoming a Cruel Past* (San Francisco: Jossey-Bass Publications, 1994).

14. Hofstede, Geert, *Culture's Consequences. International Differences in Work-Related Values*, Abridged Edition (California: Sage Publications, 1984).

15. Hollnsteiner, Mary R., "Reciprocity in the Lowland Philippines", Frank X. Lynch and Alfonso de Guzman II (Eds.), in *Four Readings on Philippine Values* (Quezon City: Ateneo de Manila University Press, 1970) pp. 65-88.

16. Jocano, F. Landa, *Management by Culture* (Quezon City: Punlad Research House, 1990).

17. Lagmay, Alfredo V., "Bahala Na", *Philippine Journal of Psychology*, 26 (1), 1993, pp. 31-36.

18. Licuanan, Patricia B., "Beyond the Economics of Overseas Employment: The Human Costs", *Philippine Studies*, 30 (Second Quarter), 1982, pp. 262-271.

19. Lynch, Frank X., "Social Acceptance Reconsidered", Frank X. Lynch and Alfonso de Guzman II (eds.), in *Four Readings on Philippine Values* (Quezon City: Ateneo de Manila University Press, 1970) pp. 1-67.

20. Manalang, Priscilla S., "Philippine Values, Local Norms, and Technological Innovation", *Philippine Social Sciences and Humanities Review*, XLVI (3-4), 1982, pp. 327-350.

21. Mangahas, Mahar, *The Philippine Social Climate* (Pasig: Anvil Publishing, Inc., 1998).

22. Medina, Belen T.G., "Issues Relating to Filipino Marriage and Family", *Social Science Information*, 23 (1-2), 1995, pp. 36-43.

23. Miralao, Virginia A., "The Family, Traditional Values and the Sociocultural Transformation of Philippine Society", *Philippine Sociological Review*, 45 (1-4), 1997, pp. 189-215.

24. Montiel, Cristina J., "Factor Analaysis of Ideological and Generational Differences in Value Orientation Among Filipino Student Activists", *Philippine Journal of Psychology*, 24 (1), 1991, pp. 12-21.

25. National Statistics Office (NSO), Department of Health, Manila Philippines, and Macro International (MI), *National Demographic and Health Survey 1998* (Manila: NSO and MI, 1999).

26. Perez, Aurora, Singh, Susheela and Wulf, Dierdre, *Clandestine Abortion: A Philipine Reality* (New York: The Alan Guttmacher Institute, 1997).

27. Pertierra, Raul (ed.), *Remittances and Returnees*, The Cultural Economy of Migration in Ilocos (Quezon City: New Day Publishers, 1992).

28. Porcalla, Delon, "More Women Judges Sought", *The Philippine Star*, March 14, 1999, pp. 1-2.

29. Quisumbing, Lourdes R. and Sta. Maria, Felice P., *Values Education Through History*. Peace & Tolerance (Pasay City: UNESCO National Commission of the Philippines, 1995).

30. Rokeach, Milton, *The Nature of Human Values* (New York: The Free Press, 1973).

31. Roque, Cesar and Posadas Roger, "Philippine Technological Dependence and Backwardness", in Roger Posadas and Celso Roque, *Toward a Scientific and Technological Self-Reliance for the Philippines* (The U.N. University, 1987).

32. Salazar, Meliton, "Comment on the Abueva Paper [What Are We in Power For?]", *Philippine Sociological Review*, 18, pp. 3-4.

33. Samonte, Elena L., *Status of Women in the Philippines* (Quezon City: Psychological Association of the Philippines, 1990).

34. _____, "Filipino Migrants in Japan: In Search of a Better Life - the Price of a Dream", *Philippine Journal of Labor and Industrial Relations*, XIII (1-2), 1991, pp. 75-122.

35. _____, *Filipino Migrant Workers in Hong Kong: Inventory of Skills and Long Term Plans* (Manila, 1997).

36. _____, (1998a) "Filipino Migrant Workers: Cost Benefit Analysis of their Sojourn and its Implications", in Allan B.I. Bernardo, Natividad A. Dayan and Allen A. Tan (eds.), *Understanding Behavior Bridging Cultures* (Manila: De La Salle University Press, Inc., 1998).

37. _____, (1998b), "Filipino Migrant Workers in Hong Kong: Inventory of Skills and Long-Term Plans" in Roswith Roth (ed.), *Psychologists Facing the Challenge of a Global Culture with Human*

Rights and Mental Health (Pabst Science Publishers, 1998).

38. SyCip, Ly, Asis, Maruja Milagros and Luna, Emmanuel, The Measurement of Filipino Well-being: Findings from the Field. Paper presented at the First International Conference on Philippine Studies. Reggio, Calabria, Italy, November 26-28, 1998.

39. SWS, *Philippine Values Survey* (Manila, 1996).

40. Tacoli, Cynthia, "Migrating 'For the Sake of the Family'? Gender, Life Course and Intra-Household Relations Among Filipino Migrants in Rome", *Philippine Sociological Review*, January-December, 44(1-4), 1996, pp. 12-32.

41. Talisayon, Serafin D., Values in our Quest for Freedom (1896-1898) and their Application for Future Development, in Lourdes R. Quisumbing and Felice P. Sta. Maria (eds.), *Values Education Through History*. Peace & Tolerance (Pasay City: UNESCO National Commission of the Philippines, 1995).

42. Torres, Amaryllis T., Work Motivation and Productivity of Government Workers, *Philippine Journal of Psychology*, 23, 1990, pp. 30-38.

43. _____, *The Filipino Woman in Focus*, A Book of Readings. 2nd Edition. (Quezon City: UP Office of Research Coordination and the UP Press, 1995).

44. Triandis, Harry C., "Cross Cultural Industrial Organizational Psychology", in Harry C. Triandis, Marvin D. Dunnette, and Leaetta M. Hough (eds.), *Handbook of Industrial and Organizational Psychology*, Second Edition, Vol. 4. (Palo Alto, California: Consulting Psychologists Press, Inc. 1994).

45. Windmiller, Nyra, Lambert Nadine, and Turiel, Elliot, *Moral Development and Socialization* (Boston: Allyn and Bacon, Inc. 1980).

Thai Social Values in Rural Development

Pirom Chantaworn
Faculty of Economics, University of Thammasat

INTRODUCTION[1]

In Thai society the social values are vital underlying values of the development of the rural community. Peoples' participation at the grass-roots level in the communities, we find, is moreover important for the development of social value in society at large. Social values constitute the basis of thinking which is derived from the basic way of life and procedure of doing things in the Thai society.

In the past, social and communal development caused some disappointment, because it tended to omit the way of development that was needed for the majority of people. The development did not consider the feelings and the indigenous intellect at all, so the outcome of Thai social development in the past resulted in the paradox of the more development, the more society became underdeveloped. This is the reason why we need to reconsider the development process, by including the social values and the local knowledge that existed in the traditional Thai community.

This paper is an attempt to identify failures of the mainstream development in Thai society. It will also present some thoughts and ideas of Pra Dhammapidok (Payutto), a member of Thai monastic order and a profound Buddhist scholar monk, who argues that the omission of traditional social values in the mainstream development thinking has caused the social vices and weaknesses in Thai society today. We should rethink the development in order to bring back the strength to society and environment in a way we may call a sustainable development.

---

[1] The author wishes to acknowledge Pra-Maha Utis Apichayo, for his research-assistantship.

SOCIAL VALUE IN THAI RURAL DEVELOPMENT

Thailand has specific characteristics when compared to other Asian countries. She is an open society and accepts outside dynamic cultures and values, and society is able to adjust the new values into her way of life in harmonious ways. Thailand has a firm belief in Buddhist principles regarding the cause and effect, logical reasons and the middle way. She has the King as a focal point of the people's mind and has upheld that belief for centuries.

Thai society enters the 21th century with a past of three decades of development planning. The economic and social transition in Thai development history has counted eight development plans, latest the eighth national economics and social plan (1997-2001). The globalisation of the world using communication technology (especially information technology) is creating a world without boundaries, a world in need of a New Economic Order. The economic and social changes and international politics will cause some disorder and thus increases the need of sustainable development in the Thai society.

In the economic arena, globalisation will widen the world market the more mobilisation factors of production and DFI (direct foreign investment). The World Trade Organisation along with a number of regional economic groupings has been established like, NAFTA (North America Free Trade Area), EU and AFTA (Asean Free Trade Area), APEC (Asia Pacific Economic Community) aiming to bring economic development and stability for their members in international trade. This organisation will speed up the transfer of technology for development among these countries. Furthermore, the creation of the networks among different economic areas will stimulate a more free trade policy, increasing competition among countries.

In the social arena, globalisation will help people in getting information according to their taste; but it will also result in more materialism, consumerism and imitationism. The disease of consumerism among youngsters will eventually influence traditional culture and social values. Furthermore, globalisation will bring new international social values as has already been seen in the 'waves' promoting democracy, human rights, gender issues, and the environmental or green wave. The latter 'green wave' may well bring about consensus and new consciousness that humanity cannot survive if human development fails to include human dimensions such as: Family, community, society and environment. What instead will happen is a seriously unbalanced development, which if not cured, will cause man and nature to live out of harmony.

170

THE IMPACT OF PAST DEVELOPMENT

After eight national economic and social plans, we can draw certain conclusions about the past three decades of development. Firstly, the record shows that Thai society has been successful in its economic development. The growth rate was at its height 7.8 percent per annum. The per capita income rose from 2,100 baht in 1961 to 68,000 baht in 1995 (at current prices). The proportion of the poor decreased and was only at 13.7 percent by 1992, quite much lower than the target of 20 percent forecast in the seventh national economic and social plan. At the time, the financial position of the country was stable and well recognised by the international community. Government investment in improving the infrastructure and in social security has continued and has brought with it a rise in the standard of living level for most Thai.

Secondly, while economic development was targeted to succeed in many areas, economic activities and wealth are still concentrated in Bangkok and its environs. The per capita income for people living in Bangkok and nearby areas is considerably higher than in other regions within the country. The north-eastern region, especially, is poor and has the lowest income per capita, in average 12 times lower than in the Bangkok area. Household income among the wealthiest 20 percent of the population increased from 54 percent of the total in 1988 to 59 percent in 1992. While for the poorest 20 percent of the household income decreased from 4.6 percent in 1988 to 3.9 percent in 1992. The widening gap between income and opportunity, which occurred during a period of economic expansion, had an impact on the quality of life the majority and will effect the country's long-term development.

Thirdly, the net effect of past development on the majority of the Thai people has been satisfactory with regards to certain social and infrastructural developments. By 1994, about 97.7 percent of all rural villages had electricity and clean water with a water supply system in place for more than 75 percent of the urban areas, in all the regions outside Bangkok, and 32 percent for all the rural villages. In transportation, there were more than 210,025 kilometres of road inter- and intraprovincial highways connecting provinces, districts and subdistricts. In addition, there were more than 123,400 kilometres of local roads in the rural areas. The effects of compulsory education on people living in rural areas was that more than 97.6 percent of children went to government schools. Meanwhile, public health developments extended the life expectancy of the average Thai from 67.6 years in 1994 compared to only 63 years in 1990.

Fourthly, the emphasis on competition to generate greater wealth and income has caused Thai people to become more materialistic. It has also caused more behavioural problems in Thai society than before: Namely, lower moral and ethical standards, weaker discipline, and increased exploitation of other human beings with the effect that the old, good and harmonious Thai social values have declined substantially. Furthermore, family institutions, the community and local cultures have begun to break down. The depression and tension arising from economic development, congestion, crowding- and environmental changes on the working peoples' mind have caused new diseases in Thai society (such as cancer, heart disease, high blood pressure). A marked increase in the number of deaths caused by accidents (both work- and road-related) has taken place. The tendency is for the rise in these social negative effects at the same time as economic development and rising incomes.

Fifth, the accelerating economic development in Thailand before 1997 caused the deterioration in the environment and declining natural resources. In the first two years of the seventh national economic and social plan (1992-92), the nation's forestry has been destroyed at a rate of more than 1 million rai (1 rai=0.40 acre) per year. One effect was soil erosion, and the quality of water in rivers and canals has deteriorated, the water has become dirty and undrinkable. The environment is spoiled by air pollution, and the quantity of dust has increased alarmingly. Noise pollution, especially in Bangkok and other main urban centres also increased greatly. All of these have had a widespread negative impact on the quality of people' life. Furthermore, development has been undertaken without consideration being given to the social costs or the need for good management of the country's natural heritage. The low priority put on the value of human development, ignoring local knowledge and insufficient care for the effect of development on the way of life of the rural people – together these are creating huge impediments to the country's future sustainable development.

It is now common knowledge that in the national economic and social plans we have placed too much emphasis on economic growth. The development strategy reliant in industrial growth and production for export has resulted in Thai society's growth in macro-economic and material terms, but this does not mean that the Thai people and society in general can expect an improved quality of life and better distribution of income. On the contrary, we are losing our simplicity and good Thai cultural traditions at a faster pace, and along with the deterioration of natural resources and increased instability of the family institution. The community and society are also in jeopardy. This is in

172

accordance with long-established international views on the spread of modern knowledge and technology to countries like Thailand that "the globalisation will bring about both an opportunity for and danger to sustainable development". The decades of this type of development have brought new problems and instability to the welfare of Thai society, a situation reflected in the economic and social crisis that Thai society has experienced now.

THE PROBLEMS FROM MAINSTREAM THEORY

The previous strategy of development has place emphasis in mainstream economic theory. As we mentioned, this Western way of development focuses on economic growth without paying much attention to Thai social values. This was considered the social cost of development, and it will have a direct impact on Thai society. Chattip Nartsupa has argued that problems of mainstream economic theory (or neo-classical theory) will have a direct impact on Thailand or Thai society in at least three ways, namely:

1. Neo-classical economic theory does not consider the economy as a system as such; it does not relate the economic system to the social and political systems.

2. Nor will it relate the economy to the social and historical facts of its setting

3. Neo-classical economic theory does not take into account the conflicts in the social systems that are caused of changes. Its models, then, are static.

As mentioned above, we have found that past development in Thailand has had the tendency to follow this mainstream economic theory, which has led to many problems for the Thai society. Furthermore, the theory of development of this kind threatens humanity in both the West, where the model originated, and the developing countries, which followed it blindly. This includes Thailand, which very much emphasises economic growth, and pays little attention to people and community participation. It is only recently, in the eighth national economic and social development plan that the focus has shifted toward including people's participation in social development. The realisation on this necessity has come much too late in Thai society.

THE VIEWPOINT ON DEVELOPMENT BY PRA DHAMMAPIDOK

Pra Dhammapidok has pointed out that development started from economic issues related to money and wealth, livelihood and consumption. Starting from the creation, of the World Bank and other UN agencies, it started with lending and assisting development, the idea being that most agencies would help underdeveloped countries with their economic development (when we talk about development here, it should be understood that we focus on economic development only, since the social concept arrived much later). By focusing on economic development as the standard type of development, the main emphasis was on industrialisation. In the past, industrial development seems to have been the essential method used by developing countries. Nowadays, although developing countries still rush to development through industrial efforts, the developed countries say that they have passed the industrial stage. In conclusion, Pra Dhammapidok has summarised the old paradigm of development as follows: Mainstream economics emphasised the factors whereby developing countries should become industrialised. Technology is needed in order to become developed, and it should be acquire by knowledge of the basic sciences, hence sciences and technologies played an essential role in industrial development. The objective of development was industrial growth or economic expansion. However, when assessing the success of this development model, we need to look back to what has been exploited, the natural resources and environment. To develop the country this way, only natural resources can be used for such economic growth and industrial development. The areas of science and technology are the most popular, although this favourite position is going to decline in some of the big industrial countries or in those few countries with opposite feelings towards science and technology.

However, over all, preference for science and technology is not declining at all. Most of the developing countries dream of economic growth through such a method. We have found that, during the process of development in newly industrialised countries, there are both positive and negative effects. The increased material prosperity is the positive effect, whereas the social problems, mental diseases, and degradation of the environment are among the negative impacts. We can tolerate the social and mental problems in society, but when environmental problems surface, the environment slowly becomes a place not fit for human beings to live in, the situation is considered serious. All countries are waking up and begin to revise the development methods of the past in order to find out how and why the negative outcome occurred. There is a fairly broad consensus that due to the failure of past developments, we need to look for new . paradigms for development. This new way of thinking is called sustainable development.

THE FRAMEWORK OF DEVELOPMENT IN THAI SOCIETY

Looking back at Thai society since the beginning of the first national economic plan in 1961, Thailand has entered a new era of economic development which is that of infrastructural development as well as the industrial activity. Besides roads and dams being built, the economy grew rapidly. Moreover, the head of government during the time declared that the success or failure of this revolution (development) depended on the economic development. At the same time he wrote his personal decree to the Buddhist monks and requested them not to preach *Suntutthi* or contentment anymore, because he was afraid that economic development for Thai society would not succeed (Pra Dhammapidok, 2, p. 409). We may accept people increasing their desire for things such as consumption, wealth, and luxurious things. That would mean that they need to work harder and eventually make economic development possible. However, if people practice *Sunthutthi*, or are satisfied with whatever they have, there would be no desire for improvement, and therefore economic development would definitely fail. To some extent, this type of logic does make sense, but problems continue at the conceptual level, especially with *Ditthi* beliefs or views (Pra Dhammapidok, 2, p. 380). All these are major factors that have caused development problems for Thailand from the very beginning when the country's development was first conceived. As the old saying goes, "well begun is half done" but in the case of the Thais, it began with a fault and the fault will continue. This proposition needs to be elaborated and discussed more.

Up until now, Thai people have not understood the real meaning of *Suntutthi*. As a result, there have been mistakes and the path of development followed has been the way previously undertaken by other developed nations. Thai society as a Buddhist community should be in the position to do some corrections to this faulty concept and not repeat them.

Besides the lack of understanding about the development of Thai society, especially in the rural areas, the lack of understanding about community characteristics and behaviour has been the downfall to rural development. Due to this misunderstanding, the rural areas cannot see the need to development and the need for improvement. An example is the rural community's belief in the basis of Karma (the Law of Karma) that is to accept differences in wealth and power. This encourages them to let their carefree attitudes continue, and will not lead to the betterment of their community. The source of this problem is the community's dependency on others' help. Furthermore, the society lacks confidence, so that nothing is initiated or advocated in the fear that to do things differently would affect the status quo and bring negative effects to bear upon them. Many will refer to *Suntutthi* and be content with hiding their laziness, although the real meaning of Dhamma is not according to one's own interpretation. Furthermore, there is a wrong interpretation in what many people say derived from the deeply rooted way of life of rural Thai society that can be traced back to the *Tripumparuang,* an old piece of Thai literature which describes the patronage system used by the ruling class to facilitate its control and subordination of the population. In fact, the literature describes the basic belief in *Samsara* - the round of existence, (or life cycle), the potentiality of humanity to develop themselves to an unlimited level without any strict constraints from the society. The main principle in considering the value of human beings is contained in the deed or the law of Karma, which is especially described only in the Buddhist principle Dhamma (Virat, V, 1-11).

THE IMPACT OF NO PARTICIPATION IN DEVELOPMENT

As mentioned, the concept of development in Thai society lacks the community's participation in the process. The elite with power at their disposition has not done the best for farmers and the rural sectors. They do not care to reform the bureaucratic system nor to reduce corruption in the government. Both of these problems hinder rural development both directly and indirectly. Furthermore, community development for Thai society is at the same developing stage. Some analysts have said that the national economic plans have not succeeded, that economic development's success is at the minimum level. Bankruptcy among medium-sized enterprises with less than 100 employees has increased. The gap between the rich and poor has also increased, with one third of the population living below the poverty line. As we develop, poverty increases because we think so much in economic development terms that we do not consider other factors. We may think that poverty is only a fault that arises from materialistic development, but actually moral or human development is the major failure. The people's lack of ideology, lack of discipline and laziness, plus the fact that there is no public consideration nor community sacrifices are factors entangling themselves more and more into the capitalism system (Chai-anant S., 1985, p. 6). We realise now that some of the effects of development are cultural and social disorder. Finally, the environmental crisis is upon us. With social and moral crisis in our hands, the world can still exist, but when environmental crises arrive, the living earth will

176

be destroyed. The need, then, for a model of sustainable development is urgent, and accordingly Thailand has looked to include the new concept in her recent eighth national economic and social plans.

PROBLEMS FROM DEVELOPMENT

Pra Dhammapidok has summarised the problems on environment in the following points:

1. All the good things on earth are being exploited and destroyed. There is a depletion of natural resources.

2. The waste has been released back to earth. He says that, as consumerism exploits all the resources and disposes the waste, the more the people consume the more waste is released back to earth.

Pra Dhammapidok's observation on development is that the failure of previous development has derived from a two-fold failure in the development method and in environment management. For the country to be able to undergo sustainable development, he makes three suggestions:

1. The population needs to be reduced by family planning.

2. The depletion of natural resources can be slowed down if the community helps conserve and prevent the destruction through reforestation, and

3. Environmental problems can be reduced by stopping pollution at its source.

The major factors in curing the problems are the same old variables used in previous development plans. The core of them is science and technology. The difference compared to earlier plans is to produce and use S&T with a new purpose, one that does not destroy the environment. Technology should be used to solve environmental problems. Economic activities of production and consumption should be designed not to destroy natural resources, nor dispose too much waste and also to consider the fair distribution of income and well being. If society has an unequal distribution of benefits among the people, they will tend to encroach upon natural resources such as forests as well as community resources. Equitable distribution of income should be able to cure the problems. These three factors suggested by Pra Dhammapidok should be considered as the basic ideas, but we should also consider other factors such as politics as well as education.

The conceptual framework in development should accordingly be based on both ideas and social values. The point is not to win against nature but to think of a way to live continuously with nature in harmony and together with self-development to achieve happiness and freedom. To develop technology we must be aware that it relies on the knowledge from science. Science itself is not perfect knowledge, nor is it holistic. As this incompleteness creates many problems, we need to change the development paradigm. Economic development needs to find the basis of thought in relation to nature. This relationship is not about destroying nor is it to win, but rather to bring nature to be a part of our living and to sustain society.

We can say that the Thai rural development has been a total failure because it has created more problems than before. The problem, however, was that there was no real effort to bring people to participate in the development process. The element of participation, however, is mentioned in the latest national economic and social plan. In addition, the earlier development process did not consider the character and behaviour of the Thai people. Based on the extreme concept of the mainstream development thinking, this did not allow development to include the basis strength of Thai society. Furthermore, the globalisation in turn could well threaten the survival of Thai society, as has been evidenced by emerging problems such as various social crises. However, the huge problems arising from the current situation has generated responses and challenges from many social reforms. There has been a change in thinking with new theories such as economic sufficiency. This responds to the failure of development that caused the deterioration of resources and weakness of the existence of the Thai society. Hence, Likit T. is stating that, Hegel suggested the dialectic principle that all things are in a state of dynamism, the presentation and resistance of presentation, and finally the synthesis. The synthesis will bring about new presentations and resistance to it will be a response, then a synthesis. Finally it will arrive at the truth, there will be no more resistance and presentation (Likit Theravekin, 1999).

The changing stream of world society has been wrought by developments in science and technology, politics, legal systems and the administration of economic production. Each era presents challenges that must be responded to in order to avoid disasters. In modern history, the strongest challenge was colonialism, which arose because of the unequal development of science and technology, and it led the Western powers to the expansion of their political power in competition with each other. The need to secure labour forces and raw

178

materials led to colonisation. Many countries were however not being colonised.

The countries that escaped to be colonised in that period met the challenge in the same way; they imitated the development pattern of the coloniser or, in other words, they tried to behave in the same way as the greater powers of that time. The challenge was colonialism or colonisation process, and the response to that is Westernisation.

The most successful countries in Asia are Siam under the King Chulalongkorn and Japan under its Meiji Emperor. Both countries avoided colonisation. After the Second World War, the conflict shifted to one between the two ideological camps, capitalism and socialism, that brought to Asia the Korea and Vietnam wars. The Cold Wars brought propaganda extolling the victims of a new (foreign) culture as well as intervention in domestic affairs by the superpowers, such as engineering coups d'etat to bring governments into the anti-communist or socialist camps. The observation is that the response to the challenge of communism was initiation of democratic and capitalist development. Most successful was the development based on science and technology that brought economic development; this seems to have been more effective when a democratic government were in place. Here, the challenge posed by the ideology of socialism and communism was responded to effectively by capitalism and liberalism.

At the present time, globalisation seems to represent the peak of capitalist development. In this, it is supported by science and technology (especially information technology), democracy, free trade, human rights and intellectual property rights. In order to protect the environment from degradation, the whole process needs to take into account the growth of borderless trade and the free flow of information due to information technology developments such as the Internet. Globalisation is the new challenge that has brought economic depression to various regions, especially Asia.

The vital variable is the unequal distribution of development in science and technology, production and management systems, and particularly international funds that manipulate capital markets and foreign exchange markets. The condition that favours the country that has a higher development has become the new imperialism. The less developed countries will have to find ways to respond to this challenge, as His Majesty the King Bhumiphol has said, there needs to be coordination between the market economy and the economy of self-sufficiency. Such coordination would allow trade and development to carry on, but with greater effectiveness and productivity together with more research and development to allow the science and technology to reach a higher level. For the rural people, who are the majority, the king suggests the economy of self-sufficiency. This would allow them to be flexible enough to survive pressures from the economic impact at both the domestic and international level. To build on this immunisation is the key for the economy of self-sufficiency within the market economy and world trade. It can extend the cooperation of trade at the regional level to achieve more bargaining power, the same path followed as the European community. This is the full and complete challenge.

In other words, globalisation and the high level of capitalism are the new challenges for the community to develop an economy that is self-sufficient and to build resistance to new forms of imperialism or colonisation. For regional economies like Thailand, the solution is to build on cooperation between regional markets, i.e. regionalisation. Westernisation is the result of the less developed countries to colonisation. In the same way, colonisation and regionalisation are results of globalisation (Likit T., 1999, p. 6).

CONCLUSION

Rural development of Thai society was emphasised in mainstream economic strategies and globalisation. It aimed to attain economic growth and capital accumulation. The strategy made some mistakes in the development process of Thai society. But, with resistance to Westernisation and new ways of thinking about the economic community or self-sufficient economy, new processes have arisen to adjust the community for its survival.

On this issue, Pra Dhammapidok has found that Thailand's social problems occurred because the country's followed a Western development model, without the holistic consideration of the process of development. The western way of development did not consider nature as a vital part of human development but as a natural resource that satisfies human needs. Humans would win over nature; we could use nature as we wish. At last, nature has readjusted itself into a new state of equilibrium. This reflects the environmental problems that the world faces. The consequences of the application of the Western concept of development as he describes have indeed been largely negative. From his point of view, sustainable development is the need to consider nature as part of the development process, to adjust to a new way of thinking and to understand the dependency of humanity and nature. We must use our potential to protect natural resources. Such a line of development is sustainable and will strengthen the real Thai society.

LITERATURE

1. Pra Dhammapidok, *Sustainable Development* (Bangkok: Sahadhammic Press, 1966).
2. Pra Dhammapidok, *Dictionary of Buddhism* (Bangkok: Mahachulalongkorn Rajvitaya, 1965).
3. Virach Virachnipavun, Problems and Obstacle for Community Development: People, Bureaucrat and Government (Bangkok: Odean Bookstore, 1987).
4. Dheraphol Arunakasikorn, et. al., Summary of the Eighth National Economic and Social Plan (Bangkok: Vinyuchon Press, 1997).
5. Amorn Raksasud, *Theory and Concept of National Development* (Bangkok: National Institute of Development and Administration, 1972).
6. Pitoon Kruekaew *Characteristics of Thai Society and Community Development* (Bangkok: Kuokun Press, 1963).
7. Nirand Jongwudveth, *Rural Development Administration* (Bangkok Odean Store Press, 1984).
8. Sunya Sunyavivat, *Community Development* (Bangkok: Thai Watana Panich Press, 1983).
9. Chattip Nartsupa, *Thai Culture and the Process of Social Changes* (Bangkok: Chulalongkorn University Press, 1991).
10. Chai-anant Smutvanich, in *Political Science Journal*, Thammasat University, Volume 1-3, January-December, Year eleventh, 1985, Bangkok.
11. Likit Theravekin, in Matichon daily paper, 2 February, 1999, Bangkok.

Gender Relation in Vietnam — Traditional and Modern

Do Thi Binh
Center for Family and Women Studies

*T*he relationship between men and women, as opposite or complementation to each other, is an issue throughout the ages, since ancient times when human came into being. In more recent times it has been a hot and controversial issue. How has this relationship in the family has changed over time? Which characters are unchanged and preserved, and which have changed in relation to the social economic development?

The study of gender relationship in the Vietnam family is necessary for the understanding of how the status and the roles of men and women have been changing over time, and how the implementation of gender equality in Vietnam society has taken place. The equality between men and women was at the agenda at an early date in Vietnam. Since 1930, Indochina's Communist Party - right after coming into being - had set up the goal of limiting and step by step abolishing the feudal vestiges (discrimination against women) in the family relations and marriage.

The Constitution – first law of the Democratic Republic of Vietnam in 1946 – confirmed: "Women are equal with men in all aspect" and it has been reconfirmed in the sequential constitutions of 1959, 1980 and 1992. In the Vietnamese constitutions there are articles, which strictly forbid "the behaviour which discriminate against women and violate the human dignity of women". *De jure* the equality between men and women has been confirmed in the Constitution of Vietnam's Socialist Republic (article 63). The Laws of Criminal affairs, Labour Code, Law for Protection of Health of Mothers and Children, and Marriage and Family Laws have exclusive chapters or the articles which define the rights of women, in order to ensure the equality between men and women.

Since the country became independent and united more than 20 years ago, Vietnam has achieved results on the way towards gender equality that we are proud of. This article only analyses a number of issues in relation to gender relationship in the traditional family and in the recent period in Vietnam.

GENDER RELATIONS IN THE TRADITIONAL FAMILY

In the behaviour of the traditional family in Vietnam, social scientists have pointed at the long time of Confucian impact on the roles of men and women in the family. The Confucian principles advocated the three relationships: The subordination and dependence of women on men - the wife to the husband, the daughter to the father and the widower to the son. In domestic life men were heads of household, the King in the family. Even if the wife was considered 'the General', she had to ask about permission in the family, and obey the decisions of her husband or her oldest son. These principles were institutionalised in the society through the family. In upper class families, the norms of behaving were abided more strictly. Women were not allowed to pass through the alter in the sitting room. They were not allowed to be head of worship ceremonies or to receive guests. Women had to avoid contact with men, their relations were limited to the family, relatives or friends of the same sex. With such principles institutionalised in society women behaved according to their subordinate status and felt inferior to the men.

Such dependent relationship, according to Confucianism, was embodied in the Yin and Yang relations, the two parts (the main and second) are indispensable and inseparable from the other. One part initiates and the other part responds; one part creates and the other fosters; Yin follows Yang and completes the works of Yang. The principles are the same for the relationship between the King and Subjects, parents and children, and between husband and wife. The head is principle, but cannot stand alone without complementation.

Confucianism takes lineage into consideration in issues like the filial piety, taking care of old parents, mourning and burial rites, and ancestor worship. There is accordingly also consideration for giving birth to and the upbringing of children. The woman – mother and the wife – was respected mainly for her housework ability. Education of children, especially the sons, was the responsibility of the father, however the mother made important contributions in the care of children.

183

The behaving principle in the well functioning family *(nê nêp)*[1] was the forgiveness of father and filial piety of children. The father, husband, brother were the authorities, while the children, wife, younger brother were subordinated and obeyed with deep affection and gratitude.

Obviously, this is an unequal relationship between men and women and there were many principles of Confucianism which were based on men oppressing women. However, according to the rites, all member were getting along with one another in a harmonious way in the well-behaved family. The man – head of the household was just an enlightened person who was respected by other family members. While the woman considered herself as servant of her husband, she took care of the housework, of production, controlled expenditures, the affairs of her husband kinship, death anniversaries and festivities, prepared for receiving guests as well as other personal relations.

In other words, in the well-behaved family, the man was the head and all their members were getting along with each other through affection and obligation. The authority of farther combined with the gentle and kind-hearted mother created the order and protection of their children. In the traditional well-behaved family, the parents were concerned to educate their children, however, for the son was responsibility of father. The mother had responsibility for educating their daughters, which was considered as the first step for preparing their daughters to take their role as wife and mother in the future.

There are two ways to look at the behaving patterns in the traditional family. From a feminist point of view, these behaving patterns were backward, because they discriminate against women in all aspects of life. However, from the social organisational point of view, this family pattern was organised in an orderly and culturally accepted way. It was a solid foundation for society and provided well-behaved and useful persons for society.

The unequal factors between men and women has to be understood as deeply rooted in the orthodox conceptions and behaviour patterns of society. However, there are some traditional attitudes and behaviours that are favourable for increasing the status and roles of women in the family and society. As Mr. Insun Yu said, that the level of freedom of Vietnamese women depended on their social status. The women who belonged to the mandarin class tended to be

---

[1] [The expression has no literary translation, but indicates an 'ideal' family which is well-behaved and well-educated in interpersonal manners, editors note].

184

placed under compulsion of their families. They were educated according to the Confucianism principles. The women in the lower classes, who took part in the farming and small trading, were, however, living under conditions where the strict control of the wife was unnecessary.[2]

High status for Vietnamese women was also embodied in some of the customs and laws of the feudal regimes. In the 17th and 18th centuries, for instance, daughters and sons inherited equally, and after marriage, daughters settled the separation from their parents themselves.[3] In addition, the man was stripped of his rights to inherit in case his wife died without given birth to a son. The relative equal status of Vietnamese women to that of men in the family was remarkable in the, 17th and 18th century. As Mr. Insun mentioned, the Chinese family was attributed by the power of father over all other family members, whereas the Vietnamese family was attributed by the almost equal position between husband and wife, and the individual was confirmed among the family members.

In Vietnam the equality between men and women has been inherent in the Vietnam tradition. Nevertheless, by taking many roles in production, housework, giving birth and bring up children, women's conditions and chances for social promoting were limited compared to men's.

GENDER RELATIONSHIP IN THE VIETNAMESE FAMILY IN THE MODERN TIME

The cause of women's liberation has created the conditions for women's equal position with men in the fields of social life. These are achievements of the revolution, and the equality between men and women was defined and confirmed by regulations in the Vietnamese constitutions and laws. For example, the marriage and family laws issued in 1959, supplemented and amended in 1986, defined the equal rights and responsibilities of men and women in marriage and family life. The marriage is defined by love and voluntariness, monogamy has been implemented, and the right to divorce was ensured by law. The law also guaranteed women's rights to property after divorce, to adopt children, inheritance of property after her husbands death, to

---

[2] Insun Yu, *The Law and the Family in Vietnam in 17-18th Century* (Hanoi: Social Sciences Publishing House, 1994) p. 76.

[3] Insun Yu, *ibid.* [The society was patrilocal, and the women moved to the husband's family after marriage, editors note].

bring up children in the marriage. Before 1945, these rights of women were not guaranteed in the laws.

In the cause of *doi moi*, the gender relationship in general and in the family in particular has clearly been changing. Besides the socio-economic transformation in all aspect, the status and roles of men and women in social life, especially in the family, has to be considered. Their roles are indispensable and supplementary to each other.

Data from surveys carried out in the countryside of Red River Delta and mid-coast reveals that women are mainly responsibility for housework, bringing up and educating their children, and taking care of elderly or sick persons in their families (Table 1).

Table 1. Who did mainly the housework, percentage. [4]

Types of works	Husband	Wife	Both	Other
Housework's	1.33	95.33	0.67	2.67
Take care of children	2.33	70.0	22.33	5.34
Education of children	15.3	41.70	24.3	18.70
Take care of elder and ill persons	1.7	24.30	56.7	17.30

The data reveals that the husbands did almost nothing of the housework. When other work done by husband increased, the tasks done frequently by husbands was often lower than their wives. This showed that up to now, regardless of the change of occupation and labour structure in rural areas under the impact of economic reform, housework is still the important domain of women. There is no indicator of a decrease of the work of rural women in the area of reproduction and housework, the tendency is rather increasing. For example, the education of children in the past was the responsibility of men, nevertheless now more women carry out this task than men. It is because that men have to earn a living far from their homes and there is no time and real conditions for them to do housework and educate their children. It is understandable as women closely connect with the reproductive roles and they

---

[4] Data from the survey in Cam Vu commune, Cam Binh district, Hai Duong province in 1996, Center for family and women studies, 1996.

have no conditions for working far from their homes over long periods. Furthermore, it implies hard work and difficult living conditions, which are not suitable for women.

Also, it is a fact that in rural areas that the households carry out many jobs for maintaining a living. In addition to the main income, there are many secondary sources of income. For example, with the farming households, besides the income from paddy and non-paddy crop, there are other sources of income from husbandry, small trading, services, and work as hire labour. Diversification of income sources is the result of diversification of occupations and crops cultivated by farming households. In order to improve the situation, it requires a redistribution of labour force in society and in the households for maximising their income. For the peasants households in the Red River Delta, the works in the agricultural production such as polishing, raking, spraying of pesticide are done by men; other works such as transplanting, weeding, fertilising, and harvesting are done by women. So women employ more work and longer working time than men, although their tasks are less heavy than the tasks done by men. According to Le Ngoc Van "For the fishing households in the coast areas, earning "in the sea" is work done by men and earning "on the land" is work done by women. For the agricultural households, earning income far from home was done by men, and earning near their houses was done by women".[5] This is regulated by a division of labour, which is considered reasonable in rural areas in order to increase the household income and stabilising the family life.

Table 2: Who decide in important issues in the family, percentage.[6]

Types of works	Husband	Wife	Both	Other
Education of children	8.0	10.3	64.3	17.3
Marriage of children	4.7	4.7	59.3	42.3
Number of children	5.0	5.3	72.3	17.3
Repair, build house	18.0	5.0	57.3	19.7

[5] The report in the workshop "Evaluation of gender study and training in Vietnam", Hanoi, 1999, p. 5.
[6] Data from the survey in Cam Vu commune, Cam Binh district, Hai Duong province, Center for family and women studies, 1996.

In order to realise more clearly the gender roles in the Vietnamese family, it is investigated who takes important decisions (Table 2). In the Vietnamese family at present, it appears that the relationship between husband and wife is a fairly democratic, equal relationship. The important issues in the family were discussed and co-decided by husband and wife, there are not arbitrary decisions of husbands as in the traditional family in the past.

For the fishing households in the mid-coast areas, 91.2 percent men and 92.2 percent women in the survey said that they exchanged their opinions and discussion with each other for deciding important issues. For example, choosing type of production, changing paddy patterns, house building, marriage of their children, education of their children are common responsibility of both husband and wife (75.9 percent of respondents).

CONCLUSION

Based on the data from many surveys which were done by the Center for Family and Women Studies in recent years, we draw some preliminary conclusions:

The gender relationship in the Vietnamese traditional family, which was influenced by Confucianism as well as many other ideas from China and other countries in the region, was not absorbed without selection. In addition, by the practical scrutiny over long time the Vietnamese people were not assimilated. In Vietnam, although the distribution of the roles and responsibility between men and women was more or less under impact by Confucianism, Buddhism, Taoism, these principles were adapted and combined with the Vietnamese culture of spirits. In the family, the man were the head who was concerned about economic growth of his household. The wife helped her husband in economic activities, taking the roles of wife, mother which no man could take. In addition, women were more concerned about the family obligations and educating children.

The attributes of gender relation in the Vietnamese family are somewhat different of that of the family in other countries in the region. In Vietnam, women in the family not only take the roles of wives and mothers, but also the role of economic – finance managers – who keep the keys of the trunks in their family (see Tran Ngọc Them).[7]

Historical and cultural traditions of Vietnamese people created the status and the roles for women which suited with their own cultural norms. Those are attributes as hard working, faithful, and sacrificing herself which was glorified as own identity. Of course, these values were impacts more or less by Confucianism, however, it is a good tradition we should continue and bring into play, and negative traditions should step by step be expelled and demolished.

In terms of laws and policies, Vietnamese women are equal with men in all aspects of social life. The cause of *doi moi* in transforming the society into a market economy, equal gender relationship in Vietnam family is ensured at a certain level. The gender relationship was reflected in the distribution of tasks for each sex in different types of activities in the family, and the division of labour by sex which was formed during very long periods of the historical process. This division creates the co-operation between men and women (different and supplementary to each other).

In general, it should exclude step by step the factors which resulted in the dependence of women on men. But it should take into consideration the harmonious division for maintaining and strengthen the development of the Vietnamese family towards equality, progress and happiness.

---

[7] See the report of Le Ngoc Lan "Study and transmission of gender issues in Vietnam from cultural point of view". The workshop "Evaluation of gender study and training in Vietnam", p. 2.

Communal Convention - Instrument of Social Administration of Rural Vietnam

Phan Dai Doan
Hanoi University for Social Sciences and Humanities

GENERAL CHARACTERISTICS OF EAST ASIA

Communal convention, an instrument of rural administration (i.e. village self-management and self-government) and a feature of administrative culture, is a popular characteristic of East Asia. In China and the Republic of Korea (ROK) and Vietnam communal conventions are found in diverse forms.

China

Long time ago, China had a communal convention that was also known as the communal regulation and people's convention –"Huong uoc" – which the "Tu Hai" Dictionary defines as the conventions that the rural community has to observe. "Tong su" (in Lui Tai-fang Story) records: "The Lu usually established communal convention for the people who were willing to help each other in doing good, setting up careers, rectifying errors, overcoming distress... with mutual love".[1]

During the Ming-Tsing Dynasties (late 14th - early 20th centuries), handicraft and trading guilds made their appearance in large numbers in the urban and rural areas in Southern China. The hamlets and the guilds had their own regulations, inscribed on paper or in wooden plaques, that their members had to comply with. In the 19th century, quite a few villages in Guang xi province still enforced their communal conventions.[2]

From 1949 until the end of the Cultural Revolution, rural China had

---

[1] Tu Hai Dictionary, Shanghai Publishing House, 1989 ed., (in Chinese) p. 108, 3rd col.

[2] See documents on farmers' uprisings in the "Thai Binh thien quoc" Revolution in Kuang-xi Province (in Chinese), ("Trung Hoa thu cuc" Publishing House, 1978) p. 20.

established people's communes, where hamlets and villages were converted into "production brigades", and communal conventions ceased to exist. A mechanism of administration called "Chinh xa phan khai" (division of power between administration and people's commune) was institutionalised after the 3rd Congress of China's Communist Party. Later on, the National People's Congress of China endorsed a Law on Organisation of Rural People's Councils and enforced it on 24 November 1987. This legal instrument saw the necessity to have communal conventions, which in their modern form China are defined as follows:

Communal Convention constitutes a regulatory framework for all rural people's community activities. It is based on the (hamlet) people's council, state laws and policies, with reference to the specific local conditions, defined by the hamlet people's congress and approved by the superior (district) people's council and executed by the hamlet people's council itself. The guiding principle and aim of the communal convention is to uphold the law, the regulations, and the constitution. The hamlet's communal convention represents an instrument of self-government, a long tradition of the Chinese people. It is not the law, but it means self-government, self-binding, self-control and inspection, which plays an important role in the establishment of the socialist material and spiritual civilisation.[3]

Japan

Japan is an island nation whose rural areas in the East and in the West are dissimilar. The traditional Japanese hamlet consists of at least 50 households and the farmers work on small plots of land to grow wet rice and other food crops. Like the villages in North and Central Vietnam, the locality of Japanese hamlets and villages is a factor of prime importance, related to a strong defence of the land. From the 17th century to the mid-19th century (during the Tukugawa period reign), Japanese hamlets and villages all had "Mura Okyte" (communal regulations), and even after the Meiji restoration, Japan has retained them. In 1960, the Japanese rural population accounted for roughly 30 percent, but the self-government mechanism was maintained in combination with the village or hamlet administration. This self-government and self-management was endorsed by the Japanese Diet in the Law on Local Self-Government,

---

[3] "Trung Quoc dan chinh tu dien" (China Dictionary of Civil Administration), (in Chinese) (1990) p. 50.

promulgated in 1947.

In September 1994, a team of researchers conducted a survey in the rural areas of Jifu - Central Japan, where we found 6 or 7 unions (of youth, women, education, old people, etc.) to protect the interests of each 'social group'. These unions are united in 'Hamlet Self-Government Association' or 'Inter-Hamlet Self-Government Association', whose president is vested with a 'Oboe Gaki' (memorandum). The hamlet of Furumiya (now Ogaki City), for instance, still keeps 3 memorandums:

- Memorandum 1, which was promulgated in 1954, has 17 signatures of the representatives of the rural unions, and defines the protection of dams and dykes.

- Memorandum 2, which was formulated in 1961, has 11 signatures of the representatives of the local families and sets terms on the irrigation and drainage of the paddy fields of the villages of Hulu Miya and Komeno.

- Lastly, "Mo tieu quy uoc thu" (Convention on cemetery boundaries) records agreement on the demarcation of the cemeteries by the people of the villages of Furumiya and Kovahami. It was promulgated in 1941 and has 73 signatures.

The above-mentioned memoranda were established much in the same way as the traditional conventions of Vietnam and observed as strictly by the villagers, with fines or punishments inflicted on the offenders.

Korea

In the Republic of Korea (ROK) in the 1960's and early 1980's, communal conventions still existed in the country. The Korean rural areas were in many respects similar to China, in that the position of the family and of ancestry was fairly strong, with ancestral conventions and regulations as a basis for communal conventions of the hamlets and villages. Up till the 1970's and 1980's, quite a few villages in the ROK still continued to operate a 'Board for Protection of Communal Convention' set up by the villagers themselves. The task of the Board was to maintain a traditional way of living.

It can thus be seen that all three of these East Asian nations had communal conventions in different forms. Essentially, however, they were similar in that they constituted an instrument for self-regulation and self-direction. The establishment of communal conventions in these countries at least three hundred years (and in some cases with traditions going back thousands of years) was arguable a natural process in harmony with the economy and culture of each nation. It is also a characteristic of the culture of administration.

Nowadays, Japan is almost completely urbanised, with shrinking rural areas, hence the communal conventions have little significance. Yet, in a few localities in Japan, the 'self-government society' still in exists, helping the households in their funeral or nuptial rites. The situation is similar in the ROK. In the 1970's, with the Korean rural areas accounting for roughly 30 percent, quite a few hamlets and villages still retained their communal conventions and their 'Board for Protection of Communal Convention.'

That China, Japan and the ROK have similarities in rural culture, is a result shaped through a long history of tradition of self-government of the community of families and ancestries, hamlets and villages. In East Asia, the family, and not the individual, is the central social unit with its complicated and intersectional relationships. In the course of rural development, the households have come to act together by virtue of socio-economic requirements - like irrigation for cultivation, defence against invaders, protection of the crops, etc - that call for some cooperation for self-direction and self-regulation, hence the appearance of communal conventions.

What, then, is the character of the communal conventions? As the Japanese put it, communal conventions are 'neutral' and not national laws (merely village rules). The Koreans see them primarily as an instrument to retain their national cultural identity in the course of national modernisation. Today, the Chinese communal conventions are aimed at forming a physical and spiritual socialist civilisation.

What may be drawn from what has been mentioned above is that the communal convention - i.e. the village rules, as a written document to be observed strictly - has helped in no small way to enhance of legal awareness among the small farm-holders. In this regard, the communal convention and state law are different in terms of level and dimension, but not in character.

Vietnam

Villages in the Red River Delta of Vietnam are administered with laws and practices. Practices represent the category of ancestral customs that mirror people's national culture with specific local and historical characteristics. It is impossible to see practices from the perspectives of time as backward, barbarous or civilised, advanced or humanitarian... In the area of the Ede ethnic group, for instance, if a baby is unfortunately born after the death of its father and the mother dies in child birth, it is customary that the baby is buried together with its mother because of a lack of support. Possibly, this practice is seen as inhuman in the eyes of the Vietnamese. Formerly in India, if the husband died, the wife would be cremated along with his corpse. Such are customs and practices, a regulatory framework for adequate actions that are accepted socially. The law has the same character: A regulatory framework for actions that are accepted nationally.

The difference between popular practices and the law lies chiefly in the forces that retain their regulatory framework. The law relies on the power of the state (with the army, police, courts, etc.), wherever customs and practices rest mainly on traditions accepted and observed by the community as a whole. The law commands external pressure, but the customs and practices originate from the internal community. The regulatory framework for behaviour in compliance with practices has been shaped out of the life experiences of people and the community, handed down, sometimes forcibly, from generation to generation. In short, the communal convention represents documented customs and practices.

Rural Vietnam

The rural areas of Vietnam consists of more than 50,000 hamlets. These account for 80 percent of the total population in the period of "pre-modernisation". The communal convention is a relic of a legacy that still plays an important role in rural administration. The guideline of the Vietnamese Government is "to encourage the formulation and execution of communal conventions and regulations on a civil way of life in the country..." It is advisable for the State to study early and enforce conventions on the roles and functions of the hamlets, in compliance with each area (Resolution of the fifth Central Committee Plenum - Session 7), which is quite relevant to the present-day rural society.

Hamlets and villages are by no means 'static'. The are in the course of change and renovation. In the old days, they were products of a closed wet-rice civilisation, but the market-oriented rural society of today is characterised by diversified trading and farming households in the course of modernisation and urbanisation. As a result, the new communal conventions should also be changed to fit the new practical situation, as a catalyst to the development of each specific hamlet or village.

The communal convention is strongly influenced by the specificity its locality. The socio-economic relations and the eco-environmental conditions of the hamlets and villages have not much in common, hence the differences in the articles of the conventions. I had the opportunity to read communal conventions that were established in the early 1990's from the provinces of Bac Ninh, Bac

194

Giang, Ha Tay, and Thanh Hoa, and found many of them were very sketchy and generalised, hence they had inevitable limitations.

Accordingly, I believe that a communal convention should be quite specific and detailed, relevant to the local socio-economic relations and eco-environmental conditions of each hamlet or village, a micro-society. Those who elaborate communal conventions should be well qualified and conversant in socio-economic administration, state laws and policies; they may be a retired official, a veteran teacher or an experienced engineer, for instance.

The communal convention should not restrict itself to cultural life, but extend to socio-economic and political realms. It should help the citizens, not only in grasping the laws, but in cultivating, with certain awareness, preservation of the cultural identity in a stabilised society and a healthy, human environment as well.

Experience shows the traditional communal conventions and the reformed ones under French colonial rule attached great importance to the question of rural security and the crops (usually making up roughly 20 percent of the articles in each convention), followed by the conciliation of civil conflicts for the sake of rural stability. The communal convention should see the household as the unit of execution. The household is the foundation of the traditional and modern village. It is a great necessity, to build a healthy economic and cultural life for every man, family and hamlet.

Vivid reality

Until now, the communal convention has been turned into an institution of rural administration in quite a few provinces in both the North, Centre and South. One of the ideas of the Resolution of the fifth Plenum (Session 7) of the Central Committee of the Vietnam Communist Party is to translate conventions into reality of rural life.

Bac Ninh, Ha Tay and Hai Duong are provinces that have adopted specific actions to specify the institutions of the administration of the hamlets and villages by means of communal conventions, most of these using the new terminology "Convention on new way of living".

As far as I know, the former province of Ha Bac was the first to apply the new 'convention'. In April 1993, the Provincial People's Council adopted Resolution No. 38 - HDND on "Convention on cultured village". In August 1995, 1,383 villages, accounting for 46 percent of the hamlets and villages in the province, elaborated on their conventions, 800 of which were regarded as completed by the Ha Bac Provincial Authority of Culture.

In the province of Ha Tay, the "Convention on cultured village" was also managed by the province's cultural authority. Today, most of the hamlets in the province have conventions of their own, either completed or in draft form, and more than 100 of them have been published and distributed for execution, for instance the "Convention on cultured village of Chau Can commune" (of Chau Can village, Phu Xuyen district,) the "Convention on cultured village of Tan Do commune" (Hong Minh village, Phu Xuyen district), the "Convention on civilized ward" (of Ha Dong provincial town).

The authorities of culture of Ha Nam, Ninh Binh, Thanh Hoa and Nghe An provinces are formulating conventions on the new way of life, or on cultured villages. In the province of Binh Dinh (in Central Vietnam), a "Board for Rural Development" has been established, with the formulation of village conventions as one of its functions.

In the ethnic minority areas, quite a few hamlets of the H'mong ethnic group in Bao Thang district (Lao Cai province) have also adopted their "Convention of new way of living of the H'mong" (in H'mong transcription). Many of the hamlets and villages in Cao Loc (Lang Son Province) have also elaborated on their village conventions. In the article titled "Achiving desires on the borderline" (People's Weekly, 26 November 1995), which portrays the dynamic development of Xuat Le village (on the border areas of Lang Son province with many ethnic groups), it is written:

It is thanks to the plans for development of gardens and forests by the districts and the province that the watershed forests and jungles and the industrial crops have been protected without any unplanned devastation. The conventions of the hamlets and villages define in specific terms the prohibition of the slash-and-burn cultivation. The people are allowed only to chop down trees not listed in the prohibited categories, or collect dried firewood. The violators are fined or punished accordingly. The offenders shall be expelled from the association for a lack of duty. The article asserts the positive effects of the convention on the socio-economic development of highland village of Xuat Le over the last few years.

Another article in People's Weekly, from 3 December 1995, entitled "Some thoughts about village rules via a new custom" by Le Van Lac discusses the convention of Co Gian hamlet (Kim Son village, Dong Trieu district, Quang Ninh province). The convention (i.e. village rules are the writer sees it) defines:

If someone, rich or poor, in the village passes away, with funeral big or small, each household is obliged to contribute one tin of rice (800 gram) upon hearing a roll of the drum, 20 percent of which is to be spent on incense joss sticks and offerings. The village shall assume the responsibility for organisation of the funeral and procession, without expensive feasts. The author concluded "Bad customs and negative customs, village practices are village rules. Such is the village life!"

And so, in the course of the history of rural development of Vietnam, for five centuries (1460-1997) since the reign of King Le Thanh Tong in North and Central Vietnam, the communal convention has been a part of the institutions of rural administration of the hamlets and villages, an important feature of the Vietnamese culture of administration, and unlike the Western culture taking God as the central and supreme norm, unlike Muslim culture regarding Allah as its supreme god and truth, the Oriental culture (the Vietnamese included) has taken man and his man-to-man relations as the central point and the yardstick of is real worth.

The renovation launched by the Party and Government restoring the hamlets and villages and regarding the family as the central entity asserts this. It has found its vivid expression in the realities of the localities in all corners of the country. It is obvious that communal conventions have gone into rural life and exerted positive effects.

In most of the villages of the North and the Centre, the "Convention of lifestyle" has been established as a type of communal convention. The provincial authorities for culture and justice are coordinating directions for the promulgation of communal conventions. And the villagers themselves are taking an active part in the undertaking, with a selective absorption of the old conventions on the basis of the specific conditions of their localities.

To summarise from what has been discussed, it is easy to see communal convention as a universal phenomenon in some nations of East Asia. It is a type of custom and practice, an instrument of self-government in the country. It is mistaken to understand the communal convention as something in contradiction with the state law or found only in the realms undefined by the law itself. In Vietnam of today, the communal convention still plays a major role in social stability and rural development.

Customary Law and Management of Natural Resources

Ngo Duc Thinh
Institute of Folklore, NCSSH

CUSTOMARY LAWS OF THE ETHNIC MINORITIES IN VIETNAM

Luat tuc (tap quan phap, le tuc) in Vietnamese, the same as English terms of customary law, folk law, traditional law, is a kind of indigenous knowledge or local knowledge, that has existed among most ethnic groups in Vietnam regardless whether they consist of a smaller or larger number.

Customary law may be definition of the as follows: It is indigenous and / local knowledge, which has been created in various forms in the process of the long history through experiences related to environment and society, transmitted from generation to generation through memory, production and social practices. The law guides, readjust and reconcile relationships between society, human beings and natural environment. The entire community acknowledge and use the standards of customary laws, which create the social unity, and balance in every community.

In each ethnic group there is a name of its customary law, for instance, *huong uoc* of the Viet, *hit khong* of the Thai, *phat kdi* of the Ede, *phat ktnoi* of the M'nong and *n'ri* of the Ma, etc. It is easily acknowledged that the customary law bears elements of the official law such as regulations of the crimes, evidences, judgement and punishments, and at the same time, it has characteristics of customary law, customs such as moral convention, admonishment, advice guiding the personal behaviours and creating public opinion to readjust those behaviours. Thus, the customary law is part of the traditional custom and at the same time it is a primitive and initial form of the official law.

With the actual knowledge obtained so far, we can classify the customary laws of ethnic groups in Vietnam according to their different forms as follows:

- Customary laws appears in the form of rhythmic verses handed down from generation to generation, for instance the customary law of Ede, M'nong, Ma, Stieng, Bana, Giarai.

- The customary laws are fixed and written in scripts; those are *huong uoc* of the Viet, *hitkhong ban muong* of the Thai, *le tuc* of the Cham.[1]

- *Luat tuc* or *le tuc* are relatively completed but not fixed in written verses or in prose, they are the memories and practices of the communities. These kinds of customary laws are popular among the most ethnic minorities and it is difficult to distinguish them from custom or traditional habits.

The customary laws of the various ethnic groups are existing in many forms, but have been lost due to the deterioration of time and to the handling by people. Many books of *huong uoc* of Vietnamese villages, law code *(hitkhong)* of the Thai were burned, lost or missing, and many oral traditional law codes of the ethnic groups in Tay Nguyen have been forgotten and not handed down. Our duty now is to restore and preserve those valuable vestiges.

According to ethnic groups, their customary laws are guiding various broad or small problems such as social and economic relationships, customs, religious rites, ceremonies, social security, and management of natural resources. In this paper, I will offer some discussions on customary laws and natural resource management.

CUSTOMARY LAW AND NATURAL RESOURCE MANAGEMENT

Studying the collected customary law codes, especially those of the ethnic groups in Tay Nguyen, we recognise the treasure of the rich popular knowledge about the natural environment and natural resources where they reside.

---

[1] Adele, *Renseignements recueillis sur les coutumes des MA de SRE*. Archives de la province du Haunt-Donnai, 1932.; Sabatier L., *Recueil des coutumeers Rhadeé du Daclac* (Hanoi: Imprimerie d'Éxtrême-Orient, 1940); Dournes, J., *Nri-Recueil des Contumer Sre du Haunt-Donnai* (Éditions "France-Asie", 1951); Gerder, Th., *Coutumier Stieng*, BEFEO, XLV, 1951; Guilleminet, P., *Coutumier de la Tribu Banar des Jarai de la Province de Kontum*, Tome Premier (Paris: E. De Boccard, Hanoi: École Française d'Extrême-Orient, 1952).
Boulbet, J., *Quelques Aspect de Coutumier N'ri des Cau Maa*, BSEI, XXXII, No 2. 1957; Lafont, P.B., *To Loi Djuat Coutumier de la Tribu Jarai* (Paris: École Francaise d'Extrême-Orient,1963); Nguyen Khac Ngu, Mau he Cham [Matrilineal System of the Cham] (Saigon, 1970).

These issues, first of all, come out from the concrete thoughts, experiences and magic. In these thoughts, humans as well as things around them have spirits; human beings and nature are regarded as equal and blended into each other. Therefore, human beings usually take sign from the natural phenomena to prepare to the human behaviours and acts. Behaviour that is suitable to the nature is found right, and if in contrast to the nature it is wrong and sinful, for instance:

Stupid pigs don't eat their piglets

Temper dogs don't eat their puppies

Furious tigers don't eat their cubs

Being human why eat ones own children?

(Ngo Duc Thinh 1998a, p. 560)

Human beings are part of nature, and the nature should be taken as point of departure to understand the relationships between people. Therefore, we can say that in the most articles of the Êdê and M'nong customary laws, there is no phenomenon of nature that is not present. The interaction of nature and natural environment is described very lively, and it shows that the knowledge of human about the nature is deep and profound. For example, when taking an animal to talk about boasting people, the customary law of the Êdê describes:

People in the morning are like male *bhi*, in the afternoon, like female *bhi*; once flying to the wood, they look for new stories.

People have voices as the sound of small bamboo in wood on fire, like the sound of earthen phoenix.

People are like grass but want to reach higher than the big tree, like the alang grass but want to come up the bamboo tree, like wild animals but want to pass high trees on mountain peak (Ngô Duc Thinh 1996, p. 47).

When relating to crimes that are not being judged, the customary laws of the M'nong compare it to:

Disagreements are not judged

They will bloom like flower of *r'tinh*

They will bloom like flower of *mpang*

They will bloom like flower of *mhay*

When talking about the honesty and objective of the judge, the customary law of the M'nong borrow the following images:

There is a catfish between rocks on the two sides

There is a new year pole between rice crops on the two sides

On one side wind, on the other side storm between which there is a kite. (Ngo Duc Thinh 1998a, p. 94)

Through the study of the customary laws, we come to understand not only ethnic society and culture but also to some extent the natural environment where they reside. In the customary law codes of the ethnic groups in Tây Nguyên, there are quite a lot of the codes characterised by the production experiences of people. In the customary laws of the M'nong, there are articles on planting crop, cultivating swidden fields, raising livestock, fishing, hunting, delivering meat, catching wild elephants, and concerned about the raising of animals such as pig, dog, buffalo, chicken. For example, different kinds of crops are cultivated according to where the land is situated:

In the low land without wind, we plant melon

In the plain land, we plant corn

Along the stream and river, we plant bananas and sugar can

On the high mountains, we plant only flax trees

Gourd we interpose with rice

Chilli and eggplant we plant in the previously swidden field

We plant rice early when land is rich in ash

We plant beans early when it is sunny.

(Ngo Duc Thinh 1998a, p. 326)

Or about animal raising:

Raising pig is to built cage

Raising buffalo is to built cage

Raising elephant is to have stakes

In the morning, we lease them on the grass

At noon, we lease them by the streams

In the afternoon, we take them home.

(Ngo Duc Thinh 1998a, p. 330)

Hunting is to:

Hiding in a hut to trap animals is done by oneself

Trapping animals is done by oneself

Hunting is done by the whole village

This person holds an arbalest, the other carries a knife

This person makes a trap, the other puts an arrow

This person takes dog, the other takes steamed rice

(Ngo Duc Thinh 1998a, p. 336)

Customary law defines the possession relationships to the natural resources. For every ethnic group, there were established regulations of possession relationships to the material resources way back in time, among them were natural resources where they reside. To respect the right of possession is basic for the community in order to be able to manage and use the natural resources in a better and more fruitful way.

The customary law codes of ethnic groups of our country have many articles to identify possession of natural resources, and along with these there are regulation of distribution and inheritance of the natural resources.

According with the developing level of society of each ethnic group, the customary laws identify the various possession relationships. In general, among the minor ethnic groups such as the Thai, Êdê, M'nong, who have not a material possession system, all natural resources and material resources belong to the whole community; every individual and family have right to own them. Among the Thai, the boundaries between communes and village are regulated clearly, and people from other communes and villages are not allowed to trespass. In Tay Nguyen, the right to forest possession, land, natural resources belong to every *buon* (commune), *play* (village). Every community member has the right to use them:

We, every of us, have right to burn swidden fields, fish anywhere

Everyone have right to climb up the tree to take honey from any low forests, bushes and shores,

Tree of *le, lo o*, thatch and bamboo are used for building houses; everyone have right to gather, do not pay anything to anyone,

202

Everyone has right to burn forest, hunt animals, fish, and does not avoid doing anything. (Ngo Duc Thinh 1996, p. 223)

Among ethnic groups of the Ede, Giarai, M'nong, matrilineal relationships hold the key roles. According to them, the blood lineage, the inheritance rights of wealth are regulated from the mother's family:

Daughter keeps grandparents' house

Son keeps house of his wife's side.

(Ngo Duc Thinh 1998a, p. 514)

Or:

Daughter is like rice grain, only daughter is a person who wears the *choang chan* (coat), a person who keep the flat winnowing and is a *lung* (support) of ancestors.

The oldest sister is a person who takes responsibility as mother, oldest brother in law takes responsibility as father. They look after land and go to visit forests. If the mango trees don't blossom perfectly, if son and daughter are born, but bad mannered, they have a right to judge them.

Any man and son don't have rights to appropriate their rolls of copper wire, of baskets of gourds.

If uncle dies, he leaves his wealth to his nephew of his blood sister, if grand mother dies, she leaves her wealth to her granddaughter on her side. (Ngo Duc Thinh 1996, pp. 221-222)

In such a matrilineal society, no one has power to own all land and natural resources, no one has rights to sell or exchange.

Grandparents' wealth belong to the whole village

Children and grandchildren inherit

If they sell and exchange

If they kill for meat

If they don't notify to community members

If they don't notify to their lineage

People who have done so is punished

(Ngo Duc Thinh 1998a, p. 515)

However, among the Êđê, the representative of the landowners is a person from the mother's side. The landowners have responsibility to look after and protect land, and they acquire some benefits, like the rights to possess the beehives made on the *ktong* tree and *kdjar* tree in forest:

Prohibit to put a stake in the *ktong* tree, prohibit to climb up on the tree of *kdjar*. Breaking these rules are as bad as the crimes like cutting down the elephant tail, breaking the bowl of tax, to woo the wife of the rich chieftain of the commune...

The rights consist of accepting gifts when they go to visit land:

Every 7 years, in the dry season, according to custom, the landowners must go to visit their land.....

All villagers, all nephews or nieces, younger sisters, brothers have to give gifts to female land owners; this person gives a bowl of rice, the other gives a basket of rice and all villagers and relatives have good health... (Ngo Duc Thinh 1996, p. 226)

The Thai in the mountainous areas have their specific social system and social relationships. First of all, the Thai communities are divided into *muong* [commune] (twelve *chau muong*), every *muong* has a number of *ban* [village]. The Thai society is build on a matrilineal system, and the society is divided into the aristocrats and the commoners. In fact, land, forest and natural resources belong to the whole *muong*, and the *chau muong* (the lord of the commune) are their representatives. The authorities and *tao ban* (the head of the village), according to their titles, are given lots of lands:

An nha are given ten acres of land in the village of Chieng di...

Thu lai are given six acres in the village of Chieng ly...

Thong lai are given five acres of land...

Phia ly are given five acres of land...

(Ngo Duc Thinh 1998b, p. 225)

Public people are given land and take responsibilities in the commune's work:

The land left over in the community is distributed to people according to the customs. Community members who are given a little work for the *muong* receive a little land; the members who are given bigger work for the *muong* receive more, the members who are not given land don't have responsibilities for the commune's work... (Ngo Duc Thinh 1998b, p. 300)

204

The resources in the forest even though it belongs to the community, everyone has right to exploit it, but there exists custom to give gifts to *an nha* and the other authoritative persons: "Please, don't eat honey so it will not be left for her (here: daughter of the landowner), don't eat deer which will not be left for *tao*; if wild animals are killed, they are divided equally." The customary law of the Thai regulates concretely the right to divide the meat of the wild animals, and honey that is gathered by villagers:

An nha are given animals living in both Xong pan (xen) and Pong

Thu lai, thong lai eat animals living in Xong ho luong

Phia lý, phia pho eat animals living in land of Pong lang

Everyone, who is a member is going hunting, catching animals according to custom, has to give the wild animal meat as gift to *an nha* and *phia* of the commune. (Ngo Duc Thinh 1998b, p. 413)

There was a long period where the traditional possession relationships were broken due to the social changes; this led to a situation where the natural resources, land and forest without an owner was left without protection (everyone thinks that he (she) is the owner but in fact, there is no owner). Therefore, the resources were destroyed and exploited randomly. Nowadays, in the new social situation with a variety of possession modes, the possession issues of the traditional society presented in the customary law still have suitable elements that should be uphold to protect and use the natural resources more fruitfully.

Customary laws are based on knowledge of management, protection and use of the natural resources

'Sacredness' of natural resources

For a long time a popular opinion existed among the smaller ethnic groups that land, forest, water resources, trees and grass have 'spirits' which are kept by Gods.

Therefore, when human beings have need to own them, they must pray, make ceremonies, follow strict customs, even if, in some cases, people are absolutely prohibited to own them. Those beliefs are presented clearly in the customary laws and these add an important contribute to the protection of natural resources. In other words, people take advantages of the supernatural world and spiritual world to protect the natural resources of their community.

The customary law of the black Thai in in Thuan Chau states clearly:

Inside *Chieng ly* in *muong Muong Muoi*, and inside and outside *muong* of *Chau Muoi*, there are all over *phi* (spirit) helping the village and commune; every *muong* has *minh*[2]; every village has *nen*[3] helping...

... *Muong Muoi* has a big pond dug long time back, by the pond a house called *don cong* was built to hang *cong muong*. When something happens to the commune and village, and they start to "startle and wake up" or when a festival is hold, the *cong muong* prays and echoes sound all over.

...*Muong Muoi* has a mountain, the Luong (dragon) mountain of Minh muong (spirit of the *muong*), where the jar of *tao*'s, the head of the *muong*, and his relatives' corpses are hidden.

At the outer part of the *muong*, there is forest of the sacred spirits called entrance of *xen* which is a large sacred forest with big trees adjoining.

The water region in some places is called Pak Bom and Pak Muoi that are prohibited areas for worship, for sacrifice of black buffalo, to pray to the water owner of the *muong*, owner of the water snake. Next to them there is prohibited forest.

The areas with forest for hunting are places that heaven gives to mundane beings to earn for living; the prohibited forest at the outer part of the resources, where the sacred spirits live, must not be exploited. (Ngo Duc Thinh 1998b, p. 407)

Among the Ede and M'nong in Tay Nguyen, the opinion on land, river, stream, plants, forest, etc. are attached to grandparents and ancestors, to sacred symbols of the polan (landowner) handed down from generation to generation:

Uncle dies, his nephew will be the owner,

Grandmother dies, her grandchild will be the owner

This person dies, the other will be the owner

Nobody dares to own it for him (her)self

Nobody dares to own it to distribute and own them in anyway

(Ngo Duc Thinh 1996, p. 222).

Thus, the land protected, forest and natural resources are holy duties of all community members:

---

[2] *minh*: the origin of spirit
[3] *nen*: as *minh*

Land, river, streams and forest plants are flat winnowing and *lung* (wealth) of grandparents

Grandparents are people who keep cave (where the Ede was born), guard forest, guard *ktong, kdjar* tree

The tree of *queo* doesn't bloom, mango tree doesn't bloom perfectly because grandchildren are bad-mannered

Therefore, grandparents try asking the chieftain

Grandparents will punish the guilty persons to pay a pig, grandparents will ask the guilty person to pay a chicken.

(Ngo Duc Thinh 1996, p. 223)

The customary law of the M'nong asserts:

... Ancestors pass away, the next generation inherits

Parents pass away, the children inherit

Selling forest, village punishes

Selling swidden field, village sues

Selling swidden field, that is lost land for rice crops

Makes next generation in trouble

There are not plants anymore to use

There is not bamboo for use

There is not shadow of trees to hide sunlight...

(Ngo Duc Thinh 1998a, p. 524)

Among the ethnic minorities in Tay Nguyen, every mistake of people, from laziness, theft to incest have the impact that land, forest and water resources are 'o ue' (filthy), it makes the spirits angry and they punish people: "Plant of *mon doc* turns yellows and dries, and water taro in pond withers because relatives commit incest and they are punished" (Ngo Duc Thinh 1996, p. 221).

In general, the opinion of 'sacredness' of these natural resources of many small ethnic minorities point out the specific features of communities about the environmental behaviours, and contribute to protect the natural resources faced with the blind destruction of human beings themselves.

Protection of the natural resources

The customary laws of the small ethnic minorities in our country have many articles concerning the natural resources such as land, forest, river and stream, and to prevent the threats of fire, epidemic, poison and pollution of the water resources. People who cause those disasters are judged of breaking the community rules.

Among the small ethnic groups, especially those cultivating swidden fields, one of the frequent threats is fire in the forest and village:

Men always make fire, women always make fire cautiously; there are people who make fire but they seem to be deaf, blind, crazy and stupid.

... The whole forest of *le* has burned, the whole *lo o* burned down completely, the cave of rabbit, the cave of weasels burned, too. Therefore, there are serious problems, they should be judged.

... Having children, one must admonish them, having grandchildren, one must admonish them, otherwise they don't know how to go to gather fire wood and take home water from streams. They might bring along a torch.

Fear that they don't know how to go to work in swidden fields, taking with them fire sticks still in flame, which may destroy the whole forest. The fire will spread to the forest and burn grass, plants, everything..

Therefore, if we know who that woman is, who that man is, we will judge them to pay a big compensation. (Ngo Duc Thinh 1996, p. 102)

Or in the customary law of the M'nong:

A shanty is burned, only one person is sad

A house is burned, the whole village is sad

A forest is burned, everyone is sad

The fire crossed stream, all varans die

The grass lots are burned, chameleons die

Forest doesn't come out naturally

... That forest belongs to ancestors

That forest belongs to children and grandchildren

That forest belongs to grandparents

That forest belongs to us

The forest is in fire, we have to stamp it out.

(Ngo Duc Thinh 1998a, p. 268)

When burning swidden fields, families have to unite, stop the fire in the swidden field and don't cause fire in the other fields:

When burning swidden fields, one should notify to each other

If burning and fire spreads out

The fire goes to other's swidden fields

Making other swidden fields and other's rice crops on fire

The swidden field burners are guilty.

(Ngo Duc Thinh 1998a, p. 270)

When seeing a village or forest in fire, everyone has duty to stamp it out:

Forest is burned, we have to stamp it out together

The water overflows, we have to prevent it

The forest is burned but not stamped

People won't have forests

People won't have land...

(Ngo Duc Thinh 1998a, p. 268)

The small ethnic groups usually raise livestock in a heard. When cows and buffaloes get sick, they usually cause an epidemic, causing large destruction. Therefore, the customary laws have strict regulations when livestock get sick, one should notify to the chieftain and has to take care of them and insulate the sick cattle; if one causes the epidemic spreading around, he will be punished:

In the years of drought, in the dry seasons, Mr. Du, Mr. Die pour water on disease, killing cows and buffaloes.

....He doesn't poke fire, he doesn't call people, he doesn't gather villagers to notify, he doesn't speak out about it, he doesn't tell the rich chieftain that cows and buffaloes are sick.

Therefore, he is guilty, he should be judged.

(Ngo Duc Thinh 1996, p. 101)

When there is an epidemic but he doesn't insulate cows and buffaloes and let them infect other creatures and villages with a disease, he is guilty:

If a person challenges tigers, requires to be higher than Gods, doesn't take admonishment into account, he still lets his cows and buffaloes be together with others'; if cows and buffaloes of other villages die, he is a guilty person; he should be judged for what he causes.

(Ngo Duc Thinh 1996, p. 102)

Exploitation and protection of the natural resources are two areas of concern. The ethnic groups burn forest to cultivate the swidden fields but still protect them, hunting wild animals, catching fish and shrimp but protecting them. The customary laws of the ethnic minorities strictly prohibit exhaustive catching, especially using poisonous leaves to catch fish.

... Streams with fish belong to everyone

Fish in streams are caught by everyone

Catching a frog, leave its mother

Cutting bamboo, one should leave the young ones

Burning a beehive one should leaves the queen bee

Poison fish is making stream poor.

... Person who poisons fish is guilty

committing fish poisoning no-one can compensate.

(Ngo Duc Thinh 1998, p. 280)

The customary laws also guarantee rights of every community member to exploit rationally the natural resources such as the water resources, catching shrimps and fish, hunting wild animals, exploiting the forest to built houses and household tools. The customary laws severely punish people who break the laws and the achievement of other's labour.

Among the Thai, the law of *muong* regulates clearly disputes about water resources to water fields, fighting for water from other's fields and stealing water pipes. The customary law of the Thai also strictly punish people who destroy fishing traps of others, stealing fish in traps of others, fighting against others for hunting places, stealing marked beehives, fishing illegally in water fields and pond of others (Ngo Duc Thinh 1998b, p. 120).

The customary laws of ethnic minorities in Tay Nguyen such as the Ede and M'nong have concrete articles regulating the guilt of people who disputed, hold and steal trapped wild animals, stealing fish, cows, buffaloes, cattle (Ngo

Duc Thinh 1996), guilt of stealing trees in forest, trapped animals and fish (Ngo Duc Thinh 1998a).

CONCLUSIONS AND DISCUSSIONS

One of the major values of the customary laws of ethnic groups is the indigenous popular knowledge about the management and exploitation of natural resources. The customary laws regulate relationships between people, but through the mirror and system of references to the natural environment. Therefore, we have feelings of the nature as 'personalised'; people and nature are inter-linked and people are combining various parts of the nature. This is a specific feature of the world-views, of thoughts and living styles of ethnic groups.

In the present social conditions, among societies of ethnic minorities dramatic changes occur: The institutions and social traditional views have been changed; a lot of new social phenomena have appeared. However, the customary laws of ethnic groups with indigenous knowledge about the environment and management methods, exploitation of the natural resources still remain their core values.

The problem here is not only to select the modern or indigenous knowledge about the exploitation, management of the natural resources but also to combine the two different sources of knowledge with the purposes to protect and exploit the natural resources in order to serve a stable development of the ethnic minorities.

LITERATURE

Ngo Duc Thinh, (ed.), 1998a, *Lôc tôc M'nong [Customary Law of the M'nong]* (Hanoi: Nha xuat ban Chinh tri Quoc gia, 1998).

Ngo Duc Thinh and Cam Trong, 1998b, *Lôc tôc Thai [Customary Law of the Thai]* (Hanoi: Nha xuat ban Dan toc hoc, 1998).

Ngo Duc Thinh, (ed.), *Lôc tôc Ede [Customary Law of the Ede]* (Hanoi: Nha xuat ban Chinh tri Quoc gia, 1996).

Some Ideas about Culture and Development in East Asia

Pham Duc Thanh
Institute for South East Asia Studies, NCSSH

*W*hen the role of culture is discussed, a good number of studies have referred to cultural values in development. Not as an expert on culture, but a researcher on the path and pattern of development for countries in the region, I pay attention more or less to Asian cultural values and the role of culture in development or even to Confucianism with development in East Asian countries. This can be domain extremely puzzling to those who have no knowledge of Han script or Chinese ideograms like myself.

In many works on the role of culture in/for development, various authors usually speak much about the positive aspects and active role of culture in development. They all realise that culture is the motive, the objective and the regulating system of development, and also admit that it would be wrong not to talk about culture in development. It seems that very few studies deal with the limitation exerted by traditional cultural values, one of the root causes of adverse affects on sustained development and a factor that some even refer to as one of the deep-seated causes of the current economic-financial crisis in the region. This is really a difficult question into which more research needs to be undertaken in the future.

The role of culture in economic development

The role of culture in general in development

In their research on Asia and the "Age of Asia and the Pacific", people all recognise that, in spite of cultural diversity in the region, there remains a common view that cultural factors have accelerated the economic development and prosperity of Asia. It is the cultural foundation that has contributed to alleviating poverty and creating an impetus to regional economic development.

Obviously, the study of Asia as a whole is very complicated, therefore the space of this analysis is limited within the region of East Asia.

East Asian countries have all achieved a high rate of economic growth since 1950 and for some countries it has developed explosively over the recent decade. This has solicited our desire to discover whether a culture in East Asia is closely connected to economic development and whether a culture really speeds up the economic development of the region perceived from the cultural angle. This issue has been rather successfully studied by scholars at home and abroad. In this article, let us analyse one of the cultural aspects in development - Confucianism in socio-economic development in East Asia.

The role of Confucianism in socio-economic development

a. Major religions with the economy of East Asia

In Asia, there are different religions including Taoism, Buddhism, Confucianism (understood as a religion), Christianism, Islamism and Hinduism. Among them, one can realise that Taoism, Buddhism and Confucianism remain the three major creeds in East Asia, having most affects on countries in the region, ranging from Japan to the Republic of Korea, Hongkong, Taiwan and Singapore.

Christianity has had positive impacts on the process of East Asian economic development, but with no great cultural influences on the whole region.

Taoism is concerned about naturalism and encourages the tendency to escape reality. It lacks social character and denies political thoughts and principles for societal structure. As such, not any modern economy can rely on pure Taoism.

Buddhism exerts much of its influence on the spiritual culture of East Asia. The Buddhist theory is esteemed with high values, but it teaches human beings to disdain materialistic life, fame and wealth. For that reason, Buddhism also does not support ideas related to economic development.

b. Confucianism and socio-economic development

Since its appearance, Confucianism has been imbued with Asian political thought. It supports principles to organise the society and educate human beings by emphasis on ethical and moral norms. On the basis of practical principles and ethics, it builds up moral rules to be applied to practical life and closely connected to the stability of a concrete political regime. Different from Taoism and Buddhism, Confucianism highlights political thoughts and ideas for organising of society. For this reason, it supports a pattern of social order necessary to economic development. Confucianism is totally suitable to any country that starts the process of economic development, because any economy, whatsoever, needs a social order related to production and consumption. Although Confucianism does not directly accelerate economic development in the manner of a religion or dogmatic form, it remains the means by which community to live in discipline and move forward to an increasingly perfect and better development. We would not be able to explain the economic development of East Asian countries without satisfactory assessments of the fundamental contents of Confucian culture related to development in those countries.

Over the past years, there have been two different remarks on the role of Confucianism in socio-economic development:

• According to the tendency to recognise the role of Confucianism, the countries influenced by Confucian culture (like 4 Asian Dragons) are able to advance quickly with sustained development.

• Meanwhile, adverse ideas hold that if so, the native land of Confucianism should be a place where speedy and sustained development has never taken place.

Let us continue the debate, but it should be realised that Confucian culture is not all but only one of the root-causes for the creation of the "Asian miracle".

It is not easy to study Confucianism so that one correctly understands it. Phan Ngoc, a researcher on Confucianism has pointed out misunderstandings of Confucianism by posterior generations. According to Prof. Phan Ngoc, at times, it was thought that Confucius did not concern himself with making people wealthy but only about self-perfection and submission to one's fate in clean poverty. This was a wrong perception as in his treatise, Confucius dealt himself much with richness and poverty and clearly stressed that the ruler's task was to make the people rich. Also in Prof. Phan Ngoc's opinion, Confucianism refers a lot to ruling skills, for example, first attention should be paid to the link of equitable distribution, and this link would help us achieve peace even in poverty. The way to promote authority is through the cultural path, to use culture to attract people from remote places to one's side and seek for peace in one's mind. Let's try by all means to avoid war for territorial expansion and for solving conflicts.[1]

A question has been posed: Let's say that Confucianism does play a role in socio-economic development in East Asian countries sharing a traditional culture based on Confucianism or having close links with countries like Japan, Republic of Korea, Taiwan, Hongkong and Singapore. How can one then understand and explain the fact that other South East Asian countries, though not directly influenced by Confucianism, have ever experienced recent decades of rather splendid development ?

c. The spreading of Confucianism

In reality, the expansion of an economic theory has resulted from the spreading of culture.

• The industrial revolution and the birth of the capitalist system, originating from England, have spread to all Europe and America. It was the spreading of ideas based on Catholicism or Protestantism.

• In the case of East Asian countries, their cultural foundation remains Confucianism, and economic development has spread on the basis of Confucianism.

This culture reflects the ability to sustain and develop communities. Initially Confucian ideas were transmitted through mutual communication of man with man and from generation to generation. Experiences were shared and secrets of success drawn from the process of economic development in one country were studied, summarised and again shared with other posterior countries.

The core Confucian countries have succeeded in managing a capitalist system imported from the outside world. The reason for this successful implantation may be attributed to their knowledge of how to make efficient use of traditional values instead of learning and copying Western individual liberalism. Although the capitalist system has its source in the West, East Asian countries have applied a totally different cultural pattern (patterns of Confucian culture) to the management of this system. Therefore, advanced Confucian countries succeeded in building and developing secrets for a new production which adjacent countries have learnt, studied and applied successfully.

The spreading of Confucianism in the transfer of capital, technology

---

[1] Phan Ngoc "Confucianism and its relation with the time", in *Vietnamese Cultural Indentity*, Culture-Information Publishing House.

215

and management system[2]

ASEAN has a cultural diversity: Buddhism in Thailand, Myanmar, and Laos, Catholicism in the Philippines and Islam in Malaysia, Indonesia and Brunei. So, how has the spreading of Confucianism proceeded to non-Confucian countries?

Transfer of capital, technology and management system

The process of industrialisation in ASEAN member countries has needed assistance in capital, technology and management system from Japan, a country which has succeeded in combining capitalism with traditional culture based on its family or community values. The taking-over of Japanese capital or application of Japanese production structure in ASEAN have brought to people of those nations a new understanding of economics and economic management.

For the past years, the transfer of technology and management systems from Japan to ASEAN have been implemented only in such domains as operation, maintenance, quality inspection, technological improvement, production, designing, and development of new products, samples and production means. The technologies of operation, maintenance and quality inspection have been transferred from Japan to ASEAN with a ratio of respectively 75%, 58.3% and 54.2%. A number of companies have moreover implemented the transfer of production technologies, technological improvement and development of samples.[3]

Over recent years, the spreading of Confucian culture has witnessed its clearer impacts when an increasing number of Japanese, Korean and Taiwanese corporations have transferred their businesses to ASEAN member countries.

The transmittal role of Chinese descents

The spreading of Confucian culture has also been implemented by the existence of people of Chinese descent in South East Asia. Traditionally, they are inhabitants with Confucian culture. They have often been living for a long time in ASEAN member countries and played a more and more important role in ASEAN economies. Though their number is not so great in each ASEAN country, they tend to be part of the local bourgeoisie and assume a guiding position with no small influence on the economic operation of South East Asian

---

[2] Kim Il Gon "The role of culture in the economic development of East Asia", *Japan's Options for the Asian Age*, Hiroshima University, 1997.
[3] See "Transfer of Japanese technology and management to ASEAN", National Political Publishing House, Hanoi.

countries. They control trade, banks and big enterprises. Actively grasping new secrets for their economic development, they have contributed in no small part to the process of economic development and industrialisation in ASEAN member countries.[4]

The process of Chinese descents' deep penetration into South East Asian economies consists of various phases. At its inception, South East Asian administrations tried to restrictive the influence of the Chinese community by discriminative measures against localisation of their capital. However, this policy brought about disadvantages for economic development and ethnical integration. So, since the 1960's, those countries have adjusted their policy, taking measures of stimulation and cooperation instead. As a result, Chinese capitalists have assumed more and more the important function to shape and develop a number of sophisticated economic sectors, speeding up the process of capital centralisation and integration, and enlarged the volume of domestic markets and international cooperation in the region.

A no less important agent of the spreading of Confucianism is the fact that a number of ASEAN governments have taken the lead to welcome this spreading. It is the case of Malaysia, an Islamic nation always with a high sense of national pride, which has volunteered to "Look East" and learn from the example of Japan. So, those governments have quickly taken over the dynamism and managerial principles and measures of the Confucian cultural.

Role of Confucianism in economic development

Confucianism in the economic order

Different from countries in the West, one of the peculiarities in the socio-economic development of South East Asian countries is the guidance of Government and the regulating role of the State in the market economy. This is a concrete policy of a centralised regime, including social principles and societal disciplines as a seal of Confucian culture in South East Asian countries.

It should be said that prior to taking the Japanese pattern of economic development, many South East Asian countries already highlighted the role of the State in socio-economic development. Particularly since "Look East" policy was adopted to learn from the example of Japan, the State's role in the development of ASEAN has been further strengthened. It is the pattern of regulated market economy in which the Government and the market are the two

---

[4] Tran Khanh, *Chinese Descents' Role in South East Asian Economies*, Da Nang Publishing House, 1992.

directly mutual interacting bodies, forming and creating institutions of the market economy.

Naturally, analysis may be taken further into the differences, especially in relation to the State's role in the two sub-patterns.

In the market economy model of the Singaporean style, the State strictly controls business operations including those of the private economic sector, but does not interfere in profitable businesses including those of State owned enterprises (some call this model one of control and non-interference). State owned enterprises in this country are operating like private enterprises with no right to enjoy any form of favours and privileges, including land lease. Meanwhile, the State does not apply any special legal restrictions on its own enterprises. The financial plans and business methods of those enterprises do not need governmental approval, their operations are totally autonomous for them to get profits or to bear losses. If they can no longer operate, they will be dissolved according to the Company Law applied to all economic sectors.

In the market economy model of the rest of ASEAN (namely Indonesia, Thailand, the Philippines and Malaysia), the Government interferes rather deeply into the administrative and financial fields of enterprises in the State economic sector. Governments in those countries usually appoint their cronies to managerial posts of State owned enterprises (SOEs) along with some favours and special obligations given to this type of enterprises. The Governments also grant privileged loans to those SOEs facing problems in their businesses. Meanwhile, the private economic sector is not closely controlled and supervised and it is left almost governed by the law of free competition.

To ensure the continued existence of SOEs, the State interferes much into their business with the hope that they will improve the business. But in reality, SOEs, of which most are large-scale industrial enterprises, are not successful in their businesses and suffer heavy losses.

In the economic field, another issue should be taken into consideration. Confucianism has extended the family mechanism and turned it into the national body with a sense of strong nationalism. Accordingly, the perception of loyalty as responsibility to the country has developed to become a common value in which the development of a country can be considered as noble result for each individual.

Economic development in East Asian countries has resulted from the principle of traditional centralisation as it is initiated by the Government and it must be considered totally different from that in the West, which is based on the

218

system of free enterprise and individualism. Governments of the countries within the area of Confucian culture centralise more power than those in areas of other cultures. In the process of economic development, the economic order of Confucian Governments appears to be more sustainable, and even when their countries become developed or industrialised countries, this sustainability is still maintained. The main characteristics of the model of government initiated economic order in Confucian countries may be the following:

- Governments have the right to intervene much stronger in the economic sector as compared with those in countries of other cultures. Governments are in administrative command of national economies. Private business operations are put under the State management.

- Governments take full authority over the selection of important industrial sectors and enterprises to be supported through the system of financial assistance and tax exemption.

- Governments resolve conflicts of interest between organisations as well as individuals. Thanks to judgement by the law, it is possible to deal with those conflicts.

- A Government with centralised power is able to make swift adjustments in various sectors in line with changes at the international and national levels.

On the other hand, enterprises in the countries with Confucian culture are usually inclined to implement governmental policies, as they always put national interests above all. Moreover, if great changes take place on the international arena, people in Confucian countries may reach a tacit unanimous agreement on a national level that individuals and enterprises in the society would together implement appropriate adjustments to adapt themselves to those changes.

Civilian obedience to governmental guidance is also a tradition of Confucian culture. Every citizen perceives that his responsibility is to contribute to national development. So, each member of the society always makes all his efforts to solve national problems thus creating a high collective efficiency.

Confucian culture in the management of enterprises

Since the system of free enterprise was applied in East Asian countries, the source of their economic achievements have been from the development of enterprises. Governments have actively managed their economies to speed up the growth of enterprises in leading sectors. Thanks to State policies, many companies have been founded and operated efficiently. Successes have been seen in such different fields as production, distribution and export, eventually creating the development of the whole economy.

It is the healthy management that has brought about the development of enterprises. This healthy management is a property inherited from the Confucian culture or in other words, this culture has granted active support to enterprise management. In Confucian-influenced countries in East Asia, the family and nation are the two core concepts for a central organisation. As the concept "enterprise as an organisation" has been imported from the West, it is an intermediate concept placed between family and nation. So, in Confucian countries, enterprises in East Asia, though imported but different from those in the West, are considered as an enlargement of the family organisation on the basis of the traditional family-community system. Therefore, while the management pattern of western countries is highly characterised by principles and functions, working people in the East pay attention to ethical values on the foundation of traditional Confucian culture, e.g. the cultural tradition of family-community is highlighted in the management of enterprises in East Asia.

Some points to be given attention in the study of the role of culture in development

Studies of the role of culture in development would be very attractive if researchers succeeded in pointing out limitations of traditional culture which adversely affect the development of contemporary society. So far, we seldom find analyses of aspects concerning the limitation of traditional culture with their impacts on the cause of industrialisation and modernisation.

Of course, sometimes we do receive papers referring to the limitations that traditional culture regarding the development of contemporary society. In this connection – apart from extremist views that totally deny Asian values while raising high Western values - there is in general a view that the current financial economic crisis can be attributed to characteristics like boastfulness, excessive ambition, long-winded speeches, a hesitation to speak straightforwardly, and to such thinking as communalism, patriarchism and family sentimentalism. Some even think that communalism in feudal society was only highly valuable to inhabitants who lived in village and hamlet communities in the spirit of mutual assistance and that "the rich helped the poor". But even now, conservatism, clannishness, kindred feelings, sectarianism, departmentalism and narrow nationalism derived from small farmers' mentality, and it has very much restrained the cooperation of countries in the region for development and these tendencies are not suitable to the formation of the sense for regional community. Such mentalities as absent-mindedness, liking for leisure and communal festivals (resulting from a way life of seasonal agricultural production) have been one of the root-causes of obstacles on the way to industrialisation and modernisation of South East Asian countries.

Within the limits of Confucianism as discussed, Vietnamese experts on Confucian study have pointed out shortcomings of Confucianism in the present modern society. From our viewpoint of today:

- Confucianism is only an ideology of a low-level agricultural civilisation concerned with the protection of a self-sufficient agricultural regime, the maintenance of a static society, and sees the consolidation of stagnation as its ideal.

- It initiates rites for the service of a monarchist order as opposed to the present democratic regime.

- It takes the remote past as an objective to strive for without concern for the current time or the future. So, it is not able to help man change his fate and catch up with the world with scientific and technological progress.

- It does not encourage individual development. Man in Confucianism is bound by ten thousand tiers of responsibilities that prevent him from changing himself and the people around, eventually becoming dependant on others and waiting for things to happen. That is why Confucian education does not create self-reliable creative people but passive rigid ones.[5]

In her article, Dr. Thu My has pointed out the close alliance between political ruling circles and big business corporations as one of the shortcomings of the ASEAN development pattern.[6] But is it not that crony capitalism results from the metamorphosis of Confucian cultural values in modern economic development as we said above? Enterprise as an organisation in an intermediate concept between the concepts of family and fatherland.

---

[5] Phan Ngoc Tai, document already mentioned.
[6] Nguyen Thu My "ASEAN: Shortcomings in the development pattern", Papers of the Seminar on *Making ASEAN a Community ofNnations with Sustainable Development, Equality and Cooperation*, Hanoi, 1998.

The Impact of Scandinavian Management in Vietnam in the Early Reform Period of the 1980s

Irene Norlund
Nordic Institute of Asian Studies

INTRODUCTION[1]

The Vietnamese way of thinking and planning started to change from the established form of central planning in a socialist economy in the early 1980s. The time coincided with the construction of a Swedish supported paper mill in Bai Bang 100 kilometres north of Hanoi. The construction of the factory started in 1974 after long discussions between the Swedish and the Vietnamese sides, and in the first phase in the 1970's the project faced numerous problems in the erection of a large factory in the remote hilly area. The mill started finally operations in 1982, and in the new phase 'operations' other types of problems had to be faced. The operation of the factory demanded huge amounts of raw materials like wood, coal, chemicals etc., which demanded new types of production in the forestry and development of infrastructure. The factory was a cooperative project, but in the early 1980s it was mainly run by the Swedish advisors, contrary to the wishes of the Swedish development agency, Sida, which was financing the project. Sida wanted a common management structure between the advisors in the newly hired consultancy firm, Scanmanagement

---

[1] The paper is based on a larger study *A Leap of Faith. A story of Swedish aid and the building and operation of the Bai Bang pulp and paper mill in Vietnam – 1969-96*, Stockholm 1999. It was commissioned by Sida and carried out by researchers at Chr. Michelsen Institute, Bergen, the Nordic Institute of Asian Studies, Copenhagen, and National Institute for Science and Technology and Strategic Studies, Hanoi. The study was presented in public in Stockholm the same day as this workshop, 24 March 1999, and translated and presented in Vietnam in November 1999, *Buoc nhay day long tin. Ve su vien tro cua Thuy Dien va viec san xuat giay o Viet Nam – du an Bai Bang, 1969-96*. Nha Xuat Ban Chinh Tri Quoc Gia, 1999.

(SM) and the Vietnamese side. But the two management systems were difficult to merged, because the worked with different logics and traditions which had to do both with the organisation at the factory and relation to the larger economic and political system.

The attention to the concept of 'Scandinavian management' increased in the Vietnamese administration, but it was a concept with many interpretations. Was it the same as Scanmanagement (the consultancy firm), capitalist management or management in accordance with Scandinavian principles? The Swedish management philosophy was based on principles of a market economy, and it was furthermore related to the idea of 'transfer of knowledge'. Transfer of knowledge was an integrated part of the management ideas of Scanmanagement, and it became even the central idea in the plan for Sida/Scanmangement to phase out of their involvement in the paper project between 1985 and 1990 in order for the Vietnamese side to take over the company. How were the concepts of Scandinavian management and transfer of knowledge linked to each other? How was Scandinavian management perceived by the Vietnamese counterpart, and how was it utilised by the Vietnamese planners. The reform ideas and partial economic reform started in the early 1980s, *before* 'renovation' (*doi moi*) was adopted at the 6th congress of the Communist Party of December 1986, and the reform process was speeded up from 1988-89. This paper will look at some of the processes taking place in the triangle between reforms in Vietnam, the Scandinavian management and the performance of the mill – an account of how the two systems and two cultures, the Vietnamese and the Swedish – were interacted in a concrete setting.

THE EARLY REFORM-IDEAS IN VIETNAM IN THE 1980s

In his speech at the inauguration of the Bai Bang paper mill in 26 November 1982, the Director General of Sida, Anders Forsse, mentioned that the project would contribute to the 'industrialisation and modernisation' of the country.[2] At that time, the Vietnamese development conceptualisation would certainly agree with the idea of industrialisation. However, a word like modernisation would never be used in the political language of that time. The main concern was still in 1982 to secure and defend the fatherland (after the conflicts with the US, China and Cambodia). As for the national development, the strategic task was to build socialism, and socialist industrialisation was the

---

[2] Archives of the Foreign Ministry, 26 November 1982.

catchword of the time, with 'large-scale' as positive characteristics.[3] Modernisation would be considered part of a 'capitalist' thinking, which was not perceived as a goal for the Vietnamese industrialisation.

THE 5TH PARTY CONGRESS AND THE NEW ORIENTATION

The 5th Party congress was the first after the announcement of the reform initiatives in August 1979. The overall strategy outlined at the 5th congress was to strengthen the cooperation with Soviet Union and the other socialist countries. China, United States and ASEAN countries were perceived as the imperialist and reactionary forces, which tried to sabotage the successful building of socialism.[4] The report by Le Duan, the late secretary general and ideologist of the Communist Party, to the 5th congress was unusually self-critical about the shortcomings of the party. It mentioned that national production was not able to meet the needs of social consumption, there being a serious shortage of food, clothing and other consumer goods. The livelihood of the working people, especially workers, public servants and peasants was seriously affected in areas hit by natural disasters and enemy destruction. Great shortages existed in the supply of energy and materials, in communication and transport.[5]

Still, in 1982, the party leader was talking with two tongues. The old socialist rhetoric was still in place, but the political line for concrete tasks and strategies had changed. It was no longer heavy industrialisation that dominated the development strategy. Now it was stressed that the country was still in a stage of small-scale production and had to build the material base from that point of departure. All types of production should be encouraged and combined, and export and consumer goods had the highest priority. The state was still leading in trade, and capitalist enterprises (in the south) should be transformed into state-private enterprises.[6]

No doubt, the reforms started earlier in the 1980s prepared the way for the *doi moi* process from 1987, but they were carried out slowly and unevenly, often brought about by initiatives at local level, as 'fence-breaking activities'. It meant that initiatives contrary to the regulations took place before the approval of changes, and maybe even as a precondition and push for the changes. The

---

[3] Communist Party of Vietnam, *5th National Congress*, Political Report, March 1982, Hanoi 1982, p. 30.
[4] Op. cit. pp. 30-31.
[5] Op. cit. p. 23.
[6] Op. cit. pp. 56, 60.

problem was that nobody knew where the limits for changes were, and when and how the political system would set limits. The bureaucratic obstacles, which often was mentioned by the Swedish advisors as one of the main constraints of the Vietnamese planning system at Bai Bang paper mill, did not become clearer or more transparent in the early 1980s. However, the Bai Bang project was increasingly perceived as an important project by the Vietnamese authorities, because it was one of the only projects which introduced Western technology and currency, both items of severely shortage and considered very attractive and necessary by the Vietnamese authorities. In the new situation of the early 1980s, it was moreover an excellent occasion to see how other types of management performed – and what could be learned.

The ideas of the secretary general, Le Duan, showed that the principles of socialist orientation of the state planned economy were still valid. However production of consumer goods was encouraged, and economic units should rely on their own resources not on government support and supply. 'Cost accounting' was a new concept in Vietnam and it meant that prices had to be calculated and determined based on market prices, contrary to the existing system of prices decided at the central political level. It also meant that a free market and a black market started to appear where goods were sold at much higher prices than the state prices, pricing determined by the demand (however irrational that might be). The Vietnamese currency had both an official exchange rate and an unofficial (black market) rate, which was much higher than the official rate. When goods were available they could be sold with much higher profits on the free market. This encouraged inflation and undermined th former stable exchange system between state and individual. The first years of reforms caused many controversies, but it meant a considerable - and necessar - increase in production.

TWO SYSTEMS, TWO CULTURES

The important point is that from 1980 the Bai Bang project with its new management consultant, *Scanmangement*, started to operate in a climate of beginning openness - and indecisiveness. It also made the Swedish suggestions much more acceptable to the Vietnamese partners than they were earlier under the management by the former consultant, *WP System*. The modern Western management style evinced by SM showed an alternative to the Vietnamese planning system. Even if it is probably not possible to prove the direct influence of the Bai Bang project on the reform process at large, the conditions for interaction were excellent. First of all, it was one of the largest projects in Vietnam; it was the only one constructed with a large number of experts from a 'capitalist' country; and it was the only one that was organised as a cooperative project between the two partners. The Swedish consultant company were furthermore allowed to continue to give direction and support in the operational period of the mill, which was unusual compared to the rules for handing over a project from a socialist country to the Vietnamese authorities. Usually it would pass from the responsibility of Technoimport under the Ministry of Foreign Trade to the relevant line ministry, when the project was finished and the foreign experts leaving. In the case of Bai Bang the foreign experts continued to manage the project even in the phase of operation. There was a beginning openness to make the two systems or two management cultures interact in a more experimental way than before.

THE ORIGIN OF "SCANDINAVIAN MANAGEMENT"

In Scandinavia there is no concept like 'Scandinavian management'. Management style vary widely in Scandinavia and within each country in the region, the example of the different management styles of WP System (the first consultancy company hired by Sida), and Scanmanagement illustrate that it is not possible to talk about one model.[7] The main difference between the Bai Bang project and other foreign projects that later came to Vietnam was not so much the Scandinavian management style. The difference was, basically, that the project was managed - or at least attempted to be managed - following market principles. It was in many respects quite different from the Vietnamese management model in the early 1980s, which was still based on the system of centrally planning.

The situation in respect of labour, infrastructure and bureaucratic organisation for the Bai Bang project was not much different from most other enterprises in 1980 in Vietnam. In some respects it was worse than for other factories, because the paper mill was situated far away from the cities in an area not prepared for the amount and skill of labour necessary to build and run the mill, and the infrastructure was insufficient to secure the most basic needs.

---

[7] The two management companies had also different functions, it should be remembered. WP System was a construction company and Scanmanagement was an operational company, where the transfer of knowledge in operations becomes even more important than in the one time construction. Moreover, SM was a company specifically set up for the Bai Bang project, and was an umbrella organisation of a number of companies. However, the management principles applied were based on the newest management principles, which included the relations to the societal environment more than earlier methods.

226

Even the supply of raw materials had not been prepared. Scanmanagement (SM), had been successful under these conditions in finishing the first paper machine for test operation in the end December 1981. The pulp mill started up in August 1982 and the second paper machine was brought into service in November 1982. The power plant had also started up operation and all construction was finished by mid-1983. The construction phase had lasted several years longer than originally planned. However, the production had started about 5 months earlier than planned after new negotiations between Sida and the Vietnamese government in November 1980, and much earlier than WP System predicted in its plans in 1979.

One of the reasons for the positive result was the right to make executive decisions in the project that SM had achieved in the 1980 agreement. This, for instance, led to a decision to send 80 erectors and other types of skilled labour from Sweden to Vietnam for 1-1 ½ year at a considerable expense. SM actually carried out much of the work using Swedish workers, although this was meant to be the task of the Vietnamese partners.[8] The cost was considerable, but it was a trade off in order to prove to the Swedish authorities and public that the project could be completed without any further delays. The 1980 agreement accepted that the Swedish side had the executive authority. However, the other demand – by Sida – to establish *one* organisation at the project site by integrating the Vietnamese and the Swedish management was agreed upon, but not implemented according to the agreement, the two styles of management and organisation were difficult to merge, because they were based on different principles.

The situation was, however, still extremely difficult at the site. With the start of the operations of the factories, new types of demands became acute. Now it concerned raw materials for the mill, wood, coal, lime, salt; procurement of spare-parts and other necessary materials from abroad; trained workers to operate the mill, and transportation of huge amounts of raw materials and products to and from the mill. 'Scandinavian management' in Scanmanagement's way of thinking was a planned and efficient system of operating a company with modern 'Western' management methods. The young, energetic planners of Scanmanagement were compared to other companies more focused on an efficient management style management, including an organisation with fairly short lines of decision-making, individual performance

---

[8] Sida archives: Utvecklingssamarbete med Vietnam 1982/83, appendix 3, 11.3.1982, p. 4. Interview with Per Gundersby, 28.8.1998.

combined with teamwork, training of the employees and high engagement. The Scandinavian management should not be seen as basically different from many other Western market-based models in a more narrow perspective (some of the Eastern systems differ more, like for instance the Japanese management system). However, Scanmanagement tried to follow some new management principles.[9] As all management concepts, they change over time, and the Bai Bang project structure also changed several times. That was part of the (new) management idea: Flexibility and adaptability.

Nevertheless, in a broader perspective the styles of management found in Scandinavia – when the role of the state and other agencies are included - did have more of an impact than the above-mentioned approach indicates. If it is considered as a system of management within a specific socio-economic and cultural structure, it is of course a different system from most others in the world. History is a factor, which cannot be repeated easily, and the state played a considerable role in the Scandinavian welfare economies. The term 'Scandinavian management' seemed to have been invented by the Vietnamese around 1982, and was probably inspired by the confusion of Scanmanagement (SM, the consultancy firm) and 'Scandinavian management' (the concept), which were considered to be the same. The term probably also implied that the type of management was based on capitalist principles (cost-benefit and the impact of the market), but at this time such an admission would have been difficult to make directly. Somehow the term indicated that it was a 'friendly capitalism' because it was Scandinavian.

For those – and maybe other – reasons, the concept of Scandinavian management was acceptable in the Vietnamese context. SM took advantage of the positive reaction of the Vietnamese to 'Scandinavian Management'. After SM now had worked some years in Vietnam, it knew the conditions in Vietnam much better and started to realise the extent of the problems they faced by working in another context, a society with a different organisation and priorities. SM took the challenge and outlined a strategy in December 1982 in which 'Scandinavian management' and 'transfer of knowledge' were the core concepts. This strategy became influential for the next phase of Sida support to the Bai Bang project 1983-85, and finally became a lead theme in the phasing

---

[9] The CIE report on Human Resources discusses also the issue if there were special attributes of Scandinavia in the 'Scandinavian management' model more than what was common to all market economies. The conclusion is that there may be some related to promotion, responsibility and effective team work, pp. 8-10.

out plan 1985-90. In the strategy the necessity to influence the Vietnamese system at other levels than the enterprise was incorporated, as a prerequisite for the Vietnamese to run the mill efficiently.[10]

The main objective for the new strategy was 'transfer of knowledge' to Vietnam so that the mill could be kept in steady operation in the time after the expatriates had have left.[11] Scanmanagement was a company with more tight and company-loyal management methods than most other Nordic companies, and it had at the same time a wish and a drive to change things through their own management strategy. The SM strategy pointed to the important role of the authorities (The Swedish authorities in the case of Sweden) in the broader definition of Scandinavian management. It also pointed to some of the most controversial issues seen from a Vietnamese point of view, the role of the Vietnamese administration and other bureaucratic structures, and the role of the individual. These two issues were embedded deeply in the Vietnamese culture, although in different ways from in Sweden, and it was issues that could not easily be changed. Scanmanagement was after all not quite aware of the size of the challenge it had faced in this respect. If Scandinavian management is understood as the management system embedded in a national culture, it has of course wider implications and is much more difficult to transfer to another society and culture than with a more narrow definition. One of the characteristics of the Scandinavian system was, evidently, that the state had a highly regulatory role for welfare and the social system. Through the social regulations and taxes the state also limited the freedom of companies. Some of the same ideas were also prevalent in Vietnam, but the rules and abilities were different.

In the Bai Bang project Sida could be compared to the state which tried to regulate SM and also was able to supply the social services it found necessary. The new side projects that were developed to support the main project - like supplementary food rations, housing, a vocational school, a large forestry programme, upgrades of the infrastructure, living standard programmes, had no doubt* not been undertaken by a commercial enterprise. Even if from time to time SM was most annoyed by the control and supervision by Sida, it was quite satisfied with all the new investments made possible by the funding from Sida. In this sense, the Scandinavian management really made a difference.[12] The

---

[10] Scanmanagement archives: Future operation of the Vinh Phu Pulp and paper mill Project. Guidelines for action, 15.12.1982, p. 24.
[11] Op. cit. p. 6.
[12] One of the few other Western projects in Vietnam at this time was the Danish supported Hoang Thach Cement factory. This project was, however, not a

difference from a fully-fledged market-based company was thus that the Bai Bang project was a development aid-financed project. It had to some extent a 'soft budget constraint' (like the Vietnamese companies) and it would not have taken into account so many social concerns, if it had been commercially financed. It depended both on the performance and negotiating power of Scanmanagement vis-à-vis Sida in some of the side-projects, and in other side-projects Sida wanted to make sure that a certain standard of living was secured, because of the accountability to the public in Sweden. On one hand, the Bai Bang company was very different from a Vietnamese company because of the outside funding and principles, but on the other hand, it was just as dependent on the funding from Sida, as a Vietnamese company was dependent on the state in Vietnam, and not a fully-fledged market based enterprise with a hard budget constraint. The company had, however, to work in a Vietnamese economic and political environment, where the market had not yet developed, the bureaucracy was inefficient, and the state decided allocations to the project. Indeed a complicated net of structures to work in!

SCANDINAVIAN MANAGEMENT AND TRANSFER OF KNOWLEDGE

Around September 1983, SM had developed a program of 'transfer of knowledge', as demanded by Sida.[13] Transfer of knowledge in its developed form was now a part of the 'Scandinavian management' idea, but was still more focused at the mill and project level than at the macro-environment. SM outlined the fundamental objectives of management (*not* called Scandinavian management by themselves), based on organisation theory, an active and integrated strategic planning as a prerequisite for a company development, both embracing values of the management system and social values of the management work. It was based on a 'socio-technical' system concept, in which business was built on three interrelated sub-systems: The technical, the administrative and the social. The *technical* subsystem included technology and working methods used for production and handling of goods and services. The *administrative* subsystem included the company organisation and managing system, and systems for communication and decision making. The *social*

---

development aid sponsored project like Bai Bang, but financed by state loans, which should be considered as support to national industries more than development projects. The projects carried out on commercial terms based on state loans were managed differently from the Bai Bag project. In the case of the cement factory, there was no interference in wages, housing and other social conditions from the Danish management.

[13] Even in its original tender, SM stressed the importance of training, and Sida and SM agreed in the principles of TOK.

subsystem was characterised by the surrounding society and individuals by whom the company was built up and included the staff's know-how, competence, values and behaviour.[14]

Some of the basic different roles and functions of a Swedish company compared to the Vietnamese company are that the Western company is an independent economic unit that makes its own decision on what to do and how to do it. The company

- Has access to own funding without approval from higher level.

- Takes independent decision about use of money and other resources at its disposal.

- Is subject to strong financial constraint.

- Takes responsibility for the outcomes of decisions.[15]

The relation between Scandinavian management and transfer of knowledge became increasingly interrelated, but the idea of transfer of knowledge was also part of Sida's original thinking and part of the agreements with Vietnam. Even back to the WP System period in the 1970s, education became quickly an integrated part of the project; when it became clear that the Vietnamese counterpart could not provide sufficiently qualified staff for the construction: Training was introduced for electricians, mechanics specialists and welders. As a considerable number of the trained Vietnamese workers disappeared during the construction phase, the training effort did not become smaller. In all, the education unit comprised 100 instructors/supervisors and 25 vocational teachers.[16] Training of process staff also started, and the training for process tasks had a fairly different character. For Sida the transfer of knowledge (TOK) was a vague idea in the beginning, but as the project developed Sida exerted increasing pressure to emphasise the TOK. Actually, training was integrated in the management, and the vocational school was under preparation as a separate project at the 1983 agreement.[17] SM was asked to outline the TOK plans in 1983, but it was still *not* connected with the departure of the Swedish advisors.

---

[14] SM archives: Vinh Phu Pulp and Paper Mill, SM, Transfer of Knowledge, n.d., ca. September 1983.

[15] The CIE report on Human Resources, p. 8-9.

[16] Gunnar Thunblad, Bai Bang – Utbildning, *WP-bladet*, December 1978, p. 14. (GT was training coordinator in the Bai Bang Sweden-organisation in the 1970's under the management of WP System).

[17] For various reasons the school was only ready for operating in the final years of the Swedish presence.

Only during the next years, the phasing-out Scanmanagement developed TOK as a special concept, under quite strong pressure and encouragement from Sida. The phasing-out TOK became suddenly much more serious, because the Vietnamese side had to be able to run the mill independently. Also in respect of the TOK, the economic reforms in Vietnam seem to have been a precondition for effective transfer of knowledge concept, because the Swedish principles were not accepted until fairly late in the 1980s.

Transfer of knowledge, especially in the mill and to a much smaller extent in the forestry program, was carried out in an almost scientific way, with the main emphasis on:

- Social competence of the employees
- Systems competence of the leaders
- Professional competence by everybody
- Planning for the individual
- Personal development and personal development program
- Company objective – individual's objective identification
- Mutual work framing
- Job description for each job
- Key tasks for everyone
- Performance standards
- Control of information and distribution of information
- Training at various levels
- Training of all department
- On the job training for some tasks
- Vocational school training for other tasks
- The counterpart system – where the Vietnamese should work with a Swedish counterpart

In all, the education, training and informal TOK was an enormous effort that was intensified in the last phase of the project. For instance in 1985 the mill training department had organised 65 courses for 684 participants and the vocational school had 2- and 3-year courses for 120 students. The progress of the Scandinavian management and TOK seems to differ from section to section in the mill. Obviously the 'Scandinavian management' in the broader version worked better when the external constraints diminished and came more in accordance with the project management towards the end of the project, along with the economic reforms.

From the Vietnamese perspective, the application of the Scandinavian management caused problems. The essence of the Vietnamese interpretation of

232

the difference between the Scandinavian and Vietnamese management systems was that Scandinavian management had higher economic efficiency, more delegation of authority, counterpart relation and a low level of bureaucracy.

Around the mid-1980's, Vietnamese historians presented the situation:

The knowledge transfer was also facing a lot of difficulties, especially in the application of Scandinavian Management model, during the beginning of this period [1980-85]. It was due to the mill operated in a central planning mechanism, so the mill had to follow the Vietnamese management system with bureaucratic, subsidy routines. And as a result, it often caused misunderstandings and unsympathy towards SM when we did things that they could not understand as well as when we could not apply their good ideas. For instance, they proposed to increase salary and bonus for the employees but we could not do it as it was out of the Mill Director's power, or like they suggested to put the wood supply enterprise into the Vinh Phu Pulp and Paper Mill, but it was impossible. When SM was going to terminate their contract (30 June 1985), all operations for the Mill and Wood Supply enterprise were going very well, but not the knowledge transfer program.[18]

In the latter part of the 1980s, the situation changed according to the Vietnamese authors. The Scandinavian model was partly applied side by side with the Vietnamese system. Internal procedures like requisitions, cost tracing, annual operational plans followed the Scandinavian way, and the external relations like reporting, statistics, financial management followed the Vietnamese system. When Decision 217, the most important decision for changing the enterprise system in Vietnam, of the Council of Ministers was issued in November 1987, the autonomy of companies was introduced and they should work on a cost-benefit basis. This helped the work in the paper company.[19] The transfer of knowledge was also greatly facilitated by these reforms taking place.

There were indications that the Swedish management had an impact on the Vietnamese system, because of an increasing openness to learn from the Swedish management principles. The transfer of knowledge developed during the whole project period and a generalisation based on the knowledge available seems to indicate that it had an important impact. However, it was not only a Swedish impact in Vietnam that took place, it was a two-way impact where both sides had to accommodate each other. The project consisted of a large

---

[18] Giay Bai Bang. Nhung chang duong/ *Bai Bang Paper Stages*, Nha Xuat Ban Lao Dong, Hanoi, 1997, pp. 58-59.
[19] Op. cit. p. 63.

number of elements, which had to work together, so it is not sufficient to look at the production figures to determine the results of improved management. The production can only be seen as an overall indicator, but one of the only indicators available (Table 1). The minimum sustainable level was a decided level by management and other authorities estimated to be a reasonable (negotiated) target. The production capacity was 50.000 tons annually.

Table 1. Minimum production, production target and actual production, 1985-90

Year	Minimum sustainable Production level, Tons of paper	Production target tons	Actual production tons
1985	22,000	24,000	22,600
1986	26,000	30,000	30,500
1987	30,000	35,000	28,000
1988	33,000	38,000	23,000
1989	33,000	40,000	26,000
1990	35,000	42-44,000	30,100

Sources: TOR for Management support to the Vinh Phu Pulp and Paper Mill Project, 22.5.1985, Sida archives, and Bai Bang Paper Stages, Hanoi 1997, p. 152.

The production did increase, but apart from 1985-86, the results were lower than the targets and even lower than the minimum sustainable level. The level of production even decreased in 1988-89, but this was during the central years of reform, with changes from one system to another caused many irregularities.

The Bai Bang project and the reforms in Vietnam

The growth of a private market and small-scale production in the early 1980s, increased step by step the pressure on the state planned activities and the difference between the prices at the private market and the state prices started inflation. The situation was aggravated in 1984-86, and severely undercut the old type of subsidies system of industrial planning. In the mid-80s a power struggle took place between the conservatives (the more traditional communist leaders), and the reformers. The larger freedom of enterprises was partly limited again in 1984. However, a decree from April 1986 (306-BBT, from the Politbureau) introduced more reforms for the state enterprises, but failed to limit the guidance from higher level. After the *doi moi* renovation policy of December 1986, a new 'reform socialism' started with a fuller recognition of the market and a private sector. The most important decision was finally approved in November 1987 (217-HDTB, Council of Ministers), when the autonomy was further encouraged and the company in principle should handle its own economy, based on cost-benefit principles. It meant that the soft budget constraint from the subsidised system was hardened and forced the companies to economic calculations. In 1989, the two-price system (state and private) was finally abandoned, wages had to be paid in money not subsidised goods, and the centrally planned economy was in principle abolished. In reality, however, the large state-owned enterprises had still less freedom than the small private ones to calculate and manage their own economy.

The Bai Bang Paper Mill received special treatment by the Vietnamese political leadership, and from the mid-1980 the company was granted a number of privileges. Some of the privileges were of little use, because the political and economic environment had not yet changed. For instance, Bai Bang was granted permission to export directly, but often the contact to foreign countries ran into obstacles caused by the middle bureaucracy which did not know the reform decrees well. Other privileges were essential to keep up production, like the supply of coal where the factory was granted special supply, and an early permission to buy raw materials at the market. Towards the end of the 1980s, the Bai Bang Company was nevertheless in severe economic troubles, and there was no help to get from the state. Sida was at this point on its way out of the project and not willing to supply more funding. For first time the company had to survive on its own resources. As the company was considered an experiment by the Vietnamese authorities to try out 'Scandinavian management', there was probably little interest from the state to support it. The Swedish advisors left in mid-1990, and only the combined efforts of the Vietnamese managers and the various market-oriented reforms saved the company from ruin. After some hard years, the situation started to improve again, so the factory by the mid-1990s reached a production level of the magical 50,000 tonnes – the planned capacity level – and even surpassed it some years.

CONCLUDING REMARKS

The ideas of the Vietnamese Party about reforms in many respects coincided with the ideas in the Swedish planning system. Why were there then so many problems making the two systems work together, it could be asked? The answer may be the simple one that it takes time to change, especially when it is not known how and what to change. The Vietnamese reform process is a good example of trial and error process. Some customs and traditions are difficult to change, whereas others change and adapt surprisingly quickly.

The introduction of the Bai Bang project into Vietnam may to be seen as a clash of two cultures in the broad definition of the word as cultures of systems. It took place at all levels from the central ministerial one down to the regional and local, and finally to the work site and the forestry area. The factory site is where the most direct confrontation took place, but it was also an area where accommodation could happen. The cultural clash was a two way process between the Vietnamese and the Swedish systems of operation. The Swedish side was in some respect the strongest, because it had the knowledge and economic resources wanted by the Vietnamese side, and because it represented a way of production which was attractive to know and learn from in Vietnam's resource-starved economy. This model became increasingly more attractive along with the economic reforms.

On the other hand, the Bai Bang project was still small compared to the Vietnamese economy and society as such, and it was the Vietnamese system that dominated the society at large. It was a huge task to have the goal of introducing a 'Scandinavian management system', which did not work well together with the rules of the Vietnamese society. Two types of planning and management system that had to cooperate, and two different cultures of thinking and even speaking. Collective thinking and trust in authority in Vietnam did not go well together with the Scandinavian value of the individual in the centre combined with self-reliance and creativity. It was moreover a period where foreigners were still looked at with great suspicion. It only made it worse that the foreigners came from capitalist countries, because people were socialised to see capitalism as the enemy of the country. At its summit of foreign expertise, around 600 foreigners - a number with families - came to Bai Bang to live under conditions that were comparable to those in Sweden, in the midst of a very poor, remote, rural area. A peaceful place in the hilly mountains where people lived from agriculture and the forest, among which there were a considerable number of ethnic minorities.

The construction of the paper mill was like a cuckoo in the nest in several ways. In the locality with the direct confrontations between the local people and environment, when huge machines came and dig out an enormous area to make the ground for the factory, and later planned and prepared the land with deep ploughing machines in order to plant trees for plantations. Secondly, the project has also to be seen as a cuckoo in a nest of the Vietnamese planning system, because of the demands to the Vietnamese side in order to fulfil its obligations to the cooperation project. The resources in the Vietnamese centrally planned, 'shortage-economy' were few.[20] The ideology still favoured ideas of equality,

---

[20] Janos Kornai launced this characterisation about the socialist planning system, which has a tendency to produce with a low level of productivity and not utilise

and the mere existence of the Swedish project created struggles and envy in the planning system as well as in the locality.

If some conclusions could be drawn, it seems that the Scandinavian management actually had some impact at the enterprise level, especially to train workers to be skilled workers with the appropriate knowledge to run the factory. At higher levels, it only really mattered when the reform thinking allowed new forms of organisation at the mill, and when the Swedes planned to leave. In a study of the Bai Bang mill today, it seems as if the Scandinavian management has survived the full take-over by the Vietnamese management. In contrast, the forestry part of the paper project was never influenced much by the Scandinavian management, and it is barely left in forestry companies today. It can be questioned if the large effort of education in the transfer of knowledge to some extent was waste of investments from the Swedish side!

When Scandinavian management is considered at higher level, the relations between the paper company and the central levels, the management system was not able to change the Vietnamese system, but it had some impact on the transformation that was already under way. The company was able to achieve some privileges, but only when the reforms were more genuinely implemented it facilitated the operation of the company. The Vietnamese managers and planners followed the company with great interest and listened to the advice given from the Swedish side. By and large, the Bai Bang project was a process where both sides had to accommodate in the 1980's. However, it was an important learning process for all parties and some of the learning from Bai Bang was taken to other enterprises in the country.

---

resources in a efficient way. The state would help the companies out of difficulties, and that is the origin of the concept of soft budget constraint. Kornai, *Economics of Shortage*. Amsterdam, North Holland, 1980; Kornai, *The Soft Budget Constraint*, Kyklos, 39 (1), 1986.

Toward an Epistemological Study of Confucius' Doctrine

Phan Ngoc
Institute of Southeast Asian Studies, NCSSH

W orks on Confucianism are countless. In Vietnam as in foreign countries, however, there exists a confusion between Confucianism, the doctrine from classical works in examination systems and the doctrine set up by Confucius. Many contradictions have therefore arisen on the appraisal.

In this symposium on Asian values, I want to examine Confucius' doctrine from the epistemological viewpoint of modern, Western philosophy in order to investigate some features of its values. Only by so doing, we can see how Confucius' doctrine has contributed to the renovation, modernisation of many regions in Asia while Confucianism, the common doctrine of three countries in Asia (China, Korea, Vietnam) was the cause of their backwardness. I think that any philosophy of Asia should be presented by closely following the requirements of Western philosophy to contribute to the mutual understanding between the East and West in this era of the global village.

CONFUCIUS' DOCTRINE AND CONFUCIANISM

A doctrine having existed through a very long time like that of Confucius inevitably underwent important changes which often lead us to an image contrary to the nature of it from its beginning. The same difference is found between the doctrine of Jesus, extolling tolerance, condemning the use of force and Catholicism. The doctrine of Confucius born 2500 years ago, in a decentralised feudal China, under a self-sufficient economy, in which relations between governors and the people essentially were direct must be of course different from Confucianism set up in 140 BC, under Han Wu-ti, in a unified

238

China under absolute monarchy with an omnipotent bureaucratic apparatus and with the ambition of ruling over the world by the use of military forces.

We know the appraisal of Hegel regarding Confucianism in his *Lectures on the History of Philosophy*, "Confucius is only a practical worldly man of wisdom. In his ideas there is not an iota of speculative philosophy but some kind of sophisticated moral doctrines from which however we can learn nothing special." To provide a serious answer, I shall make use of German philosophy by reducing everything to relations and showing that there existed a very high speculative philosophy hidden under apparently quite practical sayings. To study the epistemological aspect of Confucius' doctrine, as Husserl had pointed out when studying Descartes, I shall not examine the content of the sayings, but only the reasons why they were expressed.

CONFUCIUS' THOUGHTS

The key to find the reasons is in *The Analects* when the Master showed us the way to grasp a man's character: "Look at the reasons a man start from, observe the means he uses and examine the aim he wants to arrive at. In what way can a man hide his character? In what way can a man hide his character?" (II,10)

The first thing in order to grasp Confucius' character is therefore to examine *the reason why* Confucius had to express his views as we find them in *The Analects*? Confucius was the first man in Chinese history and probably in the world to open a private school and to earn his living by teaching. This fact proves he had an independent spirit, and wanted to live an independent life. To earn his living by this job, of course he had to teach students the necessary knowledge to become officials, because at his time, an intellectual could not earn his living otherwise. Knowledge was formerly taught to nobles in public schools of the government, but it was taught very scatteredly, a school taught only a discipline, in an esoteric manner. Therefore *The Book of Poetry, The Book of Documents, The Book of Music, The Book of Rites* have no relations with his doctrine. They represent the culture of ancient China.

But he had a burning conviction: To renovate his society, to bring concord and peace to everybody not by being based on an illumination from God, on a change in economy, in social organisation. He only asked governors to accept another way of governing, in which they would not lose anything regarding their interest and hierarchy. They had only to accept the conception of governing by virtue and practise of self - improvement. He did not act as a saver and did not affirm his superiority in any aspects: Intelligence, family situation, even moral virtue. He wanted to educate a new outlook, which could bring happiness to everybody while not creating great confusions. He did not ask any sacrifice from anybody. He did not point out a paradise or a future life to console anybody and uphold his cause. He did not ask men to live a superhuman or ascetic life and make use of superhuman faculties. He accepted man as the latter is, and made use of the most common human faculties. These reasons make him the most original, even the most modern philosopher of China. Unhappily, his disciples when recording his sayings had done it in a most chaotic, confused manner, which created too great losses to a most consistent, speculative thinking.

WHAT HAD CONFUCIUS DONE TOWARD THE ANCIENT CULTURE?

First, he had epitomised all ancient cultural knowledge in a few books whose assimilation becomes very easy. For example, three thousand poems were reduced to three hundred ones to give birth to *The Book of Poetry*. He had paved the way to the cultural synthesis of the Confucian tradition, the main reason for explaining the existence of Confucianism through centuries, despite political changes, as the unique inheritor of past culture, for apart from Confucianism no doctrines have ever played this role. We have to admit that the continuity of culture, very typical of China, Korea, Japan and Vietnam, compared with other regions on the earth was due to Confucianism.

Second, he had given out a new interpretation of the ancient culture. This is the contribution which makes up his doctrine. The culture of ancient China essentially dealt with relations between man and Gods, between politics and cosmogony, divination with numberless projects for seizing up the political power. It did not speak of self-improvement but only taught of techniques for practising a job (as a priest, a diviner, a scribe, a judge, a historian, a governor...).

Third, he had transformed the education for teaching different jobs into a doctrine for self-improvement to become 'gentlemen' and contribute to political renovation.

To grasp the differential feature of a doctrine, the first thing is not to examine what it contains, but to find out what it does not contain, the meaningful absence compared with other doctrines. In Confucius' doctrine there exists many absences determining his great contribution.

As a specialist of ancient Chinese culture, I am quite astonished when I in *The Analects* find no mentions of Yin - Yang, The Five Elements, the Eight Trigrams, astrology, divination, relations between man and the universe, spirits,

240

as I find in any posterior Confucian works. The unique mention on *Yi Jing* had been refuted by Qing scholars in which 'Yi' was replaced by its homonym meaning 'also'. The English translation by D.C. Lau is:

The Master said: "Grant me a few years more so that I may study at the age of fifty and I shall be free from major errors" (VII, 17).

The content of his education, according to what was recorded by his disciples is quite different form any teachers at his time.

Zi Gong said: "One can hear from the Master about his culture but one cannot hear his views on man's nature and the Way of Heaven" (V, 13). "The Master did not speak of extraordinary things, force, disorders and spiritual beings" (VII, 21).

Zi Lu asked about serving the spirits of the dead. The Master said: "We are not able even to serve men, how are we able to serve the spirits?" Zi Lu asked, "May I venture to ask about death?" The Master said: "We do not understand even life, how can we understand death" (XI, 12).

Confucius might be considered as the first agnostic in world philosophy. He often spoke about ceremonies but his attitude was pragmatic, he "respected spirits but stood afar from them".

His teaching of *The Book of Poetry* was typical of his education. This work as an anthology of popular poetry is full of myths, demons, spirits, Gods, and relations between man and Gods. But in his teaching he rejected any extraordinary things. *The Book of Poetry* though three hundred in number can be summed up in one phrase: "Don't think evil" (II, 2).

"Thinking evil" is to pay attention on superstitions. He asserted that "paying attention on superstitions is only harmful", and taught this work in a purely practical way:

The Master said: "My children, why do you not study *The Book of Poetry?* It may serve to stimulate the mind, to help you in observation, in organising a collectivity, in expressing resentment. Inside the family it helps you to serve your father, outside, it helps you to serve your lord. Moreover, you can know the names of birds, beasts and plants" (XVII, 9).

His teaching of *The Book of Rites* and *The Book of Music* was contrary to the normal education paying attention on the form:

The Master said: "People speak. It is according to rites. But rites do not merely mean silk and jade." People said: "It is according to music, it is according to music." But music does not merely mean bells and drums (XVII, 11).

Confucius taught four topics: Culture, moral conduct, doing one's best [lit. Loyalty] and confidence (VII, 25).

Different from Grecian philosophers inventing myths to assert their teaching, he annihilated any myth to draw toward human relations. We shall speak below of his teaching method.

Some sayings have been quoted to prove that Confucius only inherited Zhou gong and Zhou culture, but did not create anything. One should understand what was said by Confucius "The reasons one started from". Confucius must inevitably play the role of an imitator to live at his time. To react against society he could live as a hermit in a forest, but in so doing how could he contribute to renovate society? He had to live between concrete men to find a way to change his society. Any philosopher in an absolute society have to make concession toward his society. Had not Hegel despite his faith in the French Revolution, extolled Prussian monarchy?

The Zhou having before it the example of the two previous dynasties, is resplendent in culture. I am for the Zhou (III, 14).

Confucius sincerely admired Zhou gong who had created the Zhou dynasty built on rites, the longest one in Chinese history from 1100 BC to 256 BC. No doubt, the doctrine of Confucius has inherited much from Zhou gong. But a strong difference still existed. Confucius found in human personality the basis of a political line independent from the universe and Gods, which constitutes the consistency of the doctrine.

FIVE PREJUDICES

Before dealing on the speculative character of the doctrine, I have to refute five prejudices ascribed to it since a very long time. To be short, in contradiction to a prejudice I quote but a saying from *The Analects*, though similar sayings are many.

First prejudice: Confucius did not think of making people rich, but only thought of submission to poverty.

The Master said, "...It is a shame to be poor and humble when the state is well governed. Inversely it is a shame to be rich and honoured when the state is ill-governed"(VIII, 13).

Second prejudice: Confucius advocated absolutism.

242

Duke Ding asked whether there was a single sentence which could make a state prosperous. Confucius answered: Such an effect cannot be expressed by a single sentence. There is, however, a saying amongst men: "It is difficult to be a prince. It is not easy to be a subject either." If the ruler understands the difficulty to be a ruler, then is it not a sentence leading the state to prosperity?" Duke Ding asked whether there was there a single sentence which could lead a state to ruin. Confucius answered: "Such an effect cannot be expected from a single saying. There exists, however, a saying amongst men. I do not enjoy at all being a ruler except for the fact that nobody can go against what I say." "If what the ruler says is good and no one goes against him, good. But if what he says is not good and nobody goes against him, may there not be a sentence leading the state to ruin?" (XIII, 15)

Third prejudice: Confucius supported the policy of invading other countries.

Two disciples of Confucius wanted to help their ruler to occupy Zhuan Yu, Confucius said:

... I have heard that the head of a state or of a noble family worries not about underpopulation but about uneven distribution, not about poverty but about instability. For when distribution is even, there will not be poverty, when harmony prevails, there will not be scarcity of people, when the state is in peace there will be no rebellious upsettings. That is why if distant subjects are not submissive, one cultivates culture and moral virtue to attract them and make them content when they come... Instead, both of you propose to resort to the use of arms within the state. I am afraid that the worries of Ji-sun family (the family the disciples served) lie not in Zhuan Yu but within the walls of his palace (XVI, 1).

Fourth prejudice: His doctrine is considered as a national doctrine.

Confucius said: "The army can be deprived of its commander, but the common man cannot be deprived of his will" (IX, 26).

Never Confucius thought of popularising his doctrine to everybody, of making of it a national one. Man loves feminine beauty, riches, official standing, fame is quite natural. Only those who are resolved to become 'gentlemen' choose a different way of life and would act as models to others.

Fifth prejudice: Confucius despised women.

Shun had five officials and the Empire was well governed, King Wu said, "I have ten able persons". The Master said, "How true it is that talents are difficult to find. The Period of Tang (Yao) and Yu (Shun) was rich in talents. With a woman (probably the mother of King Wen), there were in fact only nine men" (VIII, 20).

The above prejudices were born from Confucianism, they are not found in *The Analects*.

THE SPECULATIVE CHARACTER OF THE DOCTRINE

Now, I have to show the speculative character of Confucius' doctrine. I shall closely follow the requirements of Confucius on the means he used.

This speculative character is manifest because we find in the doctrine all the requirements of a speculative philosophy, but because of the lack of an epistemological analysis on *The Analects* many contradictions have arisen in the interpretations and translations.

The first consistency consists in the existence of a unique, changeless essence. This essence is different among different philosophies. It might be, subject, conscience, Absolute Idea, God, and so on. Philosophers differ on the unique changeless essence, but are similar in asserting this unique changeless essence, in making use of this essence to interpret reality. Let us see whether in Confucius' doctrine there exists a similar unique changeless essence.

For Confucius, relations between human beings are the unique changeless essence.

Zi Zhang thought that his Master was a kind of prophet able to know the future, asked whether he can know ten generations hence. Confucius answered:

The Yin Dynasty followed the rites of the Xia. The Zhou dynasty followed the rites of the Yin. What was added and what was omitted can be known. Should there be a successor to the Zhou, even a hundred generations hence can be known (II, 23).

Some sayings look quite trivial but their philosophical value can be found by basing on the unique changeless essence:

He who by revising what is ancient knows what is new is worthy to be called a Master (II, 11).

Here, 'Master' means a philosopher like Confucius and not an ordinary teacher. If by revising what is old we know what is new, it is because there exists a changeless essence. Teaching as Confucius did, as we shall point out below, was to show the changeless essence under any changes we find in *The*

Book of Poetry, The Book of Documents.... Only a philosopher knows this teaching method.

Any person must have parents, therefore there must exist rules governing relations between children and parents. These rules make what is called 'filial piety', he must have brothers and sisters, therefore there must exists 'concession', he must have friends, therefore there must exist 'confidence'. In a society there must exist relations between superiors and inferiors based on 'loyalty', relations between members of a community based on 'confidence'. The circumstances being very various, one must have 'intelligence' to find the appropriate behaviour. The unique criterion a person has to follow in different behaviours is *'li'* (propriety). They are words and not concepts because one cannot dogmatically reduce these behaviours to unique definitions, but has to examine them concretely in concrete situations. We understand why Confucius did not give ready answers for these words, his replies differed according to different persons in different situations. When a person perfectly realises all these above relations he reaches what is called *'ren'*, whose meaning is near to benevolence, but in fact is the expression of perfect virtue.

The second consistency is expressed in the tool for grasping this changeless essence. This tool might be intelligence, reason, experimental sciences, supernatural feelings, numbers, dialectics... but a philosophy as such has to make use of a unique tool. The unique tool used by Confucius is learning by making use of senses and thinking. No doubt, senses never give us the truth, therefore after perceiving by the senses one has to think to find the changeless essence. Perceiving by the senses sometimes was called learning and reflecting to attain the changeless essence was called thinking. In his doctrine learning and thinking were the two faces of an indivisible unity. Many very profound sayings look quite common for they have not been interpreted from the epistemological viewpoint.

Confucius said to Zi Lu:

"Yu, shall I tell you what it is the meaning of knowledge?" Confucius wanted to explain the philosophical meaning of knowledge, and not to speak of a trivial topic. Then, he explained his conception on knowledge.

What you grasp by the senses [lit. you know] is called knowledge, what you do not grasp by the senses [lit. you do not know] is called unknown [lit. you do not know]. That is knowledge (II,17).

This view explains why Confucius refused to admit that he knew Gods, spirits, divination, Yin-Yang, relations between politics and the universe, When he said, "At fifty he knew the will of Heaven", it only shows that at fifty he was conscious of his limits to give up too high ambitions in his youth, a consciousness common to people over fifty.

CONFUCIUS AND LEARNING

Each doctrine has an operation to approach the truth. Buddhism speaks of the heart, many religions speak of a divine illumination...A systematic and often hard practice is necessary to lead to this operation. Confucius made use of senses, something common to anybody to attain the truth, therefore he did not ask any superhuman effort. He proposed learning, i.e. to make use of the senses then to think of relations and come to the truth.

For Confucius, learning is the aim of life, the deepest source of human pleasure. It is no accidence that *The Analects* begins by a saying on learning as a source of pleasure.

The Master said, "Is it not a pleasure to learn something and to practise it when time comes?"(I,1)

He did not ascribe to himself anything special, He differed from common people by learning without flagging and teaching without growing weary (VIII, 34).

This learning bears philosophical features different from the ordinary conception on learning:

First, one should learn from everybody. Everybody is one's master. If somebody walks with two persons, one has already found one's teachers:

The Master said: "When we walk along with two others, they may serve us as our teachers. We will select their good qualities and follow them, their bad qualities to correct in ourselves" (VII, 27).

Second, in learning we must have the mind in a complete blank. Despite his great erudition, Confucius said:

Do I possess knowledge? No, I do not. When a mean person asked me, my mind was a completely blank. I kept hammering at the two sides of the question to exhaust it (IX, 8).

There were four things from which the Master was entirely free: Predicted conclusions, arbitrary predetermination, obstinacy, egoism (IX, 8).

Only a philosopher has this kind of learning. And his teaching was that of a philosopher: He did not give out the answer, the answer should be drawn out after the disciple had examined the relations. Truth lies in human· heart, everybody has to find it for himself.

I do not enlighten anyone who was not eager to get knowledge, or is not anxious to know. When I have pointed out a corner (of a square) to someone and the latter does not give out the three remaining corners, I do not repeat my lesson (VII, 7).

His teaching is therefore quite different from stuffing pupils with knowledge, learning by heart, in the manner of Confucianism. One must acknowledge this is a modern way, reserved to the most competent teachers.

Third, learning decides of anything, a truth which is evident only in the post-industrial era.

The Master said: "Yu, have you heard about the six qualities and the six errors?" Yu answered, "Not yet." "Sit down and I shall tell you, the Master said." "To love benevolence without loving learning is liable to foolishness. To love wisdom without loving learning is liable to deviate from the right path. To love confidence without loving learning is liable to lead to harmful behaviour. To love straightforwardness without loving learning is liable to be rude. To love courage without loving learning is liable to be insubordinate. To love firmness without loving learning is liable to be undisciplined" (XVII, 8).

Fourth, learning is not only a way to get profits. No doubt, when learning one has the aim to become an official, but the duty of an official is to bring concord to society and not to be rich. On the contrary, the greatest happiness must be found in learning. Learning brings us an inner peace which can dissipate any worries:

The Master said: "I often spent the whole day without eating and the whole night without sleeping, buried in thoughts, but it was of no use. The better way is to learn" (XV, 31).

Fifth, when by learning one knows the Way, the aim of one's life is reached:

The Master said: "He has not live in vain who dies in the evening after being told about the Way in the morning" (IV,7).

Sixth, when reaching the utmost degree in learning one could grasp the all-pervading unity to bind together all knowledge.

The Master said: "Zi do you think that I have learnt many things and keep them in memory?" Zi Gong answered: "Yes, I do. Is it not so?" The Master answered, "No, I have an all pervading unity" (XV.3).

We see that *The Analects* is an exhaustible source for speculation.

UNITY IN MAN

The third consistency consists of finding the all-pervading unity in man, even in the humblest man Confucius has to start from a common need of anybody. That is *'shu'* which is the starting point of his philosophy.

Confucius said: "Shen [Cengzi's name]. My doctrine has an one-pervading unity". Cengzi replied, "Yes." The Master went out, the other disciples asked, "What did he mean?" Cengzi answered, "The doctrine of our Master consists in doing one's best [lit. *Zhong*] and in taking oneself as a measure to gauge others [lit, *shu*]. That is all" (IV,15).

The meaning of *'shu'* was given by Confucius himself:

Zi Gong asked: "Is there a single word which can be a guide throughout one's life?" The Master said, "Probably, it is the word *'shu'*. Do not do to others what you would not like being done to yourself" (XV, 24).

"What one wants for oneself, one should do to others, what one does not want for oneself one should not do to others." Probably any language has a similar maxim and there is no denying that this need is universal. The differential feature of Confucius' doctrine is it focuses on this universal truth. For Confucius, a man has to save himself, he cannot wait salvation from anything else. Man has therefore to find the key to self-salvation in the common need of mankind.

THE CORE OF THE DOCTRINE

But it is so difficult to realise this common need for oneself and for others, because anybody is carried away by bodily desires, wealth, beauty, high station, power, fame...and anybody easily performs acts for his own selfish interests. Has human history not proved that this truth, though existing in human mind, has never been implemented? To realise this truth, therefore, there must exist four different steps constituting the fourth consistency.

The first step is to formalise it in concrete rules, called *'li'* evident to anybody. The second step is to transform *li* into a governing principle called 'Rectification of names'. The third step is to form men different from the common people, called *'gentlemen'*, adopting and upholding the doctrine. They must adopt a line for self-improvement to bring concord and peace to society by their own examples in words and actions. The fourth step is a political line based on confidence and virtue.

Now, I have to examine each step one by one. My epistemological interpretation may have points not fully in accordance with the tradition.

What is the focus of the doctrine? Researchers have told that it is *'ren'* (benevolence). I don't think so, benevolence is the ideal the gentleman aims at, but this gentleman must have a concrete criterion to reach the ideal. I think the focus is *'li'*. This word has been translated by 'rites' as we find in works ascribed to Zhou gong, and Zhou gong used the word with a meaning expressing the formal aspect. Confucius sometimes used the word with this meaning, especially when he criticised somebody for having violated the rites reserved to the emperor or to the king. The philosophical meaning of *'li'* does not lie in the form but in the content expressing "the conformance with the concrete situation from the requirement of making oneself as a gauge". From *'shu'* to *'li'* we have but one unique content, but on the one hand *'shu'* speaks of the feeling in the human mind, and on the other side *'li'* speaks of the adapted form for everybody to express this feeling. The translation by 'propriety' would be appropriate. I think that Xun Zi is right when making of *'li'* the content of Confucius' doctrine, though his interpretation is somewhat near to law. But between 'propriety' and just laws, answering human mind, relations are organic.

In the following sayings, *'li'* does not mean 'rites' but 'propriety'.

Yan Yuan asked Confucius about benevolence. The Master said: "To overcome the self and follow propriety means benevolence. If for one day a man can follow propriety through overcoming himself, then the whole Empire would return to benevolence. Benevolence depends on oneself alone, and not on others." Yen Yuan said, "I beg you to show the steps." The Master said, "Don't look at what is contrary to propriety, don't listen to what is contrary to propriety, don't speak what is contrary to propriety, don't do any movement which is contrary to propriety" (XII,1).

We see with a surprising clarity that 'propriety' is the unavoidable criterion. Confucius makes use of 'propriety' to reach 'benevolence' when dealing on self-improvement, but when speaking of governing a state, he starts from propriety to initiate the theory of "name rectification". To use modern terms, he asks that laws, and men exercising laws, should follow human heart and the concrete situation. I don't understand why this viewpoint is in contradiction to the modern conception maintaining the observance of laws and to the revolutionary viewpoint of the mass standpoint. Legalists had absolutised 'rites' by rejecting human mind to serve absolutism and military expansion. But nothing proves we cannot maintain the form and content when following democracy and socialism.

Only when we have recognised the importance of 'propriety' we know why Confucius did not give out strict definitions regarding the content of the words 'filial piety', 'concession', 'loyalty', 'confidence', 'righteousness', 'benevolence'.., like Greece philosophers. From a methodological viewpoint, Greece philosophers started from an unprovable axiom like God, Absolute Goodness, Absolute Truth, as the basis of their speculations. This way cannot be accepted as logical for it starts from an unknown premise beyond human knowledge. Confucius starts from the self, which may be known, though this knowledge might be very difficult, he therefore asks that these words must be appropriate to the concrete situation. That is why he can point out practical requirements to be followed for the implementation. Three requirements prove necessary:

First, they should be appropriate to each man and each concrete situation, i.e. to 'the opportunity';

Second, there should exist reciprocity or conditions to be implemented. He does not absolutise any word and does not ask an one-sided behaviour;

Third, He asked a measure, i.e. the golden mean.

Supreme indeed is the mean as a moral virtue. For quite a long time, it has not been practised among the people (VI.27).

Zi Gong asked, "Who is superior Shi or Zhang?" The Master said, "Shi goes beyond the mean, and Zhang does not come up to it", Zi Gong said. "Then is Shi in fact better?" The Master answered, "To go beyond is as wrong as to fall short" (XI,16).

Starting from the senses, making use of thinking to know oneself and to come to the one-pervading unity by accepting oneself as a gauge, then coming to 'propriety' in behaviour, to 'rectification of names' in government, the consistency is of surprising clarity. Unhappily, 'rectification of names' has ever been separated from 'propriety' and 'making oneself as a gauge', that is why the doctrine becomes utopian and diffuse. The following passage is very typical:

250

Zi Lu asked, "If the ruler of Wei confers the government to you, what would you do first?" The Master said, "If it be so, probably the first thing is to rectify names."

The answer astonished Zi Lu, it looked quite utopian. Zi Lu said:

"Is this so? Why are you so utopian? Why is rectification of names necessary?"

The answer of Confucius not only applied to Zi Lu, it applies also to us after more than two thousand years:

Yu, how rustic you are! A gentleman, in regard to where he is ignorant, keeps a cautious attitude. When names are not correct, words will not be in accordance with the truth, when words are not in accordance with the truth, affairs will not be carried out with success. When affairs cannot be carried out with success, rites and music will not flourish. When rites and music do not flourish, punishments will not be properly awarded. When punishments are not properly awarded, the people will not know where to put hand and foot. That is why when a gentleman names something, the name must be appropriate, when he says something this is sure to be practicable. A gentleman thinks above all to be cautious in speech (XIII, 3).

In modern meaning, the first thing is that every official should be worthy of his position and laws should be appropriate to reality and human mind. Why can't such a government bring concord to society?

GOVERNANCE

When rectification of names has been carried out, one can speak of three topics: First, confidence considered as the basis for safeguarding the country. Good examples as a means for attracting the people, virtue as a new governing principle. This is the fifth consistency.

Different from politicians advocating politics based on intrigues, schemes, ploys, Confucius speaks of confidence:

Zi Gong asked about politics. The Master said: "The people must have food, arms and confidence." Zi Gong asked. "If one had to give up one of these three, which should you give up first?" The master said, "Give up arms". Zi Gong asked, "If one had to give up one of the remaining two, which of them should be given up first?" The Master answered, "Give up food. Death is common to men, but when the people has no confidence a state cannot stand up" (XII, 9).

The governor should set himself as an example to the people. Zi Lu asked about government.

The Master said: "Set yourself as an example and be laborious in your affairs". Zi Lu asked for more. The Master said: "Don't slacken in your efforts"(XIII, 1).

When rectification of names has been carried out and governors has set themselves as examples, government by virtue could be reached:

The Master said: "Guide them by laws, keep them in line by punishments, people will try to avoid trouble but have no sense of shame. Guide them by virtue, keep them in line with the rules of propriety, then they will have a sense of shame and reform themselves" (II, 3).

SOCIETY IN PEACE AND CONCORD

Now we can speak of the aim Confucius wanted to arrive at. His aim is to create a society based on peace and concord. The summing up is not found in *The Analects* but in *The great Learning*. I leave the word to the father of Chinese Revolution, Sun Yatsen:

We think that recently European and American countries are very progressive. But their culture is not so perfect as our political philosophy. China has a very systematic saying on political philosophy, no foreign great philosophers have ever so clearly seen and spoken. This is the saying in *The Great Learning: Ge wu, zhi zhi,* heart rectification, thought sincerity, self-improvement, family regulation, state government, concord of empire. No foreign politicians has ever seen, or formulated a so developed, sophisticated theory. This is the special treasure in our political philosophy to be preserved (*The Principles of the People,* Lecture 5).

Explanations on the conceptions 'Ge wu, zhi zhi' have been lost. Later on scholars came up with different interpretations. As a professional translator, I find that the interpretations are not appropriate. Zhu Xi translate it "carrying our knowledge to the utmost extent, with the desire that there may be nothing which it shall not embrace" and that by Wang Yangming says, "exterminating material desires to attain the enlightened conscience". They are both too difficult to grasp, far beyond the normal abilities and moreover, no sayings in *The Analects* remind us of these formulations. According to me 'ge wu' will be "to approach objects by the senses" synonymous with 'learning' (in the *Book of Documents*, chapter I, we find this meaning for *ge* for a light reaching the four

252

directions) and 'zhi zhi' will be "to come to the one-pervading unity" expressed by the word 'shu'.

Thus, the eight principles constituting the consistency of the doctrine are:

First, approaching the objects by the senses (learning).

Second, attaining the one-unifying knowledge (utmost thinking).

Third, reaching the unity between one's mind and the people's mind (heart rectification).

Fourth, reaching sincerity in any desires and reflections (or thought sincerity).

Fifth, cultivating one's personality to set an example for others (self-improvement).

Sixth, self-improvement can bring concord to the family (family regulation).

Seventh, the concord in the family will enable us to carry out concord in the state (state government).

Eight, when a state has a resplendent culture, it will attract other states and bring concord to the Empire (Empire concord).

CONCLUSION

My article only deals with the consistency and speculative character of Confucius' doctrine. It deals neither with its changes when it became Confucianism nor on its appropriateness or non-appropriateness to our present time. Nevertheless, its existence among a third of human beings through two thousand years, despite some distortions, remains a value keeping in with the requirements of this symposium, not only of Asia but of the whole mankind, in the present era when Asia has to know of the world and the world has to know of Asia. I hope that *The Analects* would be rearranged in a consistent manner with consistent interpretations to avoid misunderstandings as we have witnessed these two thousand years. In this era of universal tolerance and concord on the basis of culture, one must pay attention to the first philosopher upholding concord and tolerance on the planet on the basis of culture, the unique example in world's philosophy as far as I know.

National Consciousness of some Asian Countries on their Road towards Global Integration - An Approach from the Standpoint of Vietnamese Tradition

Dang Thanh Le
Hanoi National University

The medieval history of the four Asian countries and development of their national consciousness

It is common knowledge that the two factors that are required of a nation that participates in the global integration process are seemingly opposite: A strong national character and a broad humanistic outlook. With this as a starting point, this paper attempts to study the national consciousness of the Vietnamese people and that of other peoples of similar cultures in the Asian region: The Chinese, Korean and Japanese, in order to see how significant it is when these peoples become a part of the globalisation trend.

The rather early beginning of the medieval period in Asia, with the emergence of many states with vast territory and strong vitality, like China, Korea, Japan and Vietnam, gave rise to their marked national character and national consciousness.

China, a large and populous country with a history of more than 3500 years and a great culture, is among those countries that rank at the top in contributions to the history of mankind's civilisation. China began its medieval history very early with its establishment as the most powerful feudal country in Asia. As early as the second century BC, its territory had become vast with such a situation where, say, the Five Lords then Seven Heroes each reigned each in a locality. In 221 BC, China became a unified feudal country for the first time under Qin Suihuang, who claimed himself to be Emperor, 'The Celestial Son'. Backed by many famous individuals, Qin Suihuang managed to control his country in a unified way in many aspects. The historian Zi Matian gave a rather good generalisation of the unified culture and technology of the Chinese society under the Qin dynasty: "Same writing script, wheel axles of the same length." During his reign, Qin Suihuang also unified laws and all units of measurement.

In the cultural field, ancient China left medieval China a great scientific, philosophical, historical and literary heritage. In the period between the 8th and 2nd centuries BC, Confucius and Mencius constructed a Confucian philosophical system - the theoretical foundation for socio-political organisation institutions and spiritual institutions in the feudal society. Lao Zi was considered the greatest Chinese philosopher. His sucessor, Zhuang Tze, introduced the Chinese philosophical influence to Europe. After the Chinese philosophers' period came the period of Chinese men of letters. *In Dialogue Between Goethe and Eckermann*, Eckermann recalled:

"In your absence", Goethe said, "I did a lot of reading. Especially there's a Chinese novel that always makes me think of it again as it deserves my special attention."

"A novel?" I asked, "it must be a very unique one."

"Not exactly as one may think", Goethe replied. "Those people think and feel nearly the same way we do, and we may immediately realise that we are like them."

"But", I said, "perhaps it is one of their special books?"

"Absolutely not", Goethe said, "the Chinese have thousands of books like this and they even had them when our ancestors still lived in jungles."

With such a great history, the assumption that the later feudal arrivals in the region like Vietnam, Korea and Japan adopted these Chinese foundations in the making of their 'nationalist' feudal states is plausible. However as Fernand Braudel stated, "A nation can only exist at the expense of its constant search for its identity" (Fernand Braudel, 1902-1985). Countries like Korea, Japan and Vietnam, with their long history of relationships with other nations, including the great powers, have constantly reaffirmed and enhanced their national identity. It is because of this that Vietnam and Korea, after about a thousand-year long period under Chinese invasion and domination, still retain their respective national territory, language and culture, while at the same time adopting some Chinese cultural values.

The history of the making and development of the medieval Korean nation and its national consciousness is based on a different foundation. Like Vietnam, the Korean people's patriotic tradition was tempered throughout a long history of struggle against foreign invasion by China, Mongolia, Manchuria and Japan, from the 2nd Century BC to mid-20th Century. Besides, Korea is a country with a rather mono-ethnic and monolingual society, a country almost without the 'ethnic minorities', with the exception that there are about 30,000 Chinese who settled there a very long time ago and have been living there ever since.

255

The Koreans speak and write a single unified language, which constitutes a firm foundation for a strong national consciousness and a profound national identity for this country of 'calm morning'.

Japan's history is different from those of other East Asian countries. Owing to many factors including the geographical one, Japan enjoyed freedom from being a dependent country in medieval time, and a colony in modern times, as were Vietnam, Korea and China. Japan, however, has also experienced many ups and downs in its history, including a big glory in the Tokugawa period through to tragedy after World War II, when this country needed "national self-criticism". However, this is a country with a vigorous "inner force" as testified by history, a "majestic and violent nature", a fine and strong cultural tradition, a taciturn yet dynamic and flexible way of life, a country that has created for itself a unique image, ability and discipline, owing to which it has endeavoured to become a modern economic power of Asia and of the world as a whole.

Observation on values and limits of medieval Asia

Early emergence of medieval Asia

A comparison can be made between medieval Asia on the one hand and Europe and Africa on the other. It is common knowledge that the emergence of the feudal society in Western Europe (with the end of the ancient Western Roman Empire in 476 AD) took place after that in China.

A comparison with Africa gives rise to many interesting scientific hypotheses and findings. The fact that many Asian countries have now successfully freed themselves from the colonial yoke, while in many African countries, civil wars and wars between neighbouring countries are still going on, has led to an observation that in some areas of Africa there still exists a tribal way of life. Jean Suret-Canale remarks: "Primarily, these state mechanisms, inherited from the colonial state mechanisms, are just an instrument of foreign domination and exploitation." Bernard Founon emphasised the above situation in his article entitled "Africa: a lack of state". So, is Africa "a problem of civilisation?" Can we speak of "a special African mode of production" as did Karl Marx, with "an Asian mode of production"?

With the emergence of the feudal society in Asia, the medieval civilisation came into existence at a rather early date and reached its somewhat full development, especially in Eastern Asia with the four countries of China, Korea, Japan and Vietnam having similar cultures.

256

With a mature system of social institutions, the region has established a system of glorious cultural values that can be preserved and developed in the modern time, in the context of global integration. It is also in Asia that three major centres came into being at the dawn of mankind's culture, namely India, China and the Arab Muslim world. The great culture of ancient and medieval China gave mankind great philosophers, political thinkers, social students and religious thinkers, such as Lao Zi-Zhuang Tze's Philosophy, Confucianism, Mo Tze Thought and Buddhism.

The patriotic tradition, national consciousness and national concept, the humanity tradition and sense of friendship and collective spirit, all constitute an ideology that has created a great strength for these four countries in particular, and all of Asia in general, to surmount all big obstacles to retain their existence.

There exist now, and will continue to do so trivial opinions among scientists in their quest for theories and explanations of Asian potentials and Asian values. However, what has been found with regard to the realistic significance of the concept on Confucianism-based family organisation institutions, the universal value of the spirit of love of Buddhism, the rational dialectic spirit of Lao Zi and the ideal of a universal society of Mo Tze school, are all Asian values and potentials that are capable of contributing to human development.

On a slow decline

History has shown that many European feudal states had only a thousand years existence, while some medieval Asian countries existed for as long as 20 centuries. Many Asian countries will have to pay for the price of the lagging of the "Asian mode of production". Although China has been named "land of discoveries and inventions", and "foreteller of modern science", and "a civilisation that originated the modern world", this top-ranking Asian country still carries the burden of its former emperors and empresses, from Qin Suihuang to Dowager Empress Cixi and Puyi.

Beside the reactionary forces of the medieval mode of economic production and the centralised totalitarianism of the emperors and empresses and the ruling feudal aristocrats that affected these Asian countries, there were also great limits imposed by a culture that was deeply influenced by Confucianism. Some values even contain an anti-value element. The Asian national and community spirits, therefore, need adjustment to become balanced and harmonious with individual emancipation. In his textbook entitled Luan Ngu used at a tertiary level course in sinology (1965-1968), Professor Cao Xuan Huy quoted Zenker as saying that Confucius made "a discovery of the personality". In Luan Ngu it is also maintained that to some extent Confucius

257

succeeded in discovering the 'personality' when he commented on the personal character of each of his close disciples like Zi Lu, Fan Ci and so on. But these positive aspects of early feudal society could not have developed in the context of the development of an institution built on the foundation of a totalitarian monarchy.

Europe used to be a 'leader' in emancipation of the individual. The Renaissance started and the 1789 bourgeois Revolution in France accomplished this glorious mission with "La couverté de l'individu". In Asia, for many objective and subjective reasons, community consciousness and the national spirit were brought into full play in the history of their national defence and construction. This is fully justifiable, since many Asian countries in the 18th and 19th centuries and afterward had to confront the attack from Western imperialism, whose scientific and military strength was as big as its ambition for conquest and exploitation. In that context, the strength, will and capability of the entire national community had to be highly mobilised. This reality, together with Confucius ideology, brought about the emergence of collectivism and egalitarianism in some Asian countries. It is worth noting that in an ideological system of two Germans, Marx and Engels, also referred to "the unique and free development of the individual because it is based on a correct concept: Society is the link of individuals".

What is mentioned above are just examples. To study 'Asian values' in a 'comparative context' is a comprehensive approach, because the Orient, the Occident, Asia, Europe, America and Africa, while contributing their potentials to the future, have certain limitations, besides values, within their respective regions and their respective historical and cultural traditions.

National and human consciousness in the Vietnamese tradition and the ability for contributing to regional and global integration

This is a comprehensive topic that requires an inter-disciplinary study. In this paper, the author only touches upon some limited issues and mainly as an introductory study.

There may be a preliminary observation that from its early days up to the present time, Vietnam has had a rather long and special history of foreign relations. History has shown that this small country has had a relationship with many big powers, including some superpowers. In this long history, from the birth to the fall of an independent feudal country and into modern times, all changes were made with "historical surprises", with alien factors playing an important role. It is because of this that Vietnam, having gone through late last century (when European-Asian relations were between the invader and the invaded), to late this century (when international relations are gradually becoming characteristic of dialogue, tolerance and acceptance for co-development), has now had a "treasure of experience in foreign relations". History has prepared Vietnam with experience gained at the expense of tears and blood of innumerable Vietnamese generations. This treasure was also created from intelligence, bravery and hearts full of love and altruism, the dignity and the soul of the Vietnamese.

From racial discrimination and 'sole egoism' to foreignism

Right from the early days when the Vietnamese began to make cross-border contacts, they met many big, strong and cruel enemies. The Chinese feudal ruling class in the past, with their 'sole egoism', always considered their southern neighbours barbarous and weak countries. It seems that there was a natural psychological reaction as an inevitable defensive reaction that there arouse such concepts as Great Viet (also Great Korea) beside the Great Han.

The second confrontation was against a distant enemy with special military, technical, economic, cultural and scientific strengths that were centuries more advanced than those of Asia. From confrontation with a big power in the mid-19th century (France), Vietnam 'advanced' to the confrontation of a superpower (the USA) in the mid- 20th century.

All the above compulsory 'integrations' brought about the thought of racial discrimination. But it is because of these 'fire sparkling' encounters with these three big countries that the Vietnamese national ability was enhanced. The Vietnamese people's epic became resounding in their counter-attacks, with all their patriotism, their fighting spirit and their intelligence, against the Chinese and their arrows, the French and their guns and the Americans and their war planes and rockets.

Apart from the above traditions, the human consciousness, the human feeling and the tolerance also constitute the Vietnamese national identity. With its own strength, the Vietnamese nation has established its historical position in its relationship with neighbouring China. As they have established their own ability and identity, the Vietnamese people can be in a position and are capable of adopting foreign cultures, to enrich their national one. Past history has also shown that Vietnam is able to go beyond the narrow-minded nationalism and monologue for their national development.

The author has more than once quoted some foreigners observing the openness and tolerance of the Vietnamese people. One of these was an Italian priest named Cristoforo Borri who said after his first contacts with the Vietnamese in Binh Dinh in 1618 - 1623:

It is because of their lovely and amicable character that the Vietnamese in Dang Trong (now Central Vietnam) are kind to foreigners. In their eyes, they accept that each individual may have his own way of life and dress himself in the way he likes. They praised foreigners' dress style, and with a very polite attitude, they expressed their appreciation of the doctrines of these foreigners and gave them a higher status than theirs.

Many other researchers also gave observations on the religious tolerance demonstrated in Vietnamese religious history. This fascinating issue is worth further study.

It is a tradition of many Asian countries, including Vietnam, to combine patriotism and national consciousness with the spirit of humanity and a tolerant and open attitude, as they have gone beyond narrow-minded nationalism, doctrinal discrimination and religious discrimination, which were a result of the past situation when they had to face constant foreign schemes for their annihilation.

By adopting the spirit of Confucianism, "As for Confucius, man is, first of all, a social living being, and unity is the guiding principle of community life", the Vietnamese people have, since time immemorial, mastered the immense love-orientation of Buddhism, "Buddha understands the sea of sufferings of man and there is no one on the sides of the great river of India who can speak of these sufferings in a more merciful tone."

But it is the life of man who experiences all the making and the defending of the nation that constitutes the basic foundation on which these qualities are tempered. The tradition of ancient time – "the beautiful childhood of mankind", the struggle and the conquest of nature, the defeat of hostile forces in the society that existed for a long time in "the long medieval night" in the Asian region including Vietnam - have contributed to the existence of the love for fellow countrymen and the whole of mankind. The clear-sightedness without any racial, doctrinal or religious discrimination not only originated from the 'Oriental philosophy' of scholars, but also from the common folk's practical mindedness. The fierce struggle for survival has given them a delicate and sharp common sense which is as correct as some Vietnamese folk sayings: "Knowing others, knowing ourselves", and "At home, mother ranks first and daughter second. But outdoors, many other women look prettier".

In wars and confrontations, the Asian and Vietnamese spirit of humanity persisted in integration for peace, happiness and development. They are sure to grow.

Acquirement of Oriental and Western Legal Values with Regard to the development of Vietnam's Legal Ideologies

Dao Tri Uc & Le Minh Thong
Institute of State and Law, NCSSH

ORIENTAL VALUES IN VIETNAM'S LAWS

Throughout its long history, the development of Vietnam legal ideologies was influenced and governed by Oriental and Western law ideologies. Generations of Vietnamese, braving the ups and downs of history, knew how to win over the ideological and cultural values in general and legal ideologies in particular - from the nations having their historical relations with Vietnam - with the purpose of building their own national character for the sake of survival and development.

The interaction between Vietnam traditional values and Oriental and Western values in the sphere of law took place in history as result of really paradoxical reasons. *First,* it was the imposition of legal viewpoints and ideologies by an invading country upon an enslaved one. Throughout a millennium of northern [Chinese] dependence, various feudal dynasties of ancient China imposed on Vietnam their legal ideologies as well as their system of law and practices. In the century of domination, the French colonialists also imposed on Vietnam the ideologies of the French legal system. *Secondly,* the acquirement of values from nations having their relations with Vietnam, these values were propagated in Vietnam to create an important ideological basis for the formation of Vietnamese legal values in each specific stage of history.

When studying Vietnamese law, researchers often come to the conclusion that Vietnam's feudal laws were deeply influenced by those from China. As a matter of fact, the influence of Chinese feudal laws on feudal Vietnam in the past took place on two aspects: Ideology itself and the system of law regulations by various dynasties, and legal ideologies and the consciousness of the Vietnam feudal dynasties, governed by Confucian ideology. Since the 12th century, Confucianism was received by the contemporary feudal class as ideological basis for the building of State and laws. Confucian values strongly governed the orientation in law building and content of the Le dynasty. In the 15th century, the penal laws of Le dynasty expressed a Confucian-oriented legal system. By regulations of the law, the kings of Le dynasty wanted to transform the society along the Confucian lines. 'Loyalty-to-the-king' viewpoints such as "Right name decides on the Fate", "Three mainstays of social order", and "Five basic virtues" were clearly expressed in the formulation of Vietnam feudal laws about social relations.

Among the five sorts of relationship: King to subject, husband to wife, father to son, brother to brother, and friend to friend, the first three relations were the most basic ones defined by Confucianism as "Three mainstays of social order". These were three major components for any other relationship: "The King to use civility in issuing his orders to subjects; the subject to preach loyalty in worshipping the King" *(Analects, Eight seclusions 19)*; "The King must behave like King, subject like subject, father like father, and son like son" *(Analects, Nhan Uyen 11)*. The "Three mainstays of social order" relationship was institutionalised into rules to be defended by the law. To defend the King-Subject relationship, Vietnam feudal laws elevated the King's position to supreme power and reverence. Any infringement on the interest of the State with the King as head might be seen as disloyalty and could be severely punished by the law. Among the ten big crimes considered as the most dangerous, 5 of them (betrayal, high treason, lack of respect, rebellion, disloyalty) were seen as infringement on the King-Subject relations, conspiring against the dynasty's security. In the "Royal court penal laws", a whole chapter containing 47 articles was reserved to the "Royal guards" whose purpose was the absolute defence of the King's life, body and ownership. Any illegal action such as trespassing in the Royal ancestors' temple, Royal citadel or palaces (articles 50-56) punishable by death in the guillotine.

Besides the law regulations adjusting the King-Subject relationship in the spirit of Confucianism, Vietnam's feudal laws had many other statutes and regulating family relations between husband and wife, father and son, all of which was deeply influenced by Confucian spirit regarding family governance. The laws institutionalised the position of women to depend on men: In the family, the daughter must obey her father; the wife must obey her husband; and the widow must obey her son. Article 360 of the Royal court penal laws compelled the husband to divorce his wife should the woman commit what was called "the end of righteousness" (including seven points: Not giving birth to a child, being lustful, not worshipping the husband's parents, being garrulous, thieving, being jealous, having an infirmity). A wife who beats her husband might be punished of detention (Article 481), but a husband who beats his wife was only punished three times less than the case of causing injury to some other people (Article 482).

The regulations of marriage and family by Vietnam's feudal laws were in fact the institutionalisation of the Confucian ideas with its principle of "managing the family - governing the country - pacifying the world". Many norms and regulations of the Le dynasty in its royal court's penal laws were the very expression of Confucian ethics and morals. Crimes such as 'undutiful', 'disloyal', 'cruel', and 'traitorous' figured among the ten big crimes defined by the Royal court's penalty laws. Institutionalising the ethics of filial piety in children, the Ly dynasty defined for children several obligations such as: Not being allowed to sue their parents (Article 511); being forced to conceal any sin committed by the parents (Article 504); and to bear punishment by rod beatings in place of their parents (A. 38).

In fact, legal ideologies in Vietnam feudal dynasties were not only influenced by Confucian religious doctrines in shaping up their Confucius-oriented legal systems, they were also influenced by the ideologies of the law-makers. Feudal dynasties made the law a tool for the consolidation of the King's power. In 1464 for instance, trying to strengthen his royal power, King Le Thanh Tong said: "The law is the public rule of the State, so everyone has to implement it, remember..."[1]

In the law-makers' ideology, the law went hand in hand with reward and punishment. According to Han Phi, "the law is the root of the King whereas punishment is the clue to compassion" *(Han Phi Tu - Eight Degrees)*. Imbued with that law-making ideology, many Kings of the Le dynasty unceasingly developed and consolidated all those laws that had been created by their predecessors and previous dynasties. King Le Hien Tong, successor of King Le Thanh Tong, was constantly concerned with the correct and prompt implementation of laws. From what he conceived, the settlement of lawsuits was most important of all as people's life was endangered. He ordered all lawsuits to be urgently tried in the first year of his reign. King Le Hien Tong constantly paid attention to the selection of local mandarins and the rejection of those who were incapable. In 1499, he reformed the Court department - a

---

[1] *Comprehensive history of the Greater Viet land*, p. 785.

justice agency which originally belonged to the "Guards in brocade dress" - into an independent agency. Military mandarins in the department were replaced by civilians whose main functions were to try criminals for penal offences.

In traditional Vietnam society, enforcement of justice was the key point for the State and people to get closer to each other. Any injustice could easily create discontent, even rebellion, among the population. According to the rule by law, it was not the task of the King to attach special attention to ethics for his self-improvement but that of clearly defining the law and having it proclaimed for everyone to know and implement. The purpose of penal law was to use penalty for punishing the law-breaker. Under this viewpoint, Vietnam feudal laws, especially those in the Ly dynasty, gave prominence to penal law, the important place which was reserved to punishment system.

From the influence of Chinese feudal laws, Vietnam feudal laws, especially those of the Ly dynasty, had applied the Tang dynasty's five-penalties system to punish those who committed offences. The five-penalties system comprise: Reprimand, rod beating, deportation, detention and death (Art. 1 - Royal court penal law) were seen as hard punishments. The same was slightly modified in the Le dynasty since rod beating was considered barbarous, as it caused painful physical injuries to the victim, staining the latter's honour and dignity.

The influence of Oriental legal ideologies on Vietnam feudal dynasties was also defined in another aspect: Imitation of Chinese feudal laws in Vietnam feudal laws. Laws in the Ly and Tran dynasties, especially those of the Le dynasty's Royal court penal code were largely imitation of those from the Chinese Tang and Ming dynasties. Later, the Gia Long penal code was also another imitation of the Tsing dynasty's penal code.

Notwithstanding the influence of Confucian ideologies, the rules by law-makers or the imitation of Chinese feudal dynasties' penal code, should by no means be understood as Vietnam's feudal dynasties lost their own character. Vietnam feudal dynasties, in building their own legal system, knew how to acquire the Chinese legal ideologies, methods and contents of the penal code to be applied to the reality of Vietnam, conforming to the local character, its socio-economic development level, culture, tradition, psychology, customs and habits. Such selected acquirement without mechanically copying the legal values of Chinese culture created a real Vietnamese legal system that expressed the nation's features. By comparing with the penal codes of Tang and Ming dynasties, it was found that the 722 articles of the (Vietnam) Royal court penal

264

code contained 261 articles borrowed from the Tang dynasty penal code and 53 other articles from the Ming dynasty penal code. Thus 408 articles of the Royal court penal code were unique to the laws of Le dynasty and had not been borrowed from any law of any other country.

In structure, the Le dynasty penal code was different from that of the Tang dynasty. The Tang dynasty penal code comprised 500 articles divided into 12 chapters. The Le dynasty penal code, for its part, was made of 722 articles divided into 13 chapters. Comparing the arrangement and the name of different chapters in these two penal codes, it was found that 6 chapters of the Le dynasty penal code did not figure in that of the Tang dynasty (namely in chapters regarding offences against the system, administration, land and property, in supplementary articles on land and property, inheritance, adultery, etc). Prof. Insun Yu was of the opinion that

The imitation and copy of China law system by the Le dynasty had a specific aspect and its own character. It was of great importance for us to understand the traditional Vietnam society. On one hand, the law makers of the Le dynasty followed the Chinese legal system, on the other, they combined it to their own conditions. [2]

In the process of law promulgation, Vietnam's feudal dynasties selectively acquired ideologies and laws from the Chinese feudal states while taking as their basis the national features to be adjusted to their own social relations in an appropriate way. Thus, the acquirement and borrowing of Chinese feudal laws by Vietnam's feudal dynasties constituted a lively picture reflecting the Vietnamese life and society at each stage of its history. The content of feudal laws, especially that of the Le dynasty, were strongly embued with its national character. It was especially so in those regulations related to family or human rights. For example, the laws of Le dynasty defended the legitimate rights of women in their marriage relations. A girl who was engaged but her marriage never happened was allowed to sue at the mandarin's office for returning all offerings in case the boy was infirm, was a criminal or was ruining properties (Article 322). When a man and a woman were married, the husband could lose his wife if he left her untouched for a period of 5 months; this period could be prolonged to one year if the wife had given birth to a child. The law was not applied to those on assignment as mandarin working away from home. A

---

[2] Insun Yu: *Law and Vietnam society in 17th, 18th centuries*. Hanoi Social

Sciences Publishing House, 1994, p. 78.

husband who deserted his wife could be tried of perjury if he tried to hamper her remarriage with somebody else (Article 308). Many regulations were made to defend the rights and interests of women. For example, girls were entitled to the same inheritance as boys were; wives were entitled to get divorce; all measures that expressed a traditional respect for women in Vietnam. This was in utter opposition to the ideology of Chinese Confucianism, which preached "respect for men and contempt for women". The laws of Le dynasty did not see as 'undutiful' any act by children to have their own properties or live away from their parents while the latter were still alive. This also meant that there was a considerable difference between Vietnam and Chinese families.

In spite of being influenced by Chinese feudal legal ideologies and models, the various Vietnam feudal dynasties refused to have their laws 'sinicised'. What was characteristics of Vietnam was constantly affirmed in its penal codes from one time to another: Its traditional character being the love for people.

The love for people in Vietnam nation was not simply a magnanimous deed of respect and compassion for people in the Ly and Tran royal dynasties; it expressed a resplendent development of legal regulations in the penal laws of the Le royal dynasty. This has been assessed by the historian Phan Huy Chu as "an example of country governance, a rule of conduct for administration over the people".[3]

Today, at any time when dealing with the heritage in terms of Vietnam legal values, we used to mention the Royal court's penal code. This is a code which went far beyond any imitation or influence by the Chinese feudal legal ideologies. It is always considered a product of Vietnam's intelligence, that of a national tradition imbued with a humanistic character throughout a long history. Professor Oliver Oldman, Chairman of the East Asian Law Division at the Harvard College of Law (USA) remarked that:

The law code of the Le dynasty in Vietnam was an immortal work of the traditional East Asian region (...) which, in its special centuries, had built up a powerful nation for the defence of the people's legal ownership by a progressive law system that could be compared in many points as equal in function to the law viewpoints of the modern West.[4]

---

[3] Phan Huy Chu, *Royal annals* (Hanoi: Social Sciences Publishing House, 1992) p. 287.

[4] Quoted from *A few problems of State control and consolidation of jurisdiction in Vietnam history* (Hanoi: National Politics Publishing House, 1995).

PROCESS OF ACQUIREMENT OF WESTERN VALUES IN VIETNAM LAWS

In its history of development, Vietnamese legal ideologies were not just influenced by Oriental legal ideologies - i.e. laws and ideologies of ancient, feudal China - they were equally influenced by Western legal ideologies from the French colonisation and rule over Vietnam in the 19th century.

First, the way for Western legal viewpoints and models to be introduced to Vietnam was the invasion by French colonialists. After the French expeditionary corps entered Vietnam in the 19th century, Western laws made their appearance in Vietnam society and step by step the French colonialists imposed the Western law model on a country that was originally alien to these sorts of legal regulations. It could be said that Vietnam's society was influenced by Western laws in a quite differently than was Japan, which quite voluntarily adopted western models. Vietnam's experience was the imposition of French laws as a result of invasion and use of force.

Since Vietnam was a French colony, the French colonialists imposed on Vietnam a legal system from France, and they partitioned Vietnam into three 'countries' under three different law systems.

In Cochinchina which acquired the status as an assimilated 'colony', the French colonialist law system was established in place of that by the Nguyen royal dynasty. A decree by the Governor General of Indochina (6 January, 1903) abolished 'the native status' in Cochinchina. Every Vietnamese or Frenchman was to be tried by the French court on the basis of a French penal code. Every civil relation was adjusted along the 'French citizen elements' as proclaimed by the French President.

In Tonkin with the status as a 'protectorate', the French colonialists maintained in the first period two sorts of courts: A Western court to try Western people and a Vietnamese court to try the natives. Later, the Southern royal court was assigned to be a Revise Council, then a sort of Supreme Court. By a decree of 2 December, 1921 from the Indochina Governor General, 4 codes were promulgated and applied in Tonkin:

- The law on tribunal proceedings (37 articles) related to organisation, authority and activities of various tribunal levels;

- The law on civil lawsuits (373 articles) related to lawsuits, trials and execution of sentence;

- The law on criminal affairs (211 articles) related to the application and trial of criminal cases;
- The penal law (328 articles) defining the principles of trial on offences and punishment.

In 1931, the Tonkin civil code proclaimed by the Governor General of Indochina was applied in Tonkin. In essence, the law system in Tonkin was decided by the French administration which basically followed the French legal model, somewhat taking into account the characteristics and habits of the natives.

In Annam, the central part of the country, the Gia Long royal code was still applied but the French colonialists gradually forced the Hue royal court to issue documents that amended a number of legal regulations in many aspects according to the rulers' desire. Since 1936, the Tonkin civil code was amended to be partly (1938) and totally (1939) applied all over the central part of the country.

For nearly one hundred years of domination, the French colonialists rejected (or in practice nullified) Vietnam's feudal laws and replaced them with a French legal system that was imposed on Vietnamese social life. The imposition of alien colonialist laws met with a strong popular opposition and created a negative psychology among people regarding Western law. It should however be seen that the introduction of Western law into a feudal country as Vietnam also created an opportunity for Vietnam to be penetrated of those Western democratic legal ideologies.

Overcoming the negative psychology and consciousness of people towards a legal system imposed by the colonialists, several Vietnamese ideologists and revolutionaries had tried to understand the real values of Western European democracy because, as a result and at different levels, they were influenced by these values, too.

It was found that the harsh legal system imposed by the French colonialists in Vietnam ran counter to Western democratic values, values, which constituted an important ideological motive force for social progress in Western countries. The consciousness of people protesting against colonialist oppression and barbarous enslavement - the traditional patriotic values of the Vietnamese nation - were once again strengthened as soon as they met with Western progressive and democratic values. Western constitutionalism - ideologies on human and civil rights with their slogans of freedom, equality, fraternity and human rights - were acquired by Vietnamese patriots who propagated them among the people and created revolutionary movements among different strata of the population to carry out their struggle for liberation. It was precisely the Western democratic values which, mixed with traditional patriotism and the historic cultural values of the Vietnamese nation, became an ideological force in the struggle against colonialism for independence, freedom and democratic liberties. Western constitutionalism, the ideologies of human and civil rights, had in these circumstances contributed to the creation of new legal ideologies for Vietnamese revolutionary forces in their struggle for national liberation.

Predecessors of the revolution, from Phan Boi Chau to Phan Chau Trinh, Huynh Thuc Khang and the great leader Ho Chi Minh, had acquired the Western legal values in various forms and applied them to the reality of Vietnam, making them a tool for a struggle that demanded the French colonialists enforce democracy in Vietnam.

Phan Boi Chau advocated that a constitution must be built in Vietnam. He said:

I think our country has never had a constitution before. Now that a constitution is to be made, it would not only mean a good thing, it is necessary, too. There must be a constitution at all cost, and that is inevitable... For my part, I always have a constitution in my heart. That of mine was adjusted along the constitution of monarchies like England or Japan. But to have constitutions like those in the US, Germany or Russia would depend on our people's level to choose what was appropriate before we could have them perfected.[5]

The civil rights ideology of Phan Boi Chau stemmed from Western ideology on civil rights. According to Phan Boi Chau, "every civil right is meant to promote equality". "First, it was the right to vote to choose representatives to the Parliament. All people are entitled to vote, whether they are noble or not, rich or poor, big or small."[6]

Phan Chau Trinh was also deeply influenced by Western constitutionalism. He thought highly of having a constitution, considering it a legal tool for the abolition of monarchy and establishment of people's governance. Phan Chau Trinh maintained that people in Europe had long practised their regime of "mutual governance by the King and people, which was translated into Chinese

---

[5] Phan Boi Chau: *Complete works,* Vol.4, p.244.

[6] Phan Boi Chau: *Complete works,* Vol.2, p.261.

as constitutional monarchy", "the regimes in England, Belgium and Japan of today."[7]

He compared and affirmed that people's governance was much better than royal governance since with such regimes, people could set up their own constitution and regulations, and decide on agencies to take care of everybody's affairs. What the people wanted could be satisfied.[8]

Phan Chau Trinh's viewpoint on civil rights was strongly influenced by the bourgeois democratic system. He advocated the abolition of feudal monarchy, implementation of democracy, freedom for improvement of people's cultural standard, expansion of industry and commerce, and practice of non violence. Here he counted not on external aid but on support from the colonialist administration itself.

Though deeply influenced by Western democratic values with the wish to establish a constitutional regime and carry out civil rights in Vietnam, both Phan Boi Chau and Phan Chau Trinh failed to succeed because they were restricted in terms of their revolutionary method. But the ideologies they propagated in Vietnam were of a great significance for the preparation of ideological bases that would lead to a new revolutionary trend as it was later promoted by the leader Nguyen Ai Quoc.

With over thirty years of itinerant life abroad in search of a way for national salvation, President Ho Chi Minh largely acquired the cultural cream of humanity, especially the values of Western legal ideologies. From Western legal values, Ho Chi Minh used it as a weapon in the struggle against the French colonialists' inhuman laws in Vietnam. He received and inherited Western law values in his own way and requirement, making them his own dream and ideal. We can see from reading his "claims for the Annamite people" written in 1919:

1. Amnesty for all native political prisoners

2. Reform justice in Indochina by providing natives the right to enjoy legal assurance as Europeans, abolish all special courts which are being used as tools of terror and oppression against the most faithful part of the Annamite people

3. Freedom of the press and speech

---

[7] Phan Boi Chau: *Complete works*, Vol.2, p.261.

[8] Phan Chau Trinh: *Complete works*, id. p. 871.

270

4. Freedom of establishing associations and meetings

5. Freedom to go abroad and of tourism abroad

6. Freedom of education, establishment of technical and vocational schools in all provinces for the natives

7. Replace the regime of issuing decrees with that of laws [constitution]

8. Permanent delegation of natives, elected by natives, at the French parliament to make it the aspirations of natives known.

In 1922, putting his "claims for the Annamite people" into plain verse called "the song of demands by Vietnam", Ho Chi Minh (then under the name of Nguyen Ai Quoc wrote): "The seventh is the request for a constitution to be proclaimed. There should be among hundred items, deities of jurisdiction."[9]

From the above, we can see that Ho Chi Minh had approached and was deeply influenced by the legal ideologies of the progressive West with it's constitutionalism, the spirit of law and viewpoints on civil and human rights by Montesquieu.

The idea of progressive constitutionalism and the aspiration to establish a democratic constitution by Ho Chi Minh was successfully expressed in the first constitution of Vietnam Democratic Republic led and built by President Ho Chi Minh himself - the 1946 Constitution.

The 1946 Constitution was a skilful expression of values both of constitutionalism and Vietnam. On one hand, it expressed the requirements of a democratic constitution and basic rights for people in the spirit of human and civil rights. On the other, it reflected the specific democratic path followed by the Vietnamese revolution, which was not stereotyped on any Western democratic model.

In the history of the Vietnamese revolution, the "Claims for the Annamite people" (1919), the poem entitled "Song of demands by Vietnam" (1922) and the "Call to the League of Nations" (1926) by Nguyen Ai Quoc were a profound application of value human values mixed to the thirst of an oppressed nation for freedom and was the first appearance of Vietnam declaration on human rights, the Declaration of Independence (1945) which was worthy of the stature of a "Declaration on human rights by the colonial people".

---

[9]Ho Chi Minh, *Complete Works* (Hanoi: National Politics Publishing House, 1995, pp. 438.

The Vietnam Declaration of Independence (1945) began with the affirmed values of the US Declaration of Independence and the Declaration on human and civil rights by the French bourgeois revolution:

All men are created equal, they are endowed by their Creator with certain unalienable Rights, that among these are Life, Liberty and the Pursuit of Happiness....[10]

These human values were acquired and brought to a new height: "Right to equality", "right to life", "right of nations to live happy and free". In Ho Chi Minh's ideology, the basic rights of men should be further elevated and assured by the basic rights of national independence and self-determination. The truth of "nothing is more precious than independence and freedom" in Ho Chi Minh's ideology was the summing up the historical values and of the Vietnamese nation in its long history to freedom and independence.

The same truth can also be generalise for the 20th century's movement for national liberation in the world. It was not only a Vietnamese constitutional platform, a Vietnamese value; it was a universal value of mankind as well.

Studying the history of the formation and development of ideologies, we can see that the values of Vietnam legal ideologies, once acquired from its contact with Eastern and Western values, were developed and elevated to other heights finally become Vietnam's own values.

It was for that reason that, in spite of having received legal ideologies from feudal China, the laws of Vietnam feudal dynasties were not 'sinicised'; they all bore Vietnam's national characters. Similarly, though having acquired and being influenced by Western law ideologies, even those imposed by a colonial law system, the Vietnamese nation always knew, once its independence recovered, how to build its own constitutions that would able to keep abreast with the times while remaining democratic and purely Vietnamese.

Today, in the cause of national renovation, the need to build and perfect a legal system demands a continued acquirement of legal values, experience building and implementation of law in the world to adapt them to the reality of our country.

Comparing the modern Vietnamese legal system with others in the world, we can see that our State laws, in their form, bear the influence of Roman-Germanic legal system (i.e. continental European), so there is a great deal of

---

[10] Ho Chi Minh, *Complete Works*, Vol.1, p.3-4.

similarity between our legal system and that of some European countries from defining the source to express special norms and principles in the field of private laws. This also constitutes an advantage for the process of studying and receiving experience from the foreign laws.

Most legal branches in our country's law system, in conditions of a market economy, are built on comparison, consultation and acceptance of those rational legal values from many countries in the world, especially from developed market-economies in Europe.

The first civil code of the Socialist Republic of Vietnam (promulgated in 1996) was not simply the reflection and definition of ownership relations in Vietnam's socio-economic conditions, it was also the acquirement of principles from the Roman-Germanic civil code which originated from the 12 law tables of ancient Rome. The acquirement of European civil legal values also finds its expression in the norms, structures and disposition of chapters in the Vietnam civil code.

The law on commerce proclaimed in 1997 was an important step forward in the efforts to bring trade relations into the adjustment of law that conforms not only to the characteristics of Vietnam's market economy and its possibility of joining in the international trade relations, but also to the law standards as affirmed in the international trade laws, international customs and laws of many other countries. Important institutions in Vietnam's trade law, businessmen (individuals and companies); properties used in business activities, commercial affairs (transactions) are all built on the basis of consultation and acquirement of values from the trade laws of many European countries.

In the process of building and proclaiming draft laws in the economic field, experiences in the outlining of laws regarding economic relations with countries in the region and the world all had been consulted in the spirit of searching for the optimal. The laws on various companies, economic contracts, in the fields of finance, banking, credit, all expressed a large acquirement of law values from many countries.

In the field of formal laws, Vietnam laws acquired the principles of democratic litigation common in the laws of countries applying the Roman-Germanic system. Penal lawsuit principles like: Public trial, equality before the court, assuring the right of defence for the defendant and the accused, not-guilty deduction etc. are being defined in Vietnamese laws regarding penal lawsuit as influenced by the principles of penal trial in various European countries.

The procedures for settlement of civil cases, especially those in economic and commercial disputes, are defined in Vietnamese laws, all on the basis of consulting experiences setting up regulations of formal legislation and activities by juridical agencies in many countries of the world. Principles and procedures in the settlement of disputes in civilian, economic and commercial fields in the form of court and arbitration of Vietnam laws have basically a content similar to those international law regulations and customs on the settlement of disputes.

The process of development of a market economy in Vietnam had on different levels integrated Vietnam's socio-economic life in that of the region, an integration of Vietnam's laws step by step to the regional and international legal life.

The basis for this legal integration was the same traits in fields of Vietnamese law towards that of countries in the region and the world. The influence and process of introduction of several Oriental and Western democratic and progressive legal institutions to Vietnam have contributed to deeply improve the legal system. The system of legal norms which were subjective and voluntaristic in the period of the centralised economic mechanism had changed towards a legal system of a market economy. It was the acquirement of foreign legal values that created similarities to the laws of countries in the region and the world, thus providing conditions for Vietnam to join the regional and international organisations, but also increased the attraction to encourage foreign investors to invest their capital in Vietnam in order to strengthen the possibilities of international cooperation.

At any rate, Western or Oriental values cannot substitute the Vietnamese values. They merely constitute as precious supplements to our own efforts in building up a Vietnamese legal system, making it both modern and national.

Contributions of Linguistic Research to the Understanding of Vietnamese Thought and Culture

Cao Xuan Hao
Institute of Social Sciences in Ho Chi Minh City

*T*he existence of a relationship between the language of a nation, which directly reflects the way it conceptualises the world, and its culture and civilisation, is certainly unquestionable. Nevertheless, it may not take place just as straightforwardly as the layman might tend to think.

What is questionable is how and to what extent one can make use of this relationship, and take linguistic data as the empirical basis for non-trivial statements about the characterising features of the culture of those who speak the language as their mother tongue. We have known too many examples of gratuitous, or quasi-gratuitous, assertions about the outstanding virtues of the Vietnamese people deduced from such facts as, for example, the world order in the noun phrase meaning 'married couple' (hai vo chong – litt. 'wife (and) husband'), which was believed to be a proof of a millenary feministic tradition.

The truth seems to lie somewhere between the two poles, by relativism, for which language is a prism through which the native speaker perceives the word and hence determines the way he thinks about it, so that each language may be said to imprison the people who speaks it in a different world, a Chomskian universalism. The languages spoken by the some thousands linguistic communities are perceived as mere regional dialects of one and the same linguistic system implementing the general principle which governs the way we conceptualise the world.

Meanwhile, even if we admit that each language represents a coherent coding system that functions chiefly by its own laws, it remains highly dubious that the different conditions, in which peoples scattered all over the world live and communicate, do not contain different extra-linguistic factors that have some relevant impact on its functioning and its evolution.

Several among the most important of those factors belong to the domain of culture, i.e. the way different ethnic groups organise their material and mental life to cope with the conditions they are faced with.

The repercussion of cultural factors on the structure of a language is highly probable, though not always verifiable. And hence at least some linguistic facts may find their explanation in the cultural traits of the community which speaks the language involved, and linguistics facts in their turn may offer helpful suggestions about the way of thinking of the native speakers and, thereby, about their culture. This is hardly a questionable fact, and for many people it sounds almost like a truism.

Different languages may resemble one another in a striking manner in what they have to express and to distinguish, i.e. in the infinite richness of the ideas and meanings their speakers use in order to convey the needs of interactive communication within their community. But they may - no less strikingly - be different from each other as for the means they make use of to convey meanings.

One and the same meaning may be conveyed by lexical means in one language and by grammatical means in another, which results in the rather strange fact that some languages demand the speakers to express things that do not bear the slightest information. To give one example, let us say that in European languages the speaker is forced to mark every event that occurs before the time of speech by the verbal form called 'the past tense', even when the hearer knows for sure in what time the event happened thanks to the situation and the context, or to the use of such time adverbials as yesterday or long ago.

One way to diminish the resolving problems concerning such apparently immotivated differences is to say, according to Saussure, that the relationship between signifier and signified is typically arbitrary, i.e. immotivated. Saussure's thesis seems to hold for the majority of cases, but it remains to explicate the remaining ones, and in recent times the efforts made in this direction in many countries seem to prove that they are not made in vain: The results obtained proved to be enlightening for the understanding not only of human language, but also of human cognition in general. We may be sure to be in our rights what we expect from linguistic research such as data that may contribute to our understanding of the culture of the community, which speaks the language under study.

276

But there are some serious difficulties that make our expectations less founded, especially in what concerns the Vietnamese language. Vietnamese is generally recognised as one of the most typical among isolating languages (if not the most). Its analyticity is almost legendary. It represents the very antipode of the Indo-European fusional synthetical inflectional language family. But its grammar is usually described almost as that of a European language, except in what concerns the monosyllabicity of its morphemes (but not of its words), and a few other details of little relevance. An accurate reading of the Vietnamese grammars so far available, including those used in grammar schools and universities, shows that the real object of the descriptions is not Vietnamese sentences and constructions as such, but their equivalents in French, English or Russian.

This is true not only of some works by foreign authors, but even of those written by Vietnamese linguists. The reason of this state of affairs is easy to point out: Not all the foreign authors know Vietnamese well enough, and not all the Vietnamese authors can overcome the eurocentric prejudices acquired during their studying of European languages, even though not everyone of them are so firmly convinced that everything that is described in European grammars is universal. It is not necessarily for all the languages of the world, particularly those which completely different typologically from European languages, or every 'civilised language' to have a grammar identified almost like that of the European language(s) he is used to. Those victims of European language, ignoring their own linguistic habits.

The most striking illustration of this is perhaps represented by the respective assignation of grammatical 'tense meaning', namely 'past', 'present' and 'future' to the three modal verbs *da* (~ already – marker of the perfect aspect), *dang* (marker of the progressive or continuative aspect), and *se* (marker of the irrealis or hypothetical modality).

However strange it may be, the complete false assignation of 'tense meaning' ('past', 'present', 'future' to these three modal verbs, which have absolutely nothing to do with the localisation of an event in time (as the concept of tense is defined in contemporary linguistics) was repeated again and again in almost all the textbooks published in Vietnam and abroad throughout almost four centuries (from the beginning of the 17th century to the end of the 20th). It was only recently, in the Summer of 1998, when a representative of the Functional Grammar Laboratories of Ho Chi Minh City published the results of his research in the Journal of the Institute of Linguistics on the true meaning and use of the three mentioned modal verbs that Vietnamese linguists realised the real state of affairs involved.

Vietnamese have no tenses at all. This does not mean that it never express temporal meanings. Rather, it is not obliged to express them when the process of communication does not demand them to be expressed. When it does, the language makes use of such time adverbial as truoc kia 'in the past', 'formerly', ngay xua 'one upon a time' bay gio 'now', sau nay 'in the future' i.e. of lexical means (which are of course also used in languages with tenses, where temporal expressions are grammaticalised and function in the code as grammatical category).

On the other hand, *da*, *dang* and *se* are used indifferently to refer to events and states situated in the past, in the future as well as in the present time (i.e. the time of speech).[1] It has been so in the Vietnamese language at least since the 14th century. It was only in the 1950's that the combined use if the three modal verbs (or of two of them) appeared in an idiomatic expression meaning "in the past, in the present and in the future", but the expression is found only in rather specific language of newspapers and political speeches, and shows no tendency to be spread further into other domains of language use. It remains a stylistic peculiarity of the *language de bois*.

This is a rare curiosity in the history of human languages, where a gross blunder of the writers of school manuals results in an innovation in language practice, enclosed indeed in a rather narrow domain and bearing a strong flavour of political jargon, but seemingly fashionable enough to be adopted by some generations of journalists and orators (though far from being approved by all of them).

If we do not take into account this special use of *da*, *dang* and *se*, the theory which interprets these modal verbs as tense markers is thoroughly false. And its falsity is not so difficult to discover. Indeed, it suffices to read two or three pages of a tale or a novel translated into Vietnamese from a European language or from the Vietnamese into an European language and compare the translation with the original text to be convinced once and for all that there is not the least regular correspondence between Vietnamese *da*, *dang* and *se* and

---

[1] Only *se* shows a more or less frequent correspondence with future time, but as in many other languages, this is more exactly a market for the irrealis or hypothetical modality, which englobes the 'future' in all these languages, and a theory which exclusively attribute to *se* the future meaning would be unable to account for numerous other cases of its use.

the tense forms of the European verbs. And even those Vietnamese linguists who explicitly defined *da, dang* and *se* as the respective markers of the past, present and the future tenses are never found to be using these words in their own writings when they refer to events and states that occur in the corresponding time. All of them always use those words to convey aspect or modal meanings, just as any of their compatriots do. Even foreigners who write in good Vietnamese never use them to convey tense meanings, even if they are used to the obligatory tense forms in their native language.

Nevertheless, for more than three centuries, almost all the manuals of Vietnamese repeated one after the other that there are three tenses in the language, marked respectively by *da, dang* and *se*. Really, it is obvious that this is not a theory this is an act of faith and faith is unfalsifiable, it is above any reality.

It needs to be pointed out that the astonishing phenomenon just mentioned is only one among hundreds of cases observable in every domain of the study of Vietnamese as a national language to be taught at school. Analogous facts, among others, can be mentioned in the syntactic analysis of the sentence, where writers stubbornly look for grammatical subject, and as only less than 20 percent of the Vietnamese sentences contain something that could be translated in a European language as a subject, they simply ignore the other 80 percent as 'irregular', 'peculiar' or 'ungrammatical', never worrying about the fact that such a great classic as Kieu[2] contains more than 200 'irregular', including subjectless, sentences (among 3,254 verses).

Another example to be pointed out is the manner in which writers delimit 'words' in Vietnamese. Guided by the 'principle' that a civilised language can not be monosyllabic, these writers struggle hard to fund a plausible argumentation for a polysyllabic polymorphemic word structure in Vietnamese, which is not an easy task. Vietnamese is really an isolating language with typically monosyllabic words, and they have to resort to such arguments as asserting that *xe dap* constitute a single word (although elsewhere they have recognised that *xe* and *dap* are independent words) because in this single polymorphemic word we have not another occurrence of the two words mentioned, but of two bound morphemes which by chance are homonymous to the two independent words. This proceeding is also used to prove the 'voidness' of such 'classifier' as *cai* 'thing' when somebody has succeeded in

---

[2] [Kim van Kieu, the Tail of Kieu, is the greatest Vietnamese classical poem, note by editors].

demonstrating its noun status: The *cai* which is proved to be a noun is simply an accidental homonym of the 'classifier'.

In fact, the arguments they advanced are always invented ad hoc. What they rely on is rather some well known fact taken from a European language: *xe dap* is surely a single word because *vélo*, *bécane*, even *bicyclette* are all single words. But this method of argumentation can hardly be explicitly confessed, and to avoid such a shameful confession, the treatment is often attributed to the 'linguistic intuition' of the native speaker (namely the author of the theory in question).

And as a result, after 12 years of study, undergraduate students of any specialty have to follow a course of 'practical Vietnamese' because they remain unable to write and to speak correctly this language, which is quite natural, given the fact that they have never studied Vietnamese as it is spoken and written by the Vietnamese, with the structures and rules that govern their linguistic behaviour though they are not explicitly conscious of them: What they learned in school is rather an abstract knowledge of how Vietnamese sentence, phrases and words can be described and analysed in accordance with the rules which govern a European language.

Such a state of affairs in linguistic researches can hardly rejoice someone who finds it possible to rely on linguistic data as a source or the raw material from which one can try to build hypotheses related to the cultural physionomy of the Vietnamese people.

Meanwhile it does not seem impossible to deduce from linguistic facts some traits of the cultural characterology of a people, provided that the linguistics facts are not distorted and made unrecognisable by the imposition of an alien model upon the original structure. Current intensive researches in the Functional Grammar of Vietnamese, among which I can mention those conducted and financed by the Linguistic Society of Ho Chi Minh City, are giving us the right to hope that in a near future linguistic data, presented in a theoretic system free from eurocentric prejudices, will be able to contribute to be a better understanding of Vietnamese thought and Vietnamese culture.

Hereafter are some of the problems or sets of problems, the solution of which seems to be promising for further discussion:

1. What may the absence of a grammatical subject with a severely limited role assignment and the prominence of a topic which can be assigned

any of the semantic roles and does not always expressed giveness suggest about the way of thinking of the Vietnamese?

2. While in European languages the syntactic structure of the sentence ('grammatical subject' + 'grammatical predicate') does not coincide with the logical structure of the proposition which it expresses ('subjectum' + 'praedicatum' or otherwise 'hypokeimenon' + 'kategoroumenon') in a 'topic-prominence' language like Vietnamese, the two do coincide: Then how can this coincidence influence Vietnamese thinking?

3. Why do the majority of the Vietnamese substantives, including nouns denoting material objects, behave grammatically as mass nouns incompatible with the number marking and with the descriptive qualifiers of the type 'epitheta ornantia'? Why do they behave as if they do not denote things?

4. What is the semantic load of the count nouns commonly called 'classifiers'? What may be the relationship between them and lexical categorisation? Are they indeed aimed at 'classifying' things, or at 'reigying' (adding thingness to something that is not a thing proper?).

5. Does the absence of grammatical tenses in Vietnamese indicate some peculiarity in the vision of time of the Vietnamese?

6. What can the system of quantifiers (including numerals) and the manner it is used in speech reveal about Vietnamese thought? Why the plural, usually marked by the 'articles' *nhung* and *cac*, cannot be used for nouns denoting parts of the body (numerals and collective nouns are used instead).

7. Why, and since when, kinship terms are used as pronouns for the first and the second persons? How can be explained the absence of a neutral pronoun in modern Vietnamese? How does this system of pronouns influence relationship in Vietnamese society?

Asian Values and Vietnam's Development in Comparative Perspectives

Responsible for Publication

Editors:

Irene Norlund

Pham Duc Thanh

Cover designer:

Nguyen Thi Hoa

Photographs taken by:

Nguyen Van Ku

Nguyen Thanh Liem – Nguyen Nhu Thiet

Printed in Ka Long Company, 800 copies, size 18x25 cm
Issue License No. 63/QĐ-CXB, dated 31/3/2000
Legal Deposit: April 2000